THE ANGEL OF HISTORY

Cultural Memory

in

the

Present

Mieke Bal and Hent de Vries, Editors

THE ANGEL OF HISTORY

Rosenzweig, Benjamin, Scholem

Stéphane Mosès

Translated by Barbara Harshav

STANFORD UNIVERSITY PRESS

STANFORD, CALIFORNIA

Stanford University Press
Stanford, California

The Angel of History: Rosenzweig, Benjamin, Scholem was originally published in
French in 1992 under the title *L'Ange de l'histoire: Rosenzweig, Benjamin, Scholem*
© 1992, Editions du Seuil.

Publication assistance for this book was provided by the French Ministry of
Culture—National Center for the Book.

Printed in the United States of America on acid-free, archival-quality paper

Library of Congress Cataloging-in-Publication Data
Mosès, Stéphane, 1931–2007.
  [Ange de l'histoire. English]
  The angel of history : Rosenzweig, Benjamin, Scholem / Stéphane Mosès ;
translated by Barbara Harshav.
    p. cm. — (Cultural memory in the present)
  "Originally published in French in 1992 under the title L'Ange de l'histoire:
Rosenzweig, Benjamin, Scholem 1992, Editions du Seuil."
  Includes bibliographical references.
  ISBN 978-0-8047-4116-3 (cloth : alk. paper) — ISBN 978-0-8047-4117-0 (pbk.
: alk. paper)
  1. History—Philosophy. 2. Rosenzweig, Franz, 1886–1929. 3. Benjamin,
Walter, 1892–1940. 4. Scholem, Gershom Gerhard, 1897–1982. 5. Philosophy,
Jewish—Germany—History—20th century. I. Title. II. Series.
  D16.8.M83513 2009
  901—dc22

                         2008032674

Typeset by Bruce Lundquist in 11/13.5 Adobe Garamond

Contents

Introduction

"At first all the arrangements for building the Tower of Babel were characterized by fairly good order; . . . as if there were centuries before one to do the work in. In fact, the general opinion at that time was that one simply could not build too slowly."[1] Thus Kafka begins the narrative of the biblical episode of the tower high enough to reach the sky that ancient generations wanted to build. The story in Genesis is set at the beginning of humanity, which, still close to its original harmony, was "of one language and of one speech." Yet that unity apparently bore the seeds of its own disunion within it. To ward off their separation, men decided to gather in one place and establish a city, mother of all civilizations. As a symbol of their harmony, they undertook to erect the tower; but the Bible—unlike Kafka's narrative—makes it clear that the work went very fast, so fast that God became alarmed at that concentration of power in the hands of a single city, which dared to want to rule the world. The unity of language—or, if you like, the transparency of communication—did not resist the division of labor demanded by that superhuman undertaking. The inhabitants of the city were divided, separated, "scattered from thence upon the face of all the earth: and they left off to build the city."[2] In sum, they had been the victims of the very evil they had wanted to avoid. Perhaps their error had been wanting to consolidate hastily (that is, violently) a unity they already possessed. Or perhaps they were overtaken in spite of themselves by a dispersion more original than any unity.

If, in the Bible, the generation of Babel seemed to have sinned out of impatience, Kafka sees it as the embodiment of hesitation. All the haste and resolve implied by the biblical text turns into slowness and procrastination in Kafka. Indeed, Kafka's narrative completely subverts the biblical fable of its model: instead of evoking the construction of the tower, it tells the history of its nonconstruction:

People argued in this way: The essential thing in the whole business is the idea of building a tower that will reach to heaven. In comparison with that idea everything else is secondary. The idea, once seized in its magnitude, can never vanish again; so long as there are men on the earth there will be also the irresistible desire to complete the building. That being so, however, one need have no anxiety about the future; on the contrary, human knowledge is increasing, the art of building has made progress and will make further progress, a piece of work which takes us a year may perhaps be done in half the time in another hundred years, and better done, too, more enduringly. So why exert oneself to the extreme limit of one's present powers? . . . Such thoughts paralyzed people's powers, and so they troubled less about the tower than the construction of a city for the workmen. Every nationality wanted the finest quarter for itself, and this gave rise to disputes, which developed into blood conflicts. These conflicts never came to an end; to the leaders they were a new proof that, in the absence of the necessary unity, the building of the tower must be done very slowly, or indeed preferably postponed until universal peace was declared. . . . In this fashion the age of the first generation went past, but none of the succeeding ones showed any difference; except that technical skill increased and with it occasion for conflict. To this must be added that the second or third generation had already recognized the senselessness of building a heaven-reaching tower; but by that time everybody was too deeply involved to leave the city.[3]

As so often in Kafka, this text presents the narrative of its own erasing: from postponement to postponement, the story it intended to tell vanishes, just as by perfecting the means of construction, it is abandoned in the end. The biblical passage turns into its opposite: no longer is it a matter of illustrating the reasons why the tower *must* not be constructed but rather the reason why it *can* not be constructed. That is, if Kafka inverted the meaning of the biblical text, he has preserved its parabolic form. For him, as in the Bible, the Tower of Babel symbolizes both the effort of humanity toward its ideal accomplishment and the failure of that effort. But whereas that failure in the Bible results mainly from the intervention of a force superior to human will, in Kafka, it originates in a deficiency inherent in humanity itself. Here, the failure of Babel somehow refers to an immanent logic of self-destruction or, if you like, to the roots of the death instinct. This seems to express a *breakdown of the link with time*, more particularly of the *link with the future*. For the men of Babel, time seemed unlimited, like a line that could be extended indefinitely or a river that would flow endlessly: "as if there were centuries before one to do the work in." A neutral time, perceived as an empty form, always available, waiting for human acts to fill it. This is why "one need have no anxiety about the future"; on the axis of time where moments are added to moments, the task to be accomplished loses all urgency; all the nuances of our mental connection to the future—expectation, hope, patience, and impatience—are wiped out in a single indifference: the future, deprived of its essential dimension, the *new*, will occur without surprise, at the stated time, as a necessary stage of an unchanging movement.

In the vision of time of the men of Babel, an allegory of the modern conception of historical temporality is easily seen.[4] A critical allegory, naturally, intended to expose the contradictions of an Enlightenment idea of history, imposed on the nineteenth century as a virtually natural fact. Philosophers of the eighteenth century saw history as a process oriented from less toward more, from confusion toward order, from darkness toward light. Of course, the existence of historical rhythms accentuating the rise and fall of empires is acknowledged. But beyond those fluctuations, history in its totality is conceived as the vector of constant progress, intended to lead humanity to its final realization. Hence, the notion of an ideal end of history, a telos it is leading to. Moreover, that telos (as in the idea of the natural finality) plays the role of an immanent principle guiding the development of history. There is some sort of historical Reason controlling the course of the human adventure from inside. In Hegel, this teleological vision culminates in the interpretation of history as a dialectical process through which the Absolute itself is realized. Hence, in comparison with that inevitable progress of Reason in the world, the function of human initiative—which must still be seen as decisive—is nevertheless reduced to being a means in the service of an end that is infinitely beyond it. Every human act is contingent; its meaning (that is, its effectiveness) depends on its conformity or nonconformity with the dynamic of Reason at work in history. The work of Reason is slow, perhaps infinite. How can we know if the time is ripe for the realization of our plans? "Such thoughts," writes Kafka, "paralyzed people's powers." Does belief in the inevitable necessity of progress not lead just as inevitably to a kind of ataraxia, or in any case to the permanent postponement of action? "So why exert oneself from today to the extreme limit of one's powers?"

Kafka's whole text revolves around that "from today." What is excluded by historic Reason is precisely the idea that telos, the completion of all things, can occur "from today." The philosophy of historic progress is based on the belief in an infinite time, the term "infinite" not referring here to the idea of a plethora, a different quality of being, but to the in-terminable, the endlessness of a series that can be extended indefinitely: "In this fashion the age of the first generation went past, but none of the succeeding ones showed any difference." A perfectly homogeneous duration made of a succession of identical units of time, neutral time, comparable to that of classical mechanics in which the sequence of causes and effects can never produce anything radically new. Significantly, in Hegel, history seems interminably to play out the same scenario of the appearance and disappearance of "historic peoples" on the stage of becoming. In this perspective, the telos of history could not be conceived as a reality that, in principle, can occur at any moment, and perhaps "from today," but rather as a postulate, a controlling idea whose realization regresses indefinitely as we move forward: "The essential thing in the whole business is the idea of building a tower that will reach to heaven. In comparison with that idea everything else is secondary. The idea, once seized in its magnitude, can never vanish again; so long as there are men on the earth there will be also the irresistible desire to complete the building."

With the indefinite postponement of all its ideals, humanity will also have to repel the utopia of a "universal peace" very far into the future. Moreover, extending expectation indefinitely is itself a source of violence. The constant perfection of means becomes an end in itself, making the end initially pursued forgotten; technical progress becomes an instrument of domination and exacerbates rivalries: "the town was embellished in the intervals, and this unfortunately enough evoked fresh envy and fresh conflict." Once utopia is defined as an asymptotic, that is, unattainable, ideal, it dissolves into pure abstraction and no longer stirs anything but discouragement: "the second or third generation had already recognized the senselessness of building a heaven-reaching tower"; the concept of utopia as an "infinite task" turns against itself here; the notion of a time that can be extended indefinitely, that is, of an endless time, a priori excludes the idea that the world will some day achieve its completion.

Can another vision of history be imagined? Kafka's text does not say so. The descendants of the men of Babel, in any case, can choose only between resignation ("by that time everybody was too deeply involved to leave the city") and the expectation of apocalypse. But no doubt two complementary aspects of a single disenchantment are at issue there: when the social compact no longer rests on anything but the disenchanted awareness that nothing essential will ever change, that is, on the frustration of all hopes, the utopian energy that henceforth has no object will be invested completely—as if in compensation—in eschatological daydreams, in the expectation of the final catastrophe that will destroy the world so that a new humanity may rise from its ruins. That is precisely what is suggested by the last paragraph of Kafka's tale:

All the legends and songs that came to birth in that city are filled with longing for a prophesied day when the city would be destroyed by five successive plows from a gigantic fist. It is for that reason that the city has a closed fist on its coat of arms.[5]

*

A novella by Jorge Luis Borges echoes Kafka's tale. The central theme of Borges's novella is also time, but perceived here in a precisely opposite form: not in its endless extension, but in its most extreme condensation. "The Secret Miracle" sometimes seems to respond (probably unbeknownst to the author) to some of the harmonics hidden in "The City Coat of Arms." First because Borges's story is set in Prague, Kafka's city, identified allegorically at the end of the tale with the biblical Babel. And then because the hero of Borges's novella, Jaromir Hladik, is presented as a writer ("Apart from a few friendships and many habits, the problematic practice of literature constituted his life") and a Jew. The denunciation of the bellicose madness of men in "The City Coat of Arms," written in 1917 in the middle of the world war, corresponds in "The Secret Miracle" (written in 1943) to the evocation of the German invasion of Prague in 1939, the virtually immediate arrest of Hladik, and his death sentence (motivated primarily by his works on Jewish mysticism: "his investigation of the work of

Jacob Boehme," and a translation of the *Sefer Yetsirah*). "The Secret Miracle" concentrates on the ten days when Hladik awaits his execution in his Prague prison. One of the ideas that torments him most is the obsession of not having had time to finish the book he is working on, a three-act tragedy in verse titled *The Enemies*: "He had already completed the first act and a scene or two of the third. The metrical nature of the work allowed him to go over it continually, rectifying the hexameters, without recourse to the manuscript. He thought of the two acts still to do, and of his coming death." The night before the execution, he asked God to grant him one more year of life: "In order to bring this drama, which may serve to justify me, to justify You, I need one more year. Grant me that year, You to whom belong the centuries and all time." The day of the execution arrives. It is March 29, 1939, at nine o'clock in the morning:

The firing squad fell in and was brought to attention. Hladik, standing against the barracks wall, waited for the volley. Someone expressed fear the wall would be splashed with blood. The condemned man was ordered to step forward a few paces. Hladik recalled, absurdly, the preliminary maneuvers of a photographer. A heavy drop of rain grazed one of Hladik's temples and slowly rolled down his cheek. The sergeant barked the final command.

The physical universe stood still.

The rifles converged upon Hladik, but the men assigned to pull the triggers were immobile. The sergeant's arm eternalized an inconclusive gesture. Upon a courtyard flagstone a bee cast a stationary shadow. The wind had halted, as in a painted picture. Hladik began a shriek, a syllable, a twist of the hand. He realized he was paralyzed. Not a sound reached him from the stricken world.

He thought: *I'm in hell, I'm dead.*

He thought: *I've gone mad.*

He thought: *Time has come to a halt.*

Then he reflected that in that case, his thought, too, would have come to a halt. He was anxious to test this possibility: he repeated (without moving his lips) the mysterious Fourth Ecologue of Virgil. He imagined that the already remote soldiers shared his anxiety; he longed to communicate with them. He was astonished that he felt no fatigue, no vertigo from his protracted immobility. After an indeterminate length of time he fell asleep. On awaking he found the world still motionless and dumb. The drop of water still clung to his cheek; the shadow of the bee still did not shift in the courtyard; the smoke from the cigarette he had thrown down did not blow away. Another "day" passed before Hladik understood.

He had asked God for an entire year in which to finish his work: His omnipotence had granted him the time. For his sake, God projected a secret miracle: German lead would kill him, at the determined hour, but in his mind a year would elapse between the command to fire and its execution. From perplexity he passed to stupor, from stupor to resignation, from resignation to sudden gratitude.

He disposed of no document but his own memory; the mastering of each hexameter as he added it, had imposed upon him a kind of fortunate discipline not imagined by those amateurs who forget their vague, ephemeral paragraphs. He did not work for posterity, nor even for God, of whose literary preferences he possessed scant knowledge. Meticulous, unmoving, secretive, he wove his lofty invisible labyrinth in time. He worked the third act over twice. He eliminated some rather too-obvious symbols. . . . There were no circumstances to constrain him. He omitted, condensed, amplified; occasionally, he chose the primitive version. He grew to love the courtyard, the barracks. . . . He brought his drama to a conclusion; he lacked only a single epithet. He found it: the drop of water slid down his cheek. He began a wild cry, moved his face aside. A quadruple blast brought him down.

Jaromir Hladik died on March 29, at 9:02 in the morning.[6]

What happened to Hladik during the tiny moment separating the order to fire given by the sergeant and the shots of the salvo? The text gives us two apparently contradictory indications: on the one hand, it tells us, "The physical universe stood still"; on the other, we learn that time goes on: "He thought: *Time has come to a halt.* Then he reflected that in that case, his thought, too, would have come to a halt." Hladik is not content to think and reflect; he imagines, he wants, he is amazed, he recites Virgil's Fourth Ecologue, he falls asleep and wakes up. Must we conclude that, in the logic of the text, stopping the physical universe would not involve stopping time? But since the sensation of time is closely linked with the perception of change, wouldn't the cessation of all movement ("[T]he men assigned to pull the triggers were immobile. The sergeant's arm eternalized an inconclusive gesture. Upon a courtyard flagstone a bee cast a stationary shadow. The wind had halted, as in a painted picture.") almost necessarily suggest the idea of time stopping? A first answer would consist of distinguishing physical time from mental time: the latter might continue unfolding even if the former were apparently interrupted at least for a brief moment. We might imagine a moment of pause in the world, a sort of fixing on an image, where nature would hold its breath, but where the consciousness of the condemned man would continue to work at a dizzying speed. Such an explanation might take account of the feeling (or the illusion) that physical time has congealed for a few seconds. But the text tells us that that stopping of the universe stretches, first for a whole day, then another day, and finally an entire year. Hence the reader's impression that this phenomenon lasts much too long to be only a simple sensory illusion. An impression reinforced by the literary procedure employed: the scene is described "externally," as if it were an objective reality, before the narrator intervenes to disclose the phenomenon as the character's mental experience. No, the physical universe did not really stop; it ceased to move only in the mind of the condemned man.

But in truth, the difference between objective and subjective is no longer relevant here. For there is no point measuring physical time itself, the time of watches and calendars, in vain in discrete quantitative units (seconds, minutes and hours, days, months and years); it is still translated into qualitative terms when the mind sees it: what counts here are the contents of awareness, their frequency, their duration, their intensity. To say "physical time has stopped" means that the mind is cut off for a moment from external reality and the instruments that measure it and withdraws completely into itself: a suspension of physical time whose counterpart is an extraordinary intensification of mental time. To speak here of a *contraction of physical time* or an *extension of mental time* amounts to the same thing. For the few seconds that separate the order to fire and the arrival of the discharge, Hladik's consciousness is exacerbated to the point of accomplishing in a few brief moments the work of an entire year. But, in his mind, it is the lived content of an entire year that is condensed in the lightning speed of a moment. "For his sake, God projected a secret miracle": a miracle for, in a flash, Hladik attains an internal intensity that projects him far beyond the usual rhythms of human time; secret, for nothing of this wonder leaks out; no one except him will ever know that the work he lived for was ended. For others, for posterity, he will always be the author of an unfinished tragedy.

*

If there is an Angel of History, he would have to stay at the intersection of the time that can be indefinitely extended of Kafka's text and that other, purely internal and qualitative time in Borges's tale. No doubt he would be one of those angels evoked by the Talmud, according to Gershom Scholem: "angels recreated constantly in countless hosts to chant their hymn to God before being destroyed and disappearing into nothingness."[7] Those are the ever-renewed angels who, according to Scholem, haunt the work of Walter Benjamin: "'Their voice that passes and flees symbolizes the anticipation of the apocalypse at the very heart of history."[8] Whether utopia can be anticipated, whether it can be lived "from now," or on the contrary, whether it can be conceived only as a simple "governing idea," an asymptotic ideal whose realization recedes indefinitely as we advance, that is what most profoundly opposes the vision of temporality implied in Borges's tale to what characterized the culture of Kafka's men of Babel. The talmudic legend that assigns each moment of time its specific angel, or even its own quality or its irreplaceable messianic potentialities, states on the historical scale the idea of time lived by Borges's character as an eminently personal experience. That paradoxical figure of thought that the end can be achieved "from today," "in the very heart of history," subverts the very foundations of historical Reason. It implies in effect that time is no longer thought of as an oriented axis, where after inevitably succeeds before, or as a river that flows from its source toward its mouth, but as a juxtaposition of unique instants each time, that cannot be summed up, and that, consequently, do not succeed each other as stages of an irreversible process. The past, present, and future no longer follow each other here on a straight line that a spectator could observe from outside, but coexist as three states of permanent awareness: in the lightning flash of the instant preceding the death of Borges's hero, the completion of the work is anticipated, which, in the normal unfolding of time, he might never have finished. Similarly, according to Kafka, the generation of Babel could no doubt have built that tower "which touched the sky" very fast if they had gone to work "from today." The present moment lived in all its intensity interrupts the tedious unfolding of the days and polarizes in its force field the utopian potentials put off very far into the future by historical Reason.

The "angels recreated constantly in countless hosts to chant their hymn to God before being destroyed and disappearing into nothingness" refers to a conception of historical time as a permanent creation, as an incessant emergence of the new. All the energy of history is concentrated here on the reality of the present. Our experience of time, said Saint Augustine, is always that of the present moment; the past (in the form of memory) and the future (in all forms of expectation: fear and hope, patience and impatience, prediction and utopia) are never anything but modalities of our sojourn in the heart of the present. The same is true of our experience of historical time: for the past to remain alive (so that it does not congeal into simple commemoration), the collective memory must constantly reinvent it; for the future not to appear as the pure forward projection of the tendencies of the past, radical novelty must be foreshadowed in it through the utopian harmonics encrypted in the present constellation. But the present here (that "present of awareness" that Walter Benjamin talks about) has nothing ephemeral: it does not refer to the fleeting passage of the past to the future. Nor it is the synchronic gathering (the re-presentation) of the three dimensions of time. Quite the contrary: that topicality, the principle of "judgment and destruction," according to Scholem,[9] undermines from within the coherence of historical time, makes it fly off the handle, crushes it into countless messianic instants. It is that form of topicality, "the only one that is true,"[10] that is embodied by the Angel of History.

*

Franz Rosenzweig, Walter Benjamin, Gershom Scholem: in Germany in the 1920s, each of these three authors formulated a new vision of history, focusing on the idea of actualizing historical time, or in other words (as Walter Benjamin put it), the idea of *now-time*. All three presented a radical critique of historical Reason and its axioms: the idea of continuity, the idea of causality, and the idea of progress. Each in his own way countered the optimistic vision of a history conceived as a permanent march toward the final realization of humanity with the idea of a discontinuous history whose different moments are not cumulative, and whose crises, ruptures, and rifts are more significant—and probably more promising—than its apparent homogeneity.

That this other vision of history appeared precisely at that period and in three Jewish thinkers is no accident. In all three, reflection on history was engendered by the direct experience of the great upheavals that marked the twentieth century. The original trauma was World War I, experienced as an irreversible rupture of the historical fabric, the catastrophe heralding an unprecedented era. For Rosenzweig, it meant the end of an idea of civilization based on belief in a Logos that could establish a rational order in the world. Benjamin had seen it as the final collapse of a world controlled by tradition, that is, by a collective memory preserving and transmitting from generation to generation an immemorial treasure of historical experiences. In his journal at that time, young Scholem spoke of the death of Europe and its "entombment."[11] What the world war had ruined for all three was an old model that had previously lent meaning to human experience.

In nineteenth-century middle-class Europe, that model had been embodied in the ideology of progress, which tends to exclude from the collective memory all the flaws and regressions, all the failures that punctuate the unfolding of history. Even in the Hegelian version, the richest and most subtle, since it puts death, the tragic, and the work of the negative at the heart of the historical process, the philosophy of progress ultimately proclaims the triumph of the positive that is destined to conclude the unfolding of history and to confer its meaning on it. What the world war teaches Rosenzweig, Benjamin, and Scholem is the impossibility of maintaining the idea of historical progress or of the meaning of history in the face of the irreducible reality of human suffering. The war, experienced as an absolute beginning, cannot be reduced to an episode of the history of Meaning. A founding experience in which the absurdity of every theodicy immanent in history is proclaimed, it wrenches thought from the schema that had been classic since the Enlightenment, of a quantitative and cumulative temporality whose moments add up according to the law of a constant perfection. The war forces us to perceive historical time in its very reality: as a juxtaposition of moments that are qualitatively different from one another and hence cannot be cumulative. Past suffering is not abolished even by a triumphant future, which claims to give them a meaning, any more than thwarted hopes are refuted by the failures that seem to sanction them.

This is a kind of return to a direct experience of historical time perceived in the qualitative difference of each of its instants, since each is loaded with a unique specificity, but hence each also opens toward a multiplicity of possible futures. As soon as the present instant stops being seen as a simple transition between the preceding one and the subsequent one, historical time can no longer be presented, like physical time, as a homogeneous sequence of formally identical units. Along with its homogeneity, the idea of its continuity also disappears, and consequently the very possibility of a causality that regulates its course. So it must be admitted that the relation of one instant to the following instant—and, more generally, of the present to the future—is not unequivocal; from the present, many divergent paths can lead to different futures. Of course, the number of these paths is not indefinite; each present brings a system of constraints that condition the future and, to a certain extent, limit its elasticity. Nevertheless, those possibles are numerous enough so that, in principle, the future remains unpredictable. What characterizes the vision of history in Rosenzweig, Benjamin, and Scholem is precisely that passage from a time of necessity to a *time of possibles.*

Conceivably, negating the idea of progress could lead those three authors to a pessimistic conception of history, since nothing any longer guarantees that history necessarily tends toward the final resolution of all contradictions. Moreover, on the horizon of their life and work all the torments and catastrophes that marked our century stand out: after the war of 1914–1918, Rosenzweig, who died in 1929, watched the gradual ruin of the Weimar Republic and the rise of Nazism; Benjamin and Scholem subsequently witnessed the collapse of German democracy, Hitler's rise to power, and the persecution of the Jews; with the German-Soviet pact, Benjamin saw the collapse of all his hopes for communism; Scholem experienced World War II, the extermination of the Jews, and with the perpetuation of the Israeli-Arab conflict, the impossibility of the spiritual Zionism he had dreamed of. In truth, it is, thus, in the heart of the civilization that had come up with the idea of the meaning of history that that idea collapsed most spectacularly. Yet, for Rosenzweig, as for Benjamin and Scholem, the end of belief in a meaning of history did not involve abolishing the idea of hope. On the contrary, it is precisely on the rubble of the paradigm of historical Reason that hope is formed as a historical category. Utopia, which can no longer be thought as belief in the necessary advent of the ideal at the mythical end of history, reemerges— through the category of *Redemption*—as the modality of its *possible* advent at each moment of time. In this model of a random time, open at any moment to the unpredictable eruption of the new, the imminent realization of the ideal becomes conceivable again, as one of the possibilities offered by the unfathomable complexity of historical processes.[12]

This vision of history cannot be reduced to the teleological model characterizing historical thought of the West, either under the religious form of Christian theodicy or under the secularized form of a dialectic of Reason immanent in history. Thus, it is on the horizon of the crisis of Western civilization that the philosophical movement of Rosenzweig, Benjamin, and Scholem must be understood, turning back to the Jewish experience of history to discover a radically different dimension of historical consciousness and its utopian dimension. Jewish messianism, in fact, always had to confront the historical experience of catastrophe, deception, and failure. All eschatological attempts known by Jewish history generally ended in bitterness and frustration. This is why Jewish messianism always tried to put the particulars of visible history into perspective so as to emphasize the utopian potentials of the *secret history*: that of procreation and generations, the even more hidden one of souls and their spiritual adventures, and those that are constantly concealed, even the most humble. The Jewish messianic hope—symbolized here by the Angel of History—does not adopt the stages of a historical finality but resides in the rifts of history, where its stitches are unraveled and the millions of threads that form its fabric are exposed.

*

On that common horizon, the reflection of those three authors opens out into three different directions, indicating the three central options offered, since the beginning of the twentieth century, to Jews who wanted to break with the spirit of assimilation: religion (Rosenzweig), Zionism (Scholem), and revolution (Benjamin). Even though all three were marginal in terms of the orthodoxy of those various currents, each in his own way still appears as a representative of the great movements of ideas that have stirred our century.

Of the three, Rosenzweig's work is presented in the most rigorously philosophical form. Constantly referring to the political thought of Hegel, which he had studied in his first work, *Hegel and the State* (written between 1911 and 1914, published in 1920), he undertakes in *The Star of Redemption* (written in 1918–1919, published in 1921) to subvert the Hegelian categories from top to bottom by *taking them literally* and showing that it is in the name of Hegelian ideas (above all, in the name of the idea of a historic mission of nations and states) that Europe has plunged into catastrophe. Rosenzweig countered modern nationalism, which he interprets as a secularized form of messianism, with the concept of a *metahistory*, that is, a sacred time, cut off from the vicissitudes of political temporality, where the Jewish people would live its religious vocation.[13]

Walter Benjamin's reflection is developed in a deliberately unsystematic way through a series of studies on the theory of language, literature, social history, and philosophy of history. Shot through with an incessant questioning about the relations of politics and theology, revolution and tradition, this reflection leads in 1940, in the collection of essays *On the Concept of History*, to a reversal of orthodox Marxist schemes, insofar as the categories of historical materialism are rethought in light of Jewish messianism. With this, Benjamin once and for all rejects all notion of historical progress by countering it with the idea of the sudden interruptions of history: breaks that are so many messianic instants.

Scholem's work, unlike that of Rosenzweig and Benjamin, belongs mainly to the realm of historiography. His innovation in terms of the "science of Judaism" as conceived by historians of the nineteenth century does not concern the legitimacy of the historical method but the nature of the object studied. Reintegrating Kabbalah into the field of historical studies is accompanied by a rehabilitation of religious thought in general as a *symbolic system*. In his interpretation of messianism, Scholem underlines the destructive and apocalyptic element of Jewish eschatology as opposed to the harmonious vision of a constant progress of humanity as conceived by Jewish historians of the nineteenth century. For Scholem, the Jewish tradition always privileged the idea of a sudden eruption of the Messiah into the unpredictable unfolding of human history.

In this sense, the idea of "now-time" is certainly in the center of the vision of history of those three thinkers. In all three, in opposition to the paradigm dominant since the Enlightenment, that idea inspired by Jewish messianism, proposes a model of history that, after the collapse of the ideologies of progress, gives a new chance for hope by locating utopia in the heart of the present.

PART I

FRANZ ROSENZWEIG:
THE OTHER SIDE OF THE WEST

1

Dissimilation

In Rosenzweig, Benjamin, and Scholem, the discovery of a radically different dimension of historical consciousness centered on the perception of "now-time" emerges on the background of a sharp critique of European civilization and research of new value systems. In all three, this revision is closely linked to their experience of the Jewish condition in Germany in the first years of the twentieth century. Although they came from families that had been assimilated for generations into the majority society, they were nevertheless marginal enough to be able to view the world around them from a distance. This world was first the family, revealed even in childhood as a site of unbearable social and intellectual contradictions.

Kafka's *Letter to His Father* could have served as a model for all three, who shared the same denunciation of the incoherence of a family milieu aspiring to merge into the dominant society while preserving sporadic vestiges of a tradition that had become incomprehensible; the same critique of a petit-bourgeois conformity eager to copy the norms of the surrounding milieu, the same condemnation of a "hybrid" lifestyle,[1] blocked halfway between a purely formal loyalty to the past and the utopia of a perfect absorption into the outside world. And above all, the same sensibility to the "spiritual fraying"[2] of a Judaism stripped of all metaphysical aura. But from their youth, Rosenzweig, Benjamin, and Scholem were led in different ways to question the models and norms their parents were trying with all their might to assimilate to. In Benjamin and Scholem, it was first of all a revolt against the bourgeois values of Wilhelmian Germany: as a high school student, Benjamin was actively involved in the "Free Commune" of Wickersdorf, established in 1906 by the theoretician and pedagogue Gustav Wyneken. Yet it did not take him long to distrust the nationalist and authoritarian tendencies of this movement and to move "somewhere to the left," after 1913.[3] For him, as for Rosenzweig and Scholem, it was the shock of World War I (and in Benjamin's case, the death of one of his best friends in combat) that was to provoke the definitive break with the henceforth condemned model of a Europe devastated by the clash of nationalisms. As for Scholem, from adolescence on, he dissociated himself from a society and a culture that seemed fundamentally corrupt. His still unpublished youthful notebooks indicate his precocious revolt against the social and political codes of his milieu. Two tendencies are blended almost indiscernibly in him: an intrinsic anarchy with a strong moral bent and a spontaneous rejection of the established order on the one hand; and on the other, a keen awareness of his Jewish identity accompanied from the start by the observation that the specificity of Judaism could only be alien to the interests and preoccupations of German society. Even before the war, young Scholem was drawn to Marxism and Socialism; but his great and genuine passion pushed him to explore Judaism and its history, to the study of Hebrew and reading the Bible, to the discovery of the Talmud and the canonical texts of the Jewish tradition.

But here, too, it was the trauma of the war that precipitated the divorce from a Germany (more generally a Europe) sinking into a bloody nightmare. In 1915, just before his graduation, the young Scholem was expelled from high school for antimilitarism and pacifism. In an open letter to the Zionist weekly *Die Jüdische Rundschau* (which refused to publish it), he wrote: "We don't believe that the cause of Germany, any more than that of any other country in the world, is ours."[4] Scholem was an advocate of "spiritual Zionism": for him the creation of a Jewish State in Palestine meant much less than the internal renaissance of the Jewish people, or in other words, its return to the sources of its collective identity in its ancestral homeland. Thus, a war in which the Jews of Europe, bound by a thousand-year-old community of fate, were killing one another in the name of the national passions of the nations they lived among proved the historical absurdity of assimilation. This Zionist-inspired pacifism was mixed with an anarchist-tinged antimilitarism (he had read Kropotkin,

Proudhon, Élisée Reclus, and especially Gustav Landauer) and was fed by his admiration for his older brother, Werner Scholem, a militant leftist Socialist influenced by Liebknecht and Rosa Luxemburg. When Werner was imprisoned for refusal to obey, Scholem openly sided with him, prompting his father, a firm German patriot, to throw him out of the family house. (Werner Scholem, elected as a Communist deputy after the war, was arrested by the Nazis in 1933, deported to Dachau and then to Buchenwald, where he was murdered in 1940.)

Scholem's notebooks describe the tormented genesis of a personality that, on the tragic background of the war and its horrors, chose to break irrevocably with a Europe on which "the Heavens today recite the prayer of the dead,"[5] and to settle "in Zion," to participate in the spiritual renaissance of the Jewish people.

It was Franz Rosenzweig who described this movement of withdrawal from Western civilization and return to the sources of Jewish identity by borrowing the concept of *dissimilation* from linguistics: the history of the Jewish people, he wrote in an entry in his journal, parallel to an evident tendency toward assimilation, has always known a permanent movement of dissimilation.[6] Like Scholem and Benjamin, Rosenzweig resisted the uncertainties and contradictions of his father's vague Judaism. Like Scholem (but unlike Benjamin), he had been fascinated in adolescence by the religious dimension of Judaism; but like Benjamin (and unlike Scholem), he had never been drawn to Zionism. The history of his formative years, marked first by the skepticism and relativism prevalent in the early twentieth century, then by the double confrontation with Hegel's philosophy of history on the one hand, and with the Christian militancy of his closest friends on the other, is the narrative of a gradual reconversion to a religious vision of the world with first a Christian tinge, then a specifically Jewish bent. In one sense, this path still seems relatively timid: no principled rejection of bourgeois society, no "leftist" political commitment as in Benjamin, no violent break with Europe as in Scholem.

Yet, in Rosenzweig, it was the shock of the war that was to lead to the most profound, most radically thematized divorce from the whole of Western civilization. In his view, what the war challenged was the whole philosophical tradition "from Ionia to Jena,"[7] a tradition based on the primacy of a Logos that was supposed to account for the totality of the real. The identification of thought and Being: this original postulate of all

Western metaphysics clashed with the irreducible facticity of death, an original violence that no logic could eliminate.[8] But Rosenzweig went much further: for him, the tradition of Logos is also a tradition of Power. Following Hegel's analyses, he considered Christianity the founding principle of a civilization presented as the ultimate historical avatar of the Absolute. As such, it is the supreme incarnation of Meaning: in it, everything becomes intelligible. Nothing can remain external to the omnipotence of the Meaning it conveys. Just as philosophy has always tried to neutralize the externality of death by trying to signify it, so the tradition of the Christian West has always sought to deny the radical otherness of Judaism by absorbing it into its own horizon. Rosenzweig's entire speculative impetus consisted of trying to wrench Judaism from that alienation to restore it to its own sovereignty. This is the central (indeed only) object of the philosophical debate that would set him against the Protestant theologian Eugen Rosenstock in the middle of the war.

*

The correspondence between Franz Rosenzweig and Eugen Rosenstock represents one of the most deeply moving episodes in the Jewish-Christian dialogue of the twentieth century. This exchange of letters took place between May and December 1916, while both were fighting in the German army, Rosenzweig in the Balkans and Rosenstock on the Somme. This dialogue is characterized by its complete candor, its undeviating freedom in the exchange of ideas, and its relentless rigor in the search for truth, going far beyond simple professions of goodwill or expression of common convictions, to which Jewish-Christian exchanges are so often reduced.

To understand all that is involved in this correspondence, we must first recall the circumstances that induced it. Rosenzweig met Rosenstock during a congress of young German historians in Baden-Baden in 1912. In 1913, he had seen him again in Leipzig, where Rosenstock was teaching constitutional history. Of Jewish origin, but a convert to Protestantism, he had become a fervent and militant Christian. While at that time Rosenzweig still shared the historical relativism of his teacher Friedrich Meinecke, Rosenstock had made belief in the absoluteness of the Revelation the center of his life. During a long nocturnal discussion, Eugen Rosenstock succeeded in shaking Rosenzweig's relativism, not so much with the strength of his arguments as by the living testimony of his faith. At that stage of their dialogue, the encounter between Rosenzweig and Rosenstock was not yet that of Jew and Christian but that of philosophy and Revelation. What Rosenzweig discovered at the end of that discussion was not the specific truth of Judaism or Christianity but the general idea of Revelation. But at the same time, as a good Hegelian, he was convinced that European civilization is basically a Christian civilization and that in that particular historical context, accepting the idea of Revelation objectively means accepting Christianity. It does seem, in fact, that as a result of that discussion, Rosenzweig decided to convert; at any rate, that is what Rosenstock seems to have understood. Three years later, when Rosenzweig decided to remain a Jew, Rosenstock was apparently ignorant of it. Then came the war; the two friends lost touch with one another. It was not until 1916, three years after their discussion in Leipzig, that Rosenstock learned—almost by chance—that Rosenzweig had meanwhile made Judaism the center of his life. Shattered, he then resumed contact with his former friend and discussed with him that inexplicable change (which must have seemed to him as a kind of betrayal). From this point of view, the real point of departure of that correspondence is the question Rosenstock asks Rosenzweig on October 4, 1916: "Why on earth did he get involved in that mess?"

The exchange of letters had begun four months earlier. Until that comment, the two correspondents had carefully avoided broaching subjects that were too personal. But Rosenstock's question—intended as a provocation and taken as such—was to transform the philosophical and theological discussion into a passionate confrontation on which both men staked the very meaning of their life. But the risk was not only intellectual; the two friends were really writing in the shadow of death. Both of them lived through what Rosenzweig would write two years later in the introduction to *The Star of Redemption*: All cognition of the All originates in death. But that anguish—pre-introspective about all else—is itself the symptom of the collective experience of the war, which Rosenzweig described as "blindly opening a chasm in every life." A rupture in the world order referring to evidence shared by both correspondents: 1914 marked the end of an epoch of universal history, for the political collapse of Europe also signified the collapse of values on which its civilization had rested until then.

For Rosenzweig as for Rosenstock, the spirit of that civilization was summed up in the name of Hegel, which became emblematic for both of them. In effect, Hegel's philosophy of history led to the thesis (in which it had an implicit part) that European civilization—which Hegel also called "Germanic"—represented the ultimate stage of universal history, the return of the absolute Spirit to itself, a moment of fulfillment in which the rational coincides with the real and the real with the rational. Even as a student, Rosenzweig had expressed doubts about elevating the present state of Western civilization to such an Absolute. The events of 1914 had definitely shown him—and Rosenstock—that the time of believing in the reign of Reason in history was over. Henceforth, the question for the two correspondents was, How is the new, post-Hegelian epoch of universal history going to look? And more precisely, in this new era of history, what would be the future of religion, or rather, of the two founding religions of the West: Judaism and Christianity?

*

Between Rosenstock's first letter, dated May 1916, and Rosenzweig's last answer, in December that year, an intellectual adventure took place, with its various episodes, its crises, clashes, and misunderstandings, but also moments of intense truth, when each of the two correspondents revealed to the other (and to himself) the ultimate implications of his spiritual choices. At the end of the dialogue, their positions had not changed, but they were definitely clarified; everything that took shelter in a sort of cultural and religious consciousness for each of them at the beginning of the correspondence gradually came to light. Rosenzweig's discourse affirms the irreducible specificity of Judaism, his refusal, in the name of his own vocation, to be absorbed by the surrounding civilization of the Christian West. Rosenstock's argumentation shows mainly Christianity's consciousness of its civilizing mission, which impelled it to be the mainspring of spiritual progress in the world, and its difficulty of allowing the existence of a Judaism that claims to play a central role in the process of salvation.

Leaving aside the wealth of subjects that intersect in this correspondence (one of the most important is certainly that of a chronosophy—a philosophy of time—based on the structure of the calendar) to concentrate on the essential issue, the Judeo-Christian debate, two principal phases can be distinguished: the first, which includes two letters from Rosenzweig (September and October 1916) and two letters from Rosenstock (October 4 and October 28–30) discussing *theology*; the second, which includes Rosenzweig's letter of November 7, Rosenstock's answer dated November 19, and another letter from Rosenzweig of November 30, concerning *history* and *political philosophy*.

In a letter during September, Rosenzweig had answered Rosenstock, who had told him of his amazement at his return to Judaism:

> You have made too light of it before (I have long been an offense to you), because you simply put "the Jew" in inverted commas and lay him on one side as a kind of personal idiosyncrasy, or at best, as a pious romantic of the posthumous influence of a dead great-uncle. You make it difficult for us both, because you ask me to lay bare my skeleton. . . . You can force a living being to commit this anatomical hara-kiri simply from a moralistic compulsion and not from friendly interest.[9]

But when Rosenstock answers him that, from his point of view, this claim of a Jewish identity that would be anything but a "hobby horse" falls under the rubric of what Christian dogma classically defines as "the stubbornness of the Jews" (*die jüdische Verstocktheit*), that he does not understand how a man like Rosenzweig could claim to follow such a "stubbornness," and that all he could do, at the sight of such an absurdity, was to wonder, like Cyrano: "Why on earth did he get involved in that mess?" In spite of himself, Rosenzweig felt forced to proceed with the "anatomical hara-kiri" that so revolted him. In his answer of October 1916, which opens the theological part of the debate as such, Rosenzweig starts with a question Rosenstock had asked him: "The stubbornness of the Jews is, so to speak, a Christian dogma. But is it, can it also be, a Jewish one?"[10]

What is remarkable in Rosenzweig's answer is the *displacement* it makes, the change of perspective it implies. To Rosenstock's obviously *rhetorical* question (no, Jewish obduracy *could not* be a Jewish dogma, for no one can boast of the error he commits), Rosenzweig could answer neither by denying the fact of "stubbornness" (since the claim of Jewish specificity *in effect* implies the rejection of Christianity), nor by justifying it (since it would be a logical contradiction to use an error as an argument), but only by questioning the question itself. Not to deny its pertinence, but to *put it in perspective*, that is, to restore the background that, implicitly, gives it meaning: within the perspective of Christianity, the autonomous existence of Judaism as a specific theological reality appears as "stubbornness," that is, as persevering in error. That same reality, placed instead in the perspective of Judaism, appears as the confirmation of its own truth, as loyalty to itself. Rosenzweig's conceptual task here consists of freeing Judaism from an external view of itself to restore its own sense of itself. Judaism and Christianity are two distinct and parallel realities; in terms of relationship to truth, Judaism has the same right as Christianity to the status and dignity of a "subject of awareness." Until then, "a dogma of Judaism about its relationship to the Church must correspond to the dogma of the Church about its relationship to Judaism."[11]

The issue here is no longer, as in Enlightenment philosophy, to ask for Christian "tolerance" for Judaism, or even, as in the famous parable of "Nathan the Wise," to base the equality of the religions on the fact that, with respect to the unknowable Truth, they are all illusions. The question is rather to show that Judaism and Christianity are equally *true*, or at least that they have equal rights in their relation to truth.

Two years later, in *The Star of Redemption*, Rosenzweig would show that there is no "objective" discourse on truth but that all knowledge refers to truth from a particular point in space and time. Truth is not present in an absolute sense but is revealed *hic et nunc*, always different, to the experience of subjects already placed in one point or another in the world. Thus, knowing would not mean identifying objects of knowledge but rather restoring the visual field in which they appear. The "dialogue" between two subjects would consist, then, not of evoking in turn a supposedly common theme but rather of reexamining the very validity of the question asked; in other words, for each of the two partners, it would be a matter of reframing the question from the various perspectives in which it should, necessarily, appear before them. This is how Rosenzweig proceeds here. For the debate of "Christianity vs. Judaism," which Rosenstock apparently wished to open, Rosenzweig substitutes a twofold putting in perspective: the *image* Christianity makes of Judaism is opposed, as in a double play of mirrors, to the *image* Judaism makes of Christianity.

Thus, Rosenzweig's answer to Rosenstock can be broken down into two logical elements: in the first place, "stubbornness" is not an "objective" attribute of the Jewish people but a category of Christian theology. As a result, the question "How can the Jews conceive of their own stubbornness?" is not relevant. On the other hand, if there is a Jewish view of the world, parallel to the Christian view—and this is certainly what Rosenzweig maintains here—the question must be asked in the following manner: "According to what category does Judaism consider Christianity?" For Rosenzweig, this category is that of the "daughter religion," charged with spreading the idea of monotheism in the world. But Rosenzweig proposed two different interpretations of that idea: one, which he apparently considered superficial, is that of nineteenth-century liberal Judaism that, beyond all dogmatic differences, the Church adopted the great ethical principles of Judaism. To this doubly reductive thesis, since it makes Christianity a simple mouthpiece of Judaism, which is itself reduced to an ethical theism, Rosenzweig seems to prefer the more complex vision presented by a talmudic legend: since the destruction of the Temple, "the Messiah wanders unknown among the peoples, and when he has wandered through them all, then the time of our redemption will have come."

But Rosenzweig's shift of concepts goes even further. It is not only a matter of contrasting two images, that of Judaism in Christianity and that of Christianity in Judaism, but also of understanding how those two images are lived, within two antagonistic consciousnesses, as *truth*. By asking, "What does the Christian theological idea of Judaism mean for the Christian?" and "What does the Jewish theological idea of Christianity mean for the Jew?"[12] Rosenzweig restored its own real-life profundity to the subjectivity of these two points of view. But by describing the Christian *experience* and the Jewish *experience* from within, as it were, Rosenzweig reveals a fundamental asymmetry: the Christian experience of Judaism does not correspond to the Jewish experience of Christianity, but rather to a Jewish experience of Judaism. In *The Star of Redemption*, this asymmetry is raised to the level of a veritable constitutive principle: the mission of outward-turning Christianity is to address the world, while the vocation of introspective Judaism is to identify with itself. This is why, according to Rosenzweig, the idea of the stubbornness of the Jews is expressed, in Christian consciousness, by hatred of the Jews, while the idea of a "daughter religion" is only a *symptom* of Judaism's consciousness of itself. "In its crude state this consciousness takes the form of pride . . . and in its noble, i.e., universal state is expressed in the idea of *election*" (letter of November 7). Because they refer to pure subjectivity, these two reactions, or these two emotions "are both equally narrow and limited."[13]

The evocation, from the very depths of Jewish and Christian subjectivity, of those two antagonistic passions certainly constitutes one of the strongest aspects of this correspondence. It does not express Rosenzweig's ultimate position, but it does represent an attempt to illuminate deeply the roots of the difference dividing Judaism and Christianity. This plunge to the bottom of the cultural unconsciousness of the two religions is no doubt designed to use language to exorcise the latent violence implicit in the rivalry of the two messianisms within the same civilization. Jewish pride, said Rosenzweig, translates the metaphysical belief in the ultimate truth of Judaism into the language of the most extreme subjectivity, just as Christian anti-Semitism expresses an instinctive frustration at Judaism's refusal to "make common cause with the world-conquering fiction of Christian dogma."[14]

It is this refusal "to make common cause" that Rosenzweig reiterated when, in answer to Rosenstock's initial question, he wrote: "Should I 'be converted' when I have been 'chosen from birth'? Is that a real alternative for me? Have I only been thrown into the galley? Is it not *my* ship? I therefore belong to it (what to do? To live and die in it)."[15]

In fact, Rosenzweig's affirmation of the self-sufficiency of Judaism, his provocative refusal to "make common cause," infuriated Rosenstock, roused his "rabies theologica." By standing aside from history, he wrote, Judaism is condemned to sterility:

The teachings and events, which through the continuous stimulus of Christianity have changed the face of the earth during the last thousand years, have as their opposite numbers in Judaism a couple of distinguished names, pressed into the service of the pride of the Synagogue, and otherwise nothing. . . .

The Synagogue has been talking for two thousand years about what she had because she really has absolutely nothing; but she does not experience and will, therefore, not experience what she is. She portrays the curse of self-assurance, or pride in her nobility, and thoughtless indifference towards the law of growth of the united universe.[16]

As for the idea of election, according to Rosenstock, Judaism merely repeats the ancient myth, common to all peoples of antiquity, that they are the center of the world. But in the Jews, that ethnocentrism is sustained by the naïve faith in a hereditary transmission of its "election":

So Israel stands upon its own inalienable rights. This naïve way of thinking that one has won inalienable rights in perpetuity against God, which by nature remain for posterity as properties inherited by bequest, is the relic of blind antiquity in Judaism. The pagan tribes cried, "Sprung from Zeus, nobly born," of themselves. Who believes them? You ought not to say that it is quite unnecessary to believe them, provided that they believed it themselves.[17]

For Rosenstock, the Jewish idea of election no longer has any pertinence in an essentially Christian civilization; it is only an illusion of Jewish consciousness. As Rosenstock sees it, Judaism is an idea that has no future:

The Jew is a paragraph of the Law. C'est tout. You may well believe you have a ship of your own. But you have no idea of the sea or you would not talk like that. You have known no shipwreck; you cannot go astray, you see God with constant clarity, and so you need no mediator, who looks at you when you can no longer look out over the edge of the world and are frustrated in failure. You do not know that the world is movement and change. The Christian says there are day and night. You are so moonstruck that you take the sight of night for the only sight there is, and take the minimum of light, the night, for the all-inclusive idea that embraces day and night! *Lasciate ogni speranza: nondum viventes jam renuntiavistis* ["Renounce all hope: before you came to life, you already have renounced it"].[18]

In this theological confrontation, Rosenstock's lines represent the climax of the crisis. It is a moment of catharsis beyond which the genuine dialogue might be resumed. In his answer (letter of November 7), Rosenzweig stated in the first place that Rosenstock's "rabies theologica" only confirmed his own diagnosis of the roots of Christian anti-Judaism. But above all he tried to calm the debate by showing that, on both sides, it is located inside the same messianic aspiration. As he did systematically in *The Star of Redemption*, Rosenzweig wanted to show that Judaism and Christianity represent two approaches, competing and complementary at the same time, to the same utopia:

For you may curse, you may swear, you may scratch yourself as much as you like, you won't get rid of us. . . . We are the internal foe; don't mix us up with the external one! Our enmity may have to be bitterer than any enmity for the external foe, but all the same—we and you are within the same frontier, in the same Kingdom.[19]

*

In his "theological" letter of October 30, Rosenstock had also approached another aspect of the Judeo-Christian confrontation, that is, the question of "emancipated," that is, secularized Judaism and its status in the economics of salvation. Could a Judaism stripped of its religious references still claim to play a role in the history of Redemption?

By raising this question, Rosenstock opened a new chapter in the development of the debate. Henceforth, the tone changed. On both sides, the theological discussion is replaced by a historical analysis of the status of religion in modern Europe. But of course, the issue was not its legal or political status but its teleological function, as it were, in an increasingly secularized society. For Rosenstock, the duality of the spiritual and the temporal had always defined the very essence of Christianity; in this sense, the modern world represented a challenge for him, but not a radical threat; it was simply that, in the ubiquitous tension between the spiritual and the temporal, the modern world tends to weigh more today. For Judaism, on the other hand, 1789 and the emancipation of the Jews meant a total upheaval. In Western Europe, once the Jews were integrated into the nations where they lived, they progressively moved further away from their beliefs and rituals. In view of the absorption of the Jews into the surrounding civilization, what meaning can the idea of election still have? Hence, in the modern world, is not the only way leading to Redemption that of Christianity?

These questions forced Rosenzweig to return to his conception of election and to specify the meaning that notion can still assume at a time when, in fact, the immense majority of European Jews had merged into the surrounding societies. Once again, Rosenzweig's action was to shift the terms of the question. His concern was to redefine the meaning of the notion of election by distinguishing within it two radically opposed meanings. One is the meaning it has assumed in the historical reality of the modern world: a purely political vision that, according to Rosenzweig, has governed the national consciousness of all European nations since 1789. Revolutionary France was the first nation that believed it was charged with a universal mission to spread the idea of freedom throughout the world. Subsequently, Fichte had wanted to see Germany as the new chosen people. Hegel gave that idea a systematic form, showing that each great civilization, each "historical people," was charged, at a certain moment of its history, with a universal mission to embody a stage of the "absolute Spirit" in the dialectical process of its realization. In this sense, Rosenzweig wrote in *The Star of Redemption*, all peoples are chosen peoples, and all modern wars are holy wars. Turning a classical argument of anti-Jewish polemics against those who used it, Rosenzweig tried here to demonstrate that politicizing the biblical notion of election is the logical consequence of the process of universalizing Jewish categories undertaken by Christianity: nationalism, as a modern form of the belief in election, means "the complete Christianizing of the concept of people."[20]

Nationalism expresses not merely the peoples' belief that they come *from* God (that, as you rightly say, the pagans also believe), but that they go *to* God. But now peoples do have this belief, and hence 1789 is followed by 1914–1917, and yet more "from . . . to's."[21]

Against the background of the world war, launched in the name of the principle of nationalities, where national sentiments, above all, confronted one another, Rosenzweig radically subverted Rosenstock's argument that the idea of election would indicate the "blind antiquity in Judaism" by showing the ravages of national mystiques in a Europe that, by Rosenstock's own admission, was shaped by the spirit of Christianity.[22]

For Rosenzweig, the Jewish concept of election, as formulated in the Bible, is diametrically opposed to that political vision. It could even be argued that it is the spectacle of the catastrophe to which Europe was led by the clash of nationalisms that gave Rosenzweig a kind of negative image of what the Jewish idea of election is *not*. The Jewish idea of election does not denote, as Rosenstock imagined, the almost hereditary transmission of an "inalienable right" but rather the uniqueness of a people that eludes the determinism of history to live the utopia of Redemption as if by anticipation, through the symbolism of its rituals and its own liturgical time. This is the relationship to the future that gives meaning to loyalty to the past; messianism precedes atavism; or, as Rosenzweig later wrote in *The Star of Redemption*, *vocation* is more primeval than *condition*.

That is why even today, when the idea of being elected has become a coloring reagent in every nation, the election of the Jews is something unique, because it is the election of the "one people," and even today our peculiar pride or peculiar modesty, the world's hatred or the world's contempt, rejects an actual comparison with other peoples. Though its content has now become something universal, it has lost nothing of its metaphysical weight. (Its atavism was only a symbol, and only Messianism had real meaning for it.) For it still remains, and will always remain, the only visible actual embodiment of the attained goal of unity [i.e., the

Kingdom] . . . whereas the peoples are only on the way to this desired goal, and must be so, if [the Kingdom] is indeed ever really to be attained.[23]

Rosenzweig answered Rosenstock's charge of ethnocentrism with regard to the Jewish idea of election that, from the beginning, the vocation of the Jewish people has been defined as universal and especially that, in all times, the Jews have paid for it with their suffering. As Rosenzweig was to write in *The Star of Redemption*, it is by testifying to its truth that its veracity is proved. It is this same idea that underlies the passage of his letter to Rosenstock, in which he linked the universality of the Jewish notion of election to the persecutions that have always been its counterpart:

To the "naïve" laying claim to an inalienable right before God corresponds, you forget, just as naïve a taking up of a yoke of inalienable sufferings, which we— "naïvely"? know is laid upon us (cf., the traditional commentary on Isaiah 53).[24]

*

Yet Rosenzweig knew very well that this definition of election as a withdrawal from the stage of history or at least as loyalty to another type of history, which is fundamental in the Jewish tradition, does not answer Rosenstock's major objection, which uses the historical reality of assimilation to claim that modern Judaism no longer has a role to play in the project of salvation. So he included in his definition of the Jewish people a distinction he was to reiterate in *The Star of Redemption*, between a *Judaism of inwardness*, characterized by loyalty to its religious vocation, and a *Judaism of outwardness*, that of the great majority of Jews who are integrated into Western society. For Rosenzweig, internal Judaism, which, in social reality, still exists only in the traditional communities of Central and Eastern Europe, represents the very substance of Judaism in its religious definition, the paradigm of a collective existence concentrated on the margins of history, with its own calendar, its liturgy, and especially its experience of a static time, congealed in waiting for the ultimate Redemption. With relation to that internal truth of Judaism, the life of the assimilated Jews in the West, in fact, represents only a kind of external wrapping, a bark stripped of substance. Rosenzweig was clear that this external Judaism has nothing to do with a metaphysics of election. But it is true that, at the same time, this Judaism never completely merges with the civilization it participates in. In the historical reality of modern Europe, assimilation is never total. And not because the Jews rejected it, but on the contrary, because the surrounding society has always known where to draw its boundaries. Since the Emancipation, those boundaries are certainly not political or legal but are, more subtly, social. It is the societies themselves that define the codes for tolerating the assimilation of the Jews.

Through this analysis, Rosenzweig revealed a contradiction in Rosenstock's argumentation. In his letter of October 30, Rosenstock had claimed on the one hand that the assimilation of the Jews in the modern world had invalidated the very idea of election, while accusing them, on the other hand, of not participating actively in Western history. In his reply, Rosenzweig resolved this contradiction by showing that the first of Rosenstock's two arguments applied to external Judaism, the second to internal Judaism. But if he did not react to the imprecision of the claim that the Jews did not participate actively in the culture of modern Europe (since 1916, he could have cited Marx and Einstein, Freud and Kafka), it is no doubt because, once again shifting Rosenstock's argumentation, he discovered in it some element of truth. It is true, said Rosenzweig, that in the very heart of assimilation, because of the implicit code that societies defined regarding them, the Jews somehow always remained strangers to the culture in which they participate:

Our whole art in the life of the peoples can only be *clam, vi, precario*. No doubt all we can do is hack's work; we must accept the verdict of what people think of us, and we cannot be our own judges (because it is not our own history at which we are working).[25]

This analysis is not very far from the Zionist diagnosis of the status of Judaism in the Europe of nation-states; but, for Rosenzweig, the distance imposed on the Jews by modern societies inadvertently re-creates the otherness that has always been their vocation. In the heart of modernity, the Jew is willy-nilly reminded of his metaphysical identity:

I as an individual take upon myself the metaphysical destiny, the "yoke of the Kingdom of Heaven" to which I have been called from my birth; whether I want to live *principaliter* and *essentialiter* as a Jew . . . , whether I want to take the natural call up into the sphere of metaphysical choice.[26]

The distinction proposed by Rosenzweig in his letter of November 7 between the historical reality of the modern world, dominated by

Christianity, and a metahistory in which the religious vocation of the Jewish people is asserted, provides Rosenstock with a conceptual model whose form he accepts but whose meaning he tries to invert. In his answer dated November 19, he makes two fundamental changes to that model. On the one hand, he rejects the identification of Christianity with the spirit of modern nationalism by adopting the method used by Rosenzweig himself with regard to Judaism, but applying it to Christianity this time: while Rosenzweig distinguished between external Judaism and internal Judaism, Rosenstock introduced an analogous distinction into the notion of Christianity. This, he says, embraces two realities, one temporal and the other spiritual. In fact, Christianity does have its temporal aspect, represented by the institution of the Church, "heir throughout the centuries of dispersion, of the political aspirations, the authority and the form of the Roman Empire." This, in turn, handed down to the nations the spirit of Roman imperialism. Thus, modern nationalism is not nourished by the Christian faith, as Rosenzweig states, but by the Roman political tradition as absorbed by the Church. But behind this external and temporal facet of Christianity was the real Christian faith, which is a spiritual essence. Just as Rosenzweig had refused to admit that the messianic vocation of Judaism had been made obsolete by the assimilation of the Jews, so Rosenstock cannot accept the idea that the spirit of Christianity should henceforth be confused with modern nationalism. Each for his own faith, both claim a status of transcendence relative to the stage of history.

But at the same time, Rosenstock tries to deny Judaism the metahistorical position he demands for Christianity, and by challenging whether, in the modern world, the Jewish people can escape in any way whatever the vast movement of secularization in which all archaisms are abolished:

Today the Western world, Europe, for instance, has come to the point (owing to 1789 and 1914) when it can forget the Old Testament, the Greeks, Romans, Jews and Persians, because it has English, Germans, popes, and so on. . . . Do you believe that Zionism is an accident? Israel's time as the people of the Bible has gone by. The Church . . . is today the Synagogue. The epoch of the eternal Jew comes to an end, just as Basque, Celts, etc., come to an end. . . . As little as Wilamowitz can rescue classical philology from death, can you rescue Hebrew in its metaphysical sense, especially if and just because it will perhaps once again become a language—that is, a national heritage planted in the soil of a people.[27]

In his letter of November 30, Rosenzweig answered Rosenstock's two major arguments, ending a central part of the correspondence, that is, the debate between Judaism and Christianity. In the first place, Rosenzweig reacted to the theory of Christianity proposed by Rosenstock, particularly his distinction between the temporal and spiritual aspects of Christianity. Rosenzweig did not negate the existence of that duality but maintained that, since the beginning of the nineteenth century, it has gradually disappeared. Adopting the model developed by Schelling in his *Philosophy of Revelation*, he distinguished three epochs in the history of Christianity, each under the rubric of the three Apostles, Peter, Paul, and John. The Peter epoch covers the history of Christianity from the establishment of the Church to the Lutheran crisis of the sixteenth century; the Paul epoch, marked by the Reformation, extends to the French Revolution; as for the John epoch, it inaugurates the final phase of the history of Christianity, that is, its realization. For Schelling, the Peter epoch had seen the establishment of the temporal power of the Church, while the Paul epoch had been characterized by a process of internalization of faith. As for the John epoch, it saw the final absorption of Christianity by society; when it has reached this stage, Christianity celebrates its triumph at the same moment when it ceases to appear as a separate religion; as a "human religion," it will henceforth animate the spirit of the modern world from inside. Now, writes Rosenzweig, this idea of Schelling's certainly takes account of the reality of our civilization:

Since 1789 the Church has no longer had a relation to the "State," but only to "Society." . . . The Church has entered on its final (and to use Schelling's own expression) Johannine epoch; that is, it has become without substance. Christianity has only now, since then, become a complete miracle. . . . But now the Church is everything; that is, it is no longer constituted as some particular entity, and it no longer has as its foil a particular reality beyond itself, by which it defines its own particular nature. There is no longer any instituted paganism, nor "Greek" wisdom, nor "Roman" empire: now there is only Christianity.[28]

If Rosenzweig reiterated here the idea supported by Rosenstock, that is, that modernity is but the total secularization of Christianity or the total Christianization of Western civilization, it is to show immediately that that analysis of modernity contradicts Rosenstock's contention that even today, Christianity opens onto two radically separate levels, a temporal level and a spiritual level. For Rosenzweig, there could not be metahistorical Christianity in modern Europe, precisely because Christianity is realized as pure spirituality in a dialectical way, that is, through its identification with the movement of modern civilization itself. This, of course, is in contrast to Judaism, which, in its most internal essence, escapes the vagaries of history; hence, the central role of "self-identification" in the spiritual destiny of the Jewish people. Unlike Christianity, whose role in the process of salvation is to enter history to accompany the nations in their march toward Redemption, the vocation of the Jewish people is essentially to remain true to itself. But for Rosenzweig, self-identification as a constitutive principle of the Jewish people does not define only its "religious" core but also that external Judaism that, since Emancipation, has participated in the history of Europe:

Christianity identifies itself with the empires (the world of today), and Judaism identifies itself with itself (the example: Zionism). So, in this Christian world, which owing to the ever-increasing fulfillment of Johannine universalism becomes more and more devoid of sensible perception and substance, Judaism is the only point of contraction and of limitation and is, thereby, the guarantee of the reality of that Christian world. If it were not so, there would merely be the "empires."[29]

Thus, at the end of the debate, nothing is resolved. But it is precisely the irrevocable otherness of Judaism and Christianity that was to become the cornerstone of the theory of truth developed in *The Star of Redemption*. Every person, every society, and every nation attest to the aspect of truth revealed through their specific condition and vocation. But the multiplicity of situations experienced is ultimately subsumed in the duality of the two great religious cultures of the West, Judaism and Christianity. Each of them embodies a particular relationship to Redemption. That there are thus two paradigms of Redemption rather than only one conveys the ultimate finitude of the human condition.

2

Hegel Taken Literally

In a letter written in 1910, eight years before the publication of *The Star of Redemption*, Franz Rosenzweig declared:

> Every act becomes guilty as soon as it penetrates into history . . . ; this is why God must save man not through history, but really as "God of religion." Hegel considers history as divine, as a theodicy, while action for him is naturally profane. . . . For us, religion is the only authentic theodicy. The struggle against history in the meaning of the 19th century is for us the same as the struggle for religion in the meaning of the 20th century.[1]

At that time, Rosenzweig was studying with Meinecke at the University of Fribourg, immersed in the study of Hegel's philosophy of history. One year later, he began writing his doctoral dissertation on "Hegel and the State," which would not be published until 1920, when he and the outside world had radically changed. The year 1913 was marked by a double spiritual crisis; in July, Rosenzweig was about to convert to Christianity; in October, he decided to remain a Jew: a dialectical movement ending in the discovery of rediscovered Judaism, beyond assimilation, rich with all the prestige of the universal. The other crucial experience was the war, which presented Rosenzweig with the two facts that formed the basis of his entire philosophy: the bloody clash of the European states in the name of the principle of nationalities, and more profoundly, in the name of the resulting national mystique, which both confirms and condemns the Hegelian vision of history as the stage on which the constitution of the universal spirit is fulfilled, through the clashes of sovereign states, just as the experience of anguish at death reveals the hidden truth of Hegelian ontology as a system of Totality, that is, the negation of the irreducible uniqueness of the person.

Thus, by the time *Hegel and the State* was published, Rosenzweig already considered his book obsolete: "In the present circumstances," he declared in a preface dated 1920, "I would never have undertaken to write it."[2] Yet, without *Hegel and the State*, *The Star of Redemption* probably could not have been conceived. Or it would have been a completely different book: for despite its almost abstract rigor, what gives that thought its real force is precisely its permanent (although often implicit) reference to the historical reality of its time.

Yet, in that 1910 text, Rosenzweig already seemed to have a premonition of the two main themes underlying the thought of *The Star of Redemption* in 1918–1919: "The battle between history in the sense of the nineteenth century," and at the same time, the battle for "religion in the sense of the twentieth century." For Rosenzweig, "history in the sense of the nineteenth century" was history as Hegel had defined it, that is, the development and realization of Spirit through the series of its metamorphoses; in other words, a history both necessary and intelligible, and whose judgments are those of Reason itself. In another form, this is the concept he rediscovered in his teacher Meinecke, who had just shown in *Cosmopolitanism and the National State* that the history of Germany in the nineteenth century had to be read as a gradual liberation from the universalism of the Enlightenment, and as a patient march toward political realism as a necessary condition of the creation of a unified German state. In 1910, it was a rejection of the Bismarckian state and its "stifling narrowness" that led to Rosenzweig's reservations about the German school of historiography, and his condemnation of Hegel's philosophy of history, which, he claimed, supports its ideology: "Every act becomes guilty as soon as it penetrates into history": Rosenzweig was probably thinking here of Bismarck's establishment of the German Empire "by iron and fire."[3] In 1919, after the collapse of Germany, it is the judgment of history—ultimate irony—that condemns Hegel: "When a world collapses, the ideas that had given birth to it, the dreams that had penetrated it, also disappear under the ruins."[4]

In 1910, did Rosenzweig counter that "history in the sense of the nineteenth century" with *another history*, "history in the sense of the twentieth century"? Apparently not. It would take the crisis of 1913, the trauma of the war, and especially the correspondence of 1916–1917 with Eugen Rosenstock for emergence of the idea of a discontinuous, nonaccumulative history to emerge, a history marked not by the sequence of great civilizations and major political events but by the unique occurrence of qualitatively significant facts endowed with a symbolic value, whose sequence, under the pomp of apparent history (and sometimes against it), outlines the invisible advent of Redemption in the world. In *The Star of Redemption*, this conception of a holy History, both immanent in profane history and different from it, is attributed to Christianity. Rosenzweig would conceive of the idea of a collective existence that is radically alien— at least in principle—to profane history that, in *The Star of Redemption*, defined the mode of being specific to the Jewish people, only a few years later, as the reverse of the Hegelian theory of history at a time when the catastrophe of 1914–1918 confirmed to him that it was correct, and thus revealed its absolute perversity.

In 1910, Rosenzweig still defined "religion in the sense of the twentieth century" in contrast to history. That probably means, in the first place, that for Rosenzweig, "religion in the sense of the twentieth century" would be the belief in history as theodicy. But to set the rulings of history as ultimate criteria of all value judgment is to renounce the transcendence of ethics, to forget that history itself can and must be judged. Thus, "religion in the sense of the twentieth century" must be understood as the personal relation of man to God, man's demand for his own irreplaceable responsibility beyond the logic that claims to make him a simple actor on the anonymous stage of history. The contrast of history and religion would find its definitive form in *The Star of Redemption* as a duality of the System and of Revelation, the System indicating the Totality of the Hegelian type where man is included as a simple object (a "he"), while Revelation is the event in which man awakens to his original reality of a personal subject.

*

In *The Star of Redemption*, the critique of history is closely connected to a critique of politics. Both can be understood only on the background of Hegel's philosophy of history as revealed particularly at the end of the *Principles of the Philosophy of Right*. The systematic nature of this reference to Hegel can be grasped by comparing the developments devoted to the critique of politics in the third part of *The Star of Redemption*[5] with the chapter on the state in *Philosophy of Right*,[6] on the one hand, and the commentary on that same chapter in *Hegel and the State*,[7] on the other. This shows that the book on Hegel mediates between *Philosophy of Right* and *The Star of Redemption*: on the one hand, Rosenzweig worked there as a historian of ideas by underlining the continuity between Hegel's metaphysics and his political philosophy; but at the same time—discreetly in the parts of the work written before 1914, openly in the conclusion dated 1920—he did not abstain from taking a position against a theory that, in the name of a metaphysics of the Absolute, seems to justify in advance the political cynicism of the Bismarckian state. In *The Star of Redemption*, the account of "messianic politics," which is that of nations—in contrast to the metahistorical existence of the Jewish people—is closely inspired, but with no direct reference to Hegel, by the sections of *Philosophy of Right* that dealt with the nature of the state (§257 and §258), war (§324 to §340), and especially universal history (§341 and §360), as Rosenzweig had commented on them in the chapter of *Hegel and the State* devoted to the metaphysics of the state in *Philosophy of Right*.

What matters here, as much as and perhaps more than the ideas developed by Rosenzweig, is his way of proceeding, the form of his reasoning, or the combination of what Emmanuel Levinas has called his "operative gestures."[8] For Rosenzweig, the issue was not to prove that the Hegelian view of history is false, but on the contrary, to show that it is true, far beyond what Hegel himself could imagine. In other words, to demonstrate the intrinsic perversity of such a philosophy, it is enough to show its workings, to follow its verification in the reality of contemporary history, in short, to take it *literally*. Here we must start from the idea that, for Rosenzweig, neither Hegel's ontology nor his philosophy of history can be grasped; his ontology as a system of Totality, his philosophy of history as a narrative of the becoming of the absolute Mind include in advance every possible contradiction by understanding it as a (necessary) element of the System. One cannot get out of this closed universe; one can only locate oneself *elsewhere*. Faced with the system of Being, this elsewhere is the I who, in the anguish at death, proclaims the evidence of his autonomous existence; as for the dialectic of universal history, it is concrete historical reality, the irrefutable horror of war experienced, that exposes its true face.

Thus, Rosenzweig's first "operative gesture" consisted of letting the Hegelian view of history be judged against the background of contemporary political reality: an exacerbated nationalism of nations, violence of states, wars, and revolutions. The spectacle of the Europe of nation-states collapsing in fire and blood provided tragic confirmation of the correctness of the Hegelian theses, a confirmation that is precisely their condemnation. Of course, between those two elements, there is a difference of logical status: the confirmation is immanent in the system (history certainly unfolds according to the principles analyzed by Hegel), while the condemnation is a moral one, hence external to the system, insofar as it rejects its axioms. These were defined by Hegel himself in a remarkable passage of *Philosophy of Right*:

Herein is to be found the ethical element in war. War is not to be regarded as an absolute evil. It is not merely external accident, having its accidental grounds in the passions of powerful individuals or nations, in acts of injustice or in anything which ought not to be. Accident befalls that which is, by nature, accidental, and this fate is a necessity. So from the standpoint of the conception and in philosophy the merely accidental vanishes, because in it, as it is a mere appearance, is recognized its essence, namely, necessity. . . . [W]ar makes short work of the vanity of temporal things. It is the element by which the idealization of what is particular receives its right and becomes an actuality. Moreover, by it, as I have elsewhere expressed it,[9] "finite pursuits are rendered unstable, and the ethical health of peoples is preserved. Just as the movement of the ocean prevents the corruption which would be the result of perpetual calm, so by war people escape the corruption which would be occasioned by a continuous or eternal peace."[10]

What Rosenzweig rejected here is not the idea that war is a necessity of history, but the fundamental axiom in Hegel that that necessity—insofar as it is assumed by the state—is the expression of morality. For Rosenzweig, the place from which war (and the universal history of which it is an element) can be judged is precisely in the contingency of the I—a contingency prior to every system. Thus, this first operative gesture rests, to some extent, on the principle of *quotation*: of taking the Hegelian discourse out of its context, that is, out of the book where it slumbers innocently, and transposing it, as is, to a radically different context, that of the reality of the world itself. A technique that is less like a reversal of Hegelian theses than a diversion of them: on the stage of history, they finally speak their real language.

Rosenzweig's second operative gesture comes from the Hegelian idea that the civilization of Christian Europe constitutes the fulfillment of universal history, or in other words, that it realizes the truth of it. If Hegel is taken literally, this truth, as revealed by the beginning of the twentieth century, is not, as he wrote at the end of *The Philosophy of Right*, "the true atonement and reconciliation . . . unfolds the state as the image and reality of reason,"[11] but on the contrary the surrender of the states to the outburst of national passions. Like many men of his generation, Rosenzweig in fact lived the war of 1914–1918 not as the most recent of military conflicts that punctuated the history of modern Europe but as the end of a civilization. If what Hegel defined as the last stage of universal history ends in catastrophe, it is—in Hegelian terms—universal history itself that is condemned.

For Rosenzweig, the world war could no longer be considered an element of the dialectic of the Mind; it is a brand-new type of war and, as such, it absolutely goes beyond, and at the same time absolutely fulfills, the Hegelian idea of universal history. By the same token, the question is raised again of the place from which that condemnation of universal history is uttered. Certainly, initially, it is the I who, in the experience of anguish at death, rebels against the idea of an intelligible All and, right there, irrevocably compromises the rebellion. And insofar as this experience, universal as it may be, is lived at its extreme in the reality of war, it is really through war—and consequently through universal history whose necessary manifestation according to Hegel it is—that the I initiates its divorce from the system of Totality. But on the other hand—and it is here that the central paradox of Rosenzweig's thought probably takes shape—this has remained too Hegelian to admit that the I, that is, the private man, can challenge the power of universal history on his own.

The whole economy of *The Star of Redemption* is based on the transition from personal existence, dominated by the experience of Revelation, to collective existence, which alone can bring Redemption.[12] This is conceived in terms of a utopia as a final condition of the world, hence of history, and there are really two collective entities, that is, Christianity and the Jewish people, who are the agents of its advent. Hence the paradox of a history that is not registered in universal history, but is located outside of it, and somehow against it. As if universal history, condemned by the catastrophe that completes and fulfills it at the same time, suddenly showed, beyond itself, its secret lining, its invisible reverse side, or its own negative image: a term-by-term reversal where everything that, in the Hegelian view of history, is "serious, sorrow, patience, and negative labor" is reversed to draw the same figure of the positive aspect.[13] This history outside history, this temporality without becoming, this sociality without wars or revolutions defined Rosenzweig's ideal space, which is that of the Jewish people.

With relation to the history of Christian Europe, marked on the one hand by the gradual formation of states, their rivalries and alliances, by battles and treaties, and on the other hand by the slow becoming of a civilization, the Jewish people seems to have lived for twenty centuries in a kind of nonhistory or antihistory, which Rosenzweig defined as a meta-history: static temporality, structured year after year by the identical cycle of religious holidays, a lived eternity, from today, in the spaces of sacred time, and that, simply because a people testifies to it, proclaims the belligerent agitation of universal history.

Hence, it would not be precise to say that the Jewish people lives outside of all history; its nonhistoricity is relative; it denotes the place of an absence in universal history, or in the consciousness the West has shaped of that history. Not because the events that mark the history of the Jewish people are different from those that constitute universal history but, more fundamentally, because the temporality underlying the collective existence of the Jewish people is radically different from that which constitutes the historical consciousness of the West. According to Rosenzweig, in the specific experience of its sacred time, the Jewish people lives a parallel history, *another history*.

*

In *Hegel and the State*, Rosenzweig emphasized the bond linking Hegel's philosophy of history with his ontology. Starting from Hegel's famous formula about the identification of the real and the rational, he underlined the ambivalence of that equation, which can in fact be interpreted in two opposite ways: either as the definition of the rational by the real or as the definition of the real by the rational, which would, on the other hand, pose an absolute idealism. Of course, it is precisely the dialectical identification of those two propositions that Hegel maintains. But Rosenzweig noted that as long as that identification remains formal, that is, *reversible*, it necessarily remains tautological. "For that equation to become applicable," he wrote, "the equal sign must be replaced by the time factor which, because it is irreversible and flows in only one direction, is alone capable of making it unequivocal."[14] Thus, for the identification of the real and the rational to be realized, it must go from a purely formal dialectic to a historical dialectic. This identification is not given from the start but is gradually constituted through the historical process: "Thus the ambivalent idea that only the rational is real but only the real is rational takes the form of an unequivocal proposition, that of universal history as universal judgment. . . . It is only because universal history is universal judgment pronouncing its irrevocable sentences in the name of the law of Reason that the real is rational."[15] That is certainly what Hegel had maintained in *The Philosophy of Right* (§342):

Moreover, world history is not a court of judgment whose principle is force, nor is it the abstract and irrational necessity of a blind fate. It is self-caused and self-realized reason and its actualized existence in spirit is knowledge. Hence, its development issuing solely out of the conception of its freedom is a necessary development of the elements of reason. It is, therefore, an unfolding of the spirit's self-consciousness and freedom. It is the exhibition and actualization of the universal spirit.[16]

Hence, in *The Star of Redemption*, criticism of universal history and criticism of ontology are connected. In the introduction to the work, it is on the background of the war that the self questions the omnipotence of the system of Totality, defined in the Hegelian manner by the identification of Being and knowing. Conversely, it is the rupture of Totality, the separation of the elements, the emergence in Revelation of man as a being outside the world, that allows the deduction (and not only the empirical description) in the third part of *The Star of Redemption* of the Jewish people as a people outside history. For Rosenzweig, the tyranny of history and the tyranny of the Logos are two sides of the same oppression.

In *Hegel and the State*, Rosenzweig shows clearly how universal history is formed through the flowering and triumph, and then the decline and obliteration of the various nations. For Hegel, history is presented as the stage of a vast metaphysical drama where each nation plays its role and disappears:

Each nation represents a stage in the process (of becoming aware of itself of the universal Spirit). . . . The flowering [of a nation] consists of reaching the stage where it becomes "universal," that is, where the essence of the universal proceeds from it.

Its decadence consists of persevering in that stage while universal history wants to continue to progress. Whether it disappears or persists painfully to survive no longer interests universal history, which has already chosen another nation as its representative.[17]

Hence, the subversion of Hegelian ideas that Rosenzweig undertook in *The Star of Redemption* can be clearly understood. Hegel is certainly right, he said: the death of nations is recorded in universal history. But only on condition that they participate in that history. Imagine a nation living outside of it: that absence, which, in Hegelian terms, would no doubt mean the renunciation of life itself, would at the same time be the only possible guarantee of eternity. Thus, in Rosenzweig, the nations of the earth, subject to the inevitable laws of the historical process, are contrasted with the Jewish people, which, living on the margins of history, thus escapes the necessity that guides it. The Jewish people, therefore, "must renounce full, active participation in their life";[18] in the timelessness of their liturgy, "it is separated from the march of those who draw near to it (redemption) in the toil of centuries." This is not through indifference to the fate of the world, but on the contrary, because through the forms of its ritual life, more particularly, its specific temporality, it anticipates from today—not historically, but symbolically—the goal toward which the nations are headed. It is this advance in the realm of the symbolic that it pays for with its historical "infertility"; but on the other hand, that is what guarantees its permanence.

This "quietist" vision of the Jewish people raises many questions. While considering *The Star of Redemption* the major work of Jewish philosophy in the twentieth century, Gershom Scholem accused Rosenzweig, not incorrectly, of transforming the Jewish people into a Church.[19] Without detailing the discussion, Rosenzweig himself brought two nuances to the discussion of his thesis. In the first place, in *The Star of Redemption*, Rosenzweig clearly distinguished between the spiritual essence of the Jewish people, defined by its religious tradition, and its concrete historical reality. He saw the first embodied in the Jewish communities before Emancipation, living apart from the surrounding society, loyal to their belief and their faith, and which, in the early twentieth century, still formed the large majority of Central and Eastern European Jewry. It is this Judaism of faith he had just discovered himself, first in the Balkans and then in Poland, that represented for Rosenzweig the paradigm of the authentic Jewish vocation. On the other hand, there is an external aspect of the Jewish people, formed by the mass of emancipated Jews who have participated in the political and social history of the West since the French Revolution. In this sense, movements like assimilation or Zionism indicate a process of secularization that is probably inevitable; but precisely because of that, this entrance into history (which, for Rosenzweig, was necessarily a Hegelian type of history) represented a new fundamental challenge to the metahistorical essence of the Jewish people.

Rosenzweig subsequently corrected that thesis: while continuing to maintain that the religious vocation of the Jewish people, in principle, transcends history, he had to admit that, in its present stage of secularization, it could probably not test that vocation in and through its historical commitments. Wondering about the theoretical status of Zionism in his own vision of history, in his correspondence between 1922 and 1927, he articulated more precisely the two realms of the political and the religious. In the modern reality, the Jewish people was not seen to lead a collective life modeled on the communities of the eighteenth century, even if such a form of life in principle embodied its highest vocation. In 1920s Germany, to claim such a radical extraterritoriality, when none of the conditions necessary for its realization were given (and, whose spiritual demands no one would be willing to assume), would only be "an excuse for our need for comfort," Rosenzweig wrote in 1924. In this sense, the idea of the metahistorical vocation of the Jewish people, as he discussed it in *The Star of Redemption*, must be understood not as the theory of a political practice—precisely that of a nonparticipation of the Jews in their own history—but as a guiding idea, that of "the limit imposed on all politics."[20] Hence, the religious vocation of the Jewish people will be interpreted less as an absence in history than as a distance taken with regard to it, less as a negation of politics than as a *critique of politics*. Its role will not consist, as in Hegel, of putting itself in the service of universal history, but on the contrary, of subjecting each of its elements to an ethical judgment.

*

Rosenzweig's critique of the Hegelian vision of history centered on the question of modern nationalism. Here, Rosenzweig parted from the notion of "national spirit" (*Volksgeist*) as Hegel developed it in *The Philosophy of Right* to expose in it the very principle of messianic nationalism in whose name the European states were tearing each other apart in the early twentieth century. In fact, for Hegel, the universal Spirit is embodied alternatively in the specific principles of the different nations; the "national spirit" of each nation is then defined as the specific form the universal spirit assumes. All "historical nations" are aware of that mission set for them; they each know at the moment destiny calls them that they are privileged agents of history and that, through their "national spirit," the universal is fulfilled. According to Hegel, this mission they know they are assigned confers on them the right to regulate their history as they like:

> To the nation, whose natural principle is one of these stages, is assigned the accomplishment of it through the process characteristic of the self-developing self-consciousness of the world spirit. In the history of the world this nation is for a given epoch dominant, although it can make an epoch but once (§346). In contrast with the absolute right of this nation to be the bearer of the current phase in the development of the world-spirit, the spirits of other existing nations are void of right, and they, like those whose epochs are gone, count no longer in the history of the world.[21]

This messianic nationalism is based on the idea that history is a fulfillment of a sense, that this sense translates an absolute truth, and that "historical nations" are somehow spontaneously initiated into that truth. History as theodicy, as an inevitable march toward the *eskatos*, but also an extreme sacralization of politics, an absolute legitimation, for the "historical nations" of their specific ambitions. In his correspondence of 1916–1917, Rosenzweig had located the origin of this messianic nationalism in the spirit of the French Revolution. In his evocation of the "dominant nation," Hegel had been inspired by Napoleonic France. As for Fichte, he had claimed for Germany the role of a new chosen people.[22] In the nineteenth century, national aspirations claimed the right of each nation to play its role on the stage of history; colonial imperialism found its legitimacy in the "civilizing mission" of the most enlightened nations; in 1914, the conflicting powers had all claimed the role of the "dominant nation" at one time or another. But Rosenzweig needed a singular clairvoyance to foresee that the twentieth century was going to be marked by an intensification of political messianisms, by the emergence of eschatological ideologies demanding the rights conferred on them by the awareness of the sense of history, and by the proliferation of "national models" with universal pretensions.

The other source of this modern nationalism is the biblical idea of *election*. And this is where the subversion of the Hegelian theses in Rosenzweig's philosophy appears in its full radicalism. For Rosenzweig, in fact, what is denoted by the concept of election (and always has been denoted in the Jewish tradition) is the *peculiarity* of the Jewish people, that is, precisely its *metahistorical* status, in contrast to the essentially historical existence of the nations. Election, as an exception to the common fate, defines this place as external to the historical stage where the Jewish people lives its specific relation to its rites and its law: not a privileged presence in history, as Hegel grants to "dominant nations," but on the contrary, an absence in history, or at least a critical distance from it. It is both the "distance that the Pharisees invented from the states of the Diaspora" and the distance introduced by the prophets who, in the period of independence of a Jewish kingdom, practiced a "revolutionary critique of their own state."[23] Initially and casually, Rosenzweig defused here a central argument in the anti-Jewish polemic of the Enlightenment (itself a certain continuation of the Christian apologetic) about the biblical notion of the "chosen people" and the idea of a historical superiority it was supposed to imply. But the essence of Rosenzweig's "operative gesture" consists of turning the idea of election on those same people who had always denounced it: in the Hegelian vision of history, all historic peoples are chosen peoples.

But if, as we shall see in the analysis of the last paragraphs of *The Philosophy of Right*, to be fulfilled throughout history, the universal Spirit successively chose the Eastern empire, Greece, then Rome, it is in Christian Europe (which Hegel calls the Germanic Empire) that the historic peoples reach the stage where they become conscious of this nomination and where they identify themselves, in that consciousness itself, with the process of the objective realization of the absolute Spirit: a final stage of the dialectic of the Spirit, which Rosenzweig summarizes as "that stage when they know how far God's will is realized in the warlike destinies of their states."[24] What Hegel described in *The Philosophy of Right* is the emergence of modern nationalism as a secularized form of the idea of election. But for Rosenzweig, this secularization was only the last avatar of a much older process linked with the transformation worked by Christianity in the central categories of Judaism. In fact, the fundamental project of Christianity is not to abolish the religious categories that come from Judaism but to universalize them. Thus, in a certain sense, Hegel remained loyal to the very inspiration of Christianity, since he stated the thesis that all nations can appear, at a given moment, as charged with a historical mission by the universal Spirit. But by the same token, he stripped the idea of election of the metahistorical connotation it had in Judaism, to thrust it, so to speak, into the immanence of history. "Nationalism," Rosenzweig wrote in 1917, "is the absolute Christianization of the idea of nation. That means that nations no longer only believe that they are of divine origin . . . but also that they are going *toward* God."[25]

In *Hegel and the State*, Rosenzweig emphasized a "strange contradiction" in the Hegelian conception of the "Germanic Empire," that is, Christian Europe, as the last stage of the history of the Spirit. In the scheme of universal history, while different nations appear and disappear in turn on the stage of history, the European world, dominated by Christianity, cannot disappear. "There is no new 'historic nation' that can come take its place as Christianity took the place of the Roman world."[26] In this sense, the European world is both historical (since it is still part of the dialectic of universal history) and metahistorical (since nothing can come after it). Formally, Hegel resolved this difficulty by maintaining that, in the case of the "Germanic world," the dialectical process takes place *inside* the community of European nations; the different Western nations do in fact appear and disappear in turn, while the community itself is destined as such to last forever. But in historical reality, ambiguity still remains: each European nation is *at the same time* both a fleeting moment in the history of Spirit and an element of a civilization in which history is accomplished.

According to Rosenzweig, this ambiguity reflects a more fundamental difficulty connected with the very postulates of Hegel's philosophy of history. In effect, for him, universal history is articulated according to the same laws as the history of religions. This leads to Christianity as its culmination. Thus, this will appear both as the historical (and somehow phenomenal) principle of a given civilization—in this case, that of Europe—and as the truth of the historical process in general. "Christianity," wrote Rosenzweig, "with its tendency to realize Reason, became [for Hegel] the archetype of the agreement between the rational and the real."[27] In other words, it is both the phenomenon to be explained and at the same time the law of its explanation. This is the crux of Rosenzweig's critique of Hegel's philosophy of history: the universal idea in Hegel is itself historically dated; it denotes simply the Christian vision of history; this is why it must necessarily leave out the realities that disturb its order—as, for example, the permanence of the Jewish people. Thus, there is the real outside the system: this real denotes, in this precise case, the metahistorical space of the Jewish people, or, if you like, the exact measure of metahistorical space the Jewish people has been able to preserve.

Utopia and Redemption

The notion of redemption is probably the central category of Rosenzweig's thought. In his system, that term denotes not the relationship between God and man, or between God and the world, but the relationship of man to the world, the movement of human initiative that turns to reality to act on it. Like the other two categories that Rosenzweig saw as structuring our experience (Creation and Revelation), Redemption is present in the forms of the language: it is through the first-person plural on the one hand and the future tense on the other that we express our nostalgia for a better world. Thus, for Rosenzweig, Redemption is a category of collective experience, and it is lived essentially in the mode of *waiting*. In fact, the world appears to us as fundamentally unfinished; the idea of a definitively accomplished reality can be given to us only in the future, as the representation of what is not yet. That final state of the world, which Rosenzweig called the Kingdom, is always conceived as an ultimate limit of what is to be attained.

But how to get to that impassible term, that to-come on a different scale from our present? Here Rosenzweig distinguished two radically different modalities of our relationship with that absolute idea: one is *historic*; the other is *symbolic*. In fact, the relationship between the present moment and the final accomplishment of all things can be imagined as a long march, a continuous process developing from one stage to another, through the time of history. This idea of a long progression of an initial condition to a final condition whose vector is historical time borrows both from the theological vision of a providential history and from the model of time of Newtonian mechanics, a time at once linear, continuous, and irreversible. It is probably no accident that the modern idea of historical progress was born in the age of Enlightenment when the Christian vision of providential history, discredited in its theological form by the attacks of philosophical criticism, was taken over by belief in a historical causality conceived on the model of physical causality. History appears here as if it is oriented, as if it is leading from a less to a more, that is, as bearing a double meaning, endowed both with an unequivocal direction and a clearly decipherable signification. In Hegel, then in Marx, history is certainly the medium through which meaning is realized, the path on which humanity marches inevitably toward its glorious completion.

But for Rosenzweig, this view of history was inspired mainly by the theory of evolution and is based on an almost organic perception of historical time; this would be animated by a finality comparable in every point to that recorded in the heart of life. And if, as we shall see, Rosenzweig refused to consider history as the privileged path to Redemption, it is precisely because he regarded it as marked by the whole impetus, but also by all the limitations of life itself. Like the Romantic theoreticians, Rosenzweig in fact thought that "institutions, societies, feelings, things, and works" participate in their way in the great current of life.[1] Yet, if this organic metaphor must be taken seriously, it implies that history, like biological evolution, is made of a permanent tension between the forces of life and the forces of death. Most profoundly, this conflict characterizes organic time and, consequently, that of history. For Rosenzweig, history is marked by an essential incompleteness, not only because of the incessant alternation of moments of life and moments of death but especially because each instant is made of a tension between those antagonistic tendencies. This is why the final victory of life will always remain uncertain; similarly, nothing guarantees that the history of humanity will end with the triumph of Good. That is certainly a hope recorded in each human act; but the realization of that hope must inevitably be postponed from day to day, as a horizon that retreats indefinitely as we approach it. It is this idea of an ideal end, an endless movement toward an impossible goal that, in contrast to the idea of Redemption, we agree to call *utopia*.

It is precisely that the idea of an end of history is inconceivable, except as a notion-limit, in other words, that it is essentially *asymptotic*, that motivates the incompatibility of historical time with the idea of Redemption. This idea, strictly considered, necessarily implies the completion of everything, the resolution of all contradictions, the end of the temporal continuum. Thus, it signifies a violent rupture of the historical fabric, the eruption into the heart of time of an absolute otherness, a form of experience radically different from everything we know. In this sense, Redemption is contrasted with utopia as a present event to an ideal end that is always postponed, as a stasis of time on an indefinitely extended line, as a sudden illumination at the endless series of moments. As a category of historical time, utopia proposes to the imagination only a new combination of elements already known; Redemption, on the other hand, rises up against all waiting, with the unpredictability of the brand-new. Hence, Rosenzweig's critique of the idea of progress, understood as infinite process, is supposed to lead humanity, almost necessarily, to its ideal flourishing. Hence, too, the rejection of Hegel's philosophy of history: not only because the vision of history as theodicy, as the stage on which God's judgment is played, justifies, in the name of the Absolute, the triumph of the victors and the disappearance of the vanquished, but also because on the horizontal axis of historical time, nothing radically new can occur, especially not that qualitative leap into an absolutely *other* reality implied by Redemption.

Rosenzweig contrasted the idea of historical time perceived as a river flowing endlessly toward an ever-fleeing estuary, or as an arrow shot at an unattainable target, on the one hand, with the human experience of the future, particularly our relationship to the idea of the end of history, on the other. A paradoxical relationship insofar as that history has no end, but where man cannot give up the idea of an end of history. The hope that someday human suffering will cease, the world will know an "eternal peace" (in Kant's terms) continues—despite everything history teaches us—to underlie the utopian aspirations of humanity. But if it does not want to remain a simple "guiding idea," such a hope implies the belief that its realization can, in principle, appear at any moment. At its most profound, human hoping will never be satisfied with the idea of an unlimited progress, an "infinite task" that never succeeds. The metaphor of the endless road indefinitely bringing us closer to a goal that is always retreating from us has always been contrasted, by human hoping, with the spontaneous conviction that the world can be regenerated "here and now." It is this "messianic impatience" that, for Rosenzweig, defines the specifically human relationship to the future. Before being a religious belief, this impatience constitutes the very essence of hoping. It would always demand somehow that the end of history can be anticipated, that it can occur at any moment, perhaps tomorrow. The idea of the ever possible imminence of Redemption is thus contrasted radically with the idea of the unlimited distance separating us from the realization of utopia. In other words, if utopia is declared at the start as a category of the imaginary (its essential function is less to anticipate the future than to declare the present situation), authentic hoping (which, for Rosenzweig, concerns the possibility of Redemption) is always lived as waiting for an upheaval that can occur at any moment.

*

Rosenzweig saw those two forms of relating to the future as referring to two contrasting conceptions of the infinite: a quantitative one in which infinity is made up of the endless addition of discrete units as a line that can be extended indefinitely; and a qualitative one in which infinity denotes an abundance, an absolute magnitude, not comparable to any measure of the senses. From this point of view, historical time is the symbol par excellence of quantitative infinity, since it can be represented as an axis that can be extended indefinitely, while qualitative infinity is incommensurate with time, and can be thought only at odds with it, as a form of radical otherness. Thus, waiting for Redemption is contrasted to utopia as the hope of suddenly seeing a radically new world occur is contrasted with the slow progression on the tedious road of time.

But how can Redemption, defined thus as an essentially *metahistorical* event, occur on the endless path of historical time? How can infinite abundance, conceived as incommensurate with the sum total of finite magnitudes, be manifested at the core of our endless infinity? Yet, the idea of Redemption implies precisely the possibility of its imminent occurrence. It is this paradox that Rosenzweig tried to resolve with a mathematical metaphor, in a letter dating from the period when he conceived *The Star of Redemption*:

What does the irrational number mean in relation to the rational? For rational numbers, infinity is an always unattainable limit, a forever *improbable* magnitude, even if it is of the order of certainty, of permanent truth. With irrational numbers, on the contrary, at each of its points, that limit comes up against rational numbers, almost physically, with the presence specific to numbers, thus liberating it from its abstract, linear and one-dimensional nature (from which its hypothetical status also proceeds), to confer a "spatial" totality and an obvious reality on it. In the form of the infinitesimal number, infinity is the secret spring, forever invisible, of the rational number and its visible reality. On the other hand, through the irrational number, infinity is manifested, becomes visible, while forever remaining an alien reality: a number that is not a number, or so to speak, a "non-number."[2]

The contrast of the rational number and the irrational number corresponds here to the antinomy of quantitative infinity and qualitative infinity, or, if you like, accumulative infinity and abundance infinity. The indefinite series of decimals of a rational number refers to the "infinite bad" of the endless progression, while, for Rosenzweig, the incommensurate nature of the irrational numbers refers to a radically different mathematical space. The specific properties of these two forms of infinity are then contrasted term by term: while the infinity of the rational number appears as an unattainable limit, the infinity of the irrational number attests to the presence of an absolutely *different* dimension within the world of numbers. On the other hand, the infinite-limit of the rational number is only an abstract notion, while infinity is concretely present in the very reality of the irrational number. Moreover, Rosenzweig contrasts the linear and one-dimensional nature of the sequence of decimals with the "spatial totality" of the irrational number. Similarly, the principle of unlimited progression, that is, of the "infinite bad" is somehow the "invisible" postulate of the rational number, while the infinite is manifested, becomes visible, through the irrational number. Nevertheless, the irrational number remains irremediably "alien" to the totality of rational numbers, just as infinity-abundance (that absolute magnitude incommensurate to all summation of relative magnitudes) is absolutely transcendent to the quantitative infinity of the endless progression.

This obviously evokes the Kantian contrast in *Critique of Judgment* between the perceptible infinity of the imagination and the authentic idea of the infinite as revealed in the experience of the mathematical sublime. What evokes the sense of the sublime in us is not what is very big or even what is bigger than anything we can know, but "something that is absolutely great," that is "beyond all comparison."[3] At the junction of the intelligible world and the perceptible world, the mathematical sublime is that feeling in which the human spirit discovers in itself the absolutely great, that is, "what goes beyond all measure of the senses." For the magnitude of perceptible objects is never appreciated except in terms of units of definite measures in relation to one another and whose series forms, in principle, an unlimited progression. All unity of magnitude is differential so that the very notion of absolute magnitude is stripped of meaning in the physical world. Yet, our mind is capable of forming the idea of an absolute magnitude. Or, more precisely, we make the effective experience of a sense—that of the sublime—which implies, as its condition of possibility, the presence in us of the idea of the Absolute. A thematic paradox at the core of the Kantian system, in the duality of a subjectivity limited in its theoretical capacities, but open at the same time to the requirement of the unconditioned. The sense of the sublime is precisely that in which our finite mind (that is, knowing only the unlimited series of relative magnitudes) awakens to the presence of the genuinely infinite in it: "The sublime is that, the mere capacity of thinking which evidences a faculty of mind transcending every standard of sense."[4] Thus, the sublime is not in the object; it is a sense that subverts subjectivity and draws it beyond itself: "The mere ability even to think the given infinite without contradiction, is something that requires presence in the human mind that is itself supersensible."[5]

Our evaluation of the orders of magnitude in nature rises from representation to representation according to the law of an indefinite progression, from the image of the most minute object to that of the galaxies and even beyond, for the imagination is endowed with an unlimited capacity to shape increasingly general representations. It is precisely on the background of that endless progression and in contrast to it that a demand for the Absolute incommensurate to all perceptible magnitude emerges—as if it came from somewhere else. Yet, beyond nature, beyond knowing, Reason, a case of the Absolute, speaks in us, opening our mind to the idea of the infinite: "because there is a striving in our imagination toward progress ad infinitum, while reason demands absolute totality, as a real idea, that same inability on the part of our faculty for the estimation of the magnitude of things of the world of sense to attain to this idea, is the awakening of a feeling of a supersensible faculty within us."[6] Thus, the bad infinity of the imagination and the authentic infinity demanded by Reason are both radically opposed to one another and, somehow, mutually condition one another. The infinite revealed in the feeling of the sublime is not the endless course of an imagination that never reaches its end; on the contrary, the demand of the infinite in us is defined precisely by its radical difference with the experience of a progression without limits.

In Kant, as in Rosenzweig, the idea of the infinite affects our sensibility while remaining absolutely alien to it: the sense of the sublime denotes a *violence* done to us by the intrusion into our world of a radically *different* order: facing the sublime, we feel the shock of the infinite against our finite nature, as a personal wound. But this shock, which resembles the trauma inflicted on our sensibility by the moral Law, is not that of morality itself; rather, it concerns an opening of the soul to infinity, an opening that predisposes us or prepares us to hear the voice of morality: "[There is] a dominion which reason exercises over sensibility with a view to extending it to the requirements of its own realm (the practical) and letting it look out beyond itself into the infinite, which for it is an abyss."[7] *The infinite as abyss*: for the sensible world (corresponding to that of historical temporality in Rosenzweig), is that not like the premonition or rather the reminder of its eternal vulnerability to the demand of the Absolute that upsets its self-sufficiency? No doubt there is an analogy between the metaphor of the irrational number in Rosenzweig and the idea of the infinite in Kant: in both cases, a world condemned to the monotony of an endless progression is struck to the quick by the shock inflicted on it by the intrusion of an absolute otherness.

*

This detour through Kantian sublimity introduces us to the allegorical reading of Rosenzweig's text. "What the irrational number means in relation to the rational number illustrates what Judaism means in relation to Christianity," he wrote.[8] In other words, the rational number refers here to Christianity (or Christian civilization), the irrational number to Judaism. Rosenzweig himself made this allegorical signification explicit at the end of his text: "[The irrational number] always remains a foreign reality: a number that isn't a number, or as it were, a 'non-number.' . . . Do you want to know who are 'non-humans'? Reading the newspaper day after day will teach you."[9] The historiosophical allegory thus hides another (tragically premonitory) allegory of a political or theological-political nature. Yet, the historiosophical signification is first: we know that, for Rosenzweig, Christianity was animated by a historical dynamic that had to lead it straight from an origin—the birth of Christ—to an ideal end, that is, the Parousia that will see the Kingdom of God established. This theological view of history is as valid for the Church as a temporal power as for the whole of Christian civilization. Henceforth, the history of the West will look like a theologically signified history and will be invested with a providential meaning. This model of history as theodicy was continued by Hegel, for whom, as we have seen, Christian Europe represented the ultimate embodiment of absolute Spirit. Hegel's philosophy of history, a secularized version of Christian historiosophy, represents the progress of Spirit as a necessary movement, where the idea of infinity plays both the role of an invisible driving force of evolution and that of an ideal limit of the historical process. All the attributes of the rational number refer to this vision of the "bad infinite," which was certainly denounced by Hegel himself, but which, according to Rosenzweig, still characterized the essence of his philosophy of history.

All the properties of the irrational number, on the other hand, illustrate the description of the Jewish people and its vision of history as proposed by *The Star of Redemption*. In the Jewish religious experience, the ideal end of history is lived, to a certain extent, in advance through the symbolism of rituals. For those who share this experience, "the end, that is, the Kingdom of God, has already begun, is already here; for every Jew, it is present as of now in his immediate and definite relation to God Himself, in his daily acceptance of the 'Yoke of the Kingdom of Heaven,' that is, in the fulfillment of the law."[10] A paradoxical inversion of the representation that each of those two religions makes for itself of its relationship to Redemption: for Rosenzweig, Christianity was still waiting for the coming of the Kingdom of God, while for Judaism, it had already arrived.

Yet, this contrast represents only one aspect of the truth. In fact, Rosenzweig could not deny that, at the core of the Christian faith is the event of the Incarnation, that is, of the coming of the Savior, while the specificity of Judaism inheres precisely in the affirmation that the Messiah has not yet come. Thus, on either side, there is the same tension between the present and the future, between a given and a lack, between an *already-there* and a *not-yet*. The central difference between these two visions of history, however, consists of the exact nature of the relationship between the point of departure and the point of arrival: for Christianity, Holy History has an origin (the birth of Christ), but it has not yet reached its end; thus, it is defined as a process, a long march from the Incarnation to the Parousia, in other words, as a transition from one condition to another. In this sense, there is in fact a history of Salvation that can pass perfectly through profane history, that of empires and civilizations, without ever being entirely merged with it.

On the other hand, for Judaism, the world is not yet finished; the reality we live in is still marked by an essential imperfection. This is why Redemption, which has not yet really begun, cannot have a history either. It remains irremediably profane, inhospitable, in its very essence, to the demand of absolute implied by the idea of Redemption. Since it cannot be thought in terms of its origin (which has not yet taken place), it can be imagined only in terms of its future. In contrast to the Christian experience of Redemption, as a presence gradually revealed in history, Judaism aims at Redemption as a beyond without a common measure with the visible order of historic time. Thus, to think Redemption, Judaism will have to *suspend time* to some extent, rise from diachrony to synchrony, from the historical order to the symbolic order. For in the order of the symbol, that is, in the timelessness of ritual, the future can be anticipated, just as the past can be replayed. Thus, the symbolic time of Judaism is distinguished from that established by most religious societies in this respect: it is less concerned with returning to the mythical time of origins than with anticipating the absolute completion of all things, through fulfilling the Law and rituals.

Clearly at the core of this symbolic time itself, there is an essential gap between what is and what will be: the idea of anticipation implies a break of pure synchrony, an aim at what is not. This gap is found in another way in the form of the abyss separating the symbolic anticipation of Redemption from its concrete advent in the reality of history. There is no common denominator between the religious experience of an immediate presence of the absolute in the practice of the Law and the finitude of a still unfinished world. To some extent, this awareness of the imperfection of the world and history moderates the "quietism" that Scholem denounced in Rosenzweig. From this perspective, the religious existence of the Jewish people, centered around the symbolic—but only symbolic—

anticipation of Redemption, and Christianity, which aims at Redemption through the vicissitudes of history, in fact appear as essentially *complementary* in Rosenzweig.

*

In all religious societies, a symbolic time runs parallel to the course of natural time: the times of celebrations and rituals that recur at a regular rhythm and that superimpose their recurrent cycle on the monotonous passing of the days. In religious awareness, time is not lived as a flow, as a line that can be extended indefinitely, but as a circle; from year to year, the cycle of sacred time tells the same story, repeats the same scenario. The periodic return of an always identical ceremony stops the flight of the days, establishes a stability in the very heart of becoming. In these caesuras of temporality, a radically different reality is revealed, preserved from change, erosion, and death. The cycle of religious time somehow projects fragments of eternity onto the continuous line of time.

The function of civil calendars is not essentially different. In our secular societies, the rhythm of holidays, religious or secular, interrupts the course of time and confers its specific syntax on the amorphous sequence of daily life. In most religious societies, stopping time functions to abolish the gap separating the present from the mythic past, from the time of origins. The identification of the believer with the founding events and the return to the primordial order are central experiences of religious life. In the case of Judaism, stopping time also, and perhaps mainly, has a completely different object: to annul the distance—no matter how incalculable—that separates the present from the extreme future, that is, from the ideal end of the historical process. Only an absolutely synchronic time can allow the actualization of the most distant future in the flash of the present instant, in other words, anticipating Redemption. This anticipation somehow equals an extraordinary *acceleration of time*, since it leads to suppressing the interval between two points that, on a horizontal axis, might be infinitely distant from one another.

This specific form of religious time then produces an extremely paradoxical effect: stopping time is somehow equal to its infinite acceleration. This paradox is, in fact, at the core of the religious experience of the Jewish people: for two thousand years, its congealed, almost anachronistic life on the margins of history has kept it in the immediate proximity not only of

its founding myths but also of the messianic end of history. Moreover, because its most distant past has always been more present to it than the most
immediate present, the realization of even its most chimerical hopes has
always seemed very close. This paradoxical effect is based on a thoroughly
specific religious experience: that of the *contraction of time*. This is what
provokes the absolute simultaneity of the past, present, and future. The
possibility of seeing messianic promises realized *today* stems from a millen-
nial spiritual technique, an ancestral familiarity with the internal experience of condensation in a single point of the three dimensions of time.

One of the central modalities of this experience, which Rosenzweig
alludes to in a passage of *The Star of Redemption*, is the reference to the ancestors. The tradition, he wrote about Rembrandt's painting *Jacob's Bless-
ing the Children of Joseph*, passes less from the father to the son than from
the grandfather to the grandson. Rosenzweig did not explain this remark,
but it is clearly based on the fundamentally *discontinuous* nature of the
tradition, whose goal is precisely to overcome oblivion. It must fight incessantly against its own decline, against the flaws and breaks of memory,
in short, against death that inevitably separates the generations and that,
at the same time, is the very condition of their succession. Death is what
threatens the substance of the tradition from one age to the next but also
what makes its permanent renewal possible. What the fathers knew may
be forgotten or denied by their children; but what the fathers had forgotten can be rediscovered by their sons. The continuous and irreversible
time postulated by historical causality is contrasted here with the *time
of the generations*, a discontinuous and reversible time symbolized by the
double bond of the grandfather to the grandson and from the grandson
to the grandfather: a discontinuity of a transmission that (as in the biblical episode evoked by Rembrandt) immediately binds the ancestor to the
generation of his grandson; the reversibility of a nonaccumulative time in
which the grandson, going above the generation of the fathers, connects
directly to the teachings of the grandfather.

To decipher historical time in terms of generations is to break its homogeneity, to subvert the fiction of its continuity. This is how traditional
societies proceed: to create the illusion that a very distant past is still very
near, they count the distance separating us from it not in years but in generations. This distance will appear even shorter if it is assessed in terms of
individual memory, which generally covers the length of two generations.

For example: a man today can say that his grandfather's grandfather knew the Napoleonic era. A numerical chronology (the count of years) is converted here into subjective values, into a sum of personal experiences, in short, into a *memory.*

This will be even more vivid if the persons evoked, who form intermediaries of memory, so to speak, are recalled by their *name.* To invoke the name of the grandfather—by leaping over the generations—is to reconstruct an ideal line that brings us close to our ancestors and brings them close to us. This procedure of collective memory creates a striking effect of a contraction of time. In the Jewish tradition, this proximity of the grandfathers extends back to the eponymous ancestors, the biblical patriarchs, founders of a line that bears their name. Conversely, very far in the future, the contraction of time thus produced will absorb the totality of conceivable historical time. In the Jewish religious experience, the last generations of the human adventure appear just as close to us as the very first. The anticipation of Redemption is absolutely symmetrical here to the immediate proximity of the time of the origins.[11]

*

Historical time and symbolic time each possess a specific form of the present. Rosenzweig defined these two modalities of the present with a felicitous formula, contrasting "today which is only a footbridge to tomorrow" to "the other today which is a springboard to eternity."[12] The *present-footbridge* is the one that, on the linear axis of time, links the past moment to the moment to come. A fleeting moment of a homogeneous continuity, it appears as a quantitative unit in a purely additive temporal process. This is the present conceived by historical Reason: an ideal point both separating and connecting two other points on an undifferentiated line that can be extended indefinitely, or else an infinitesimal unit of time on a vector oriented toward an ideal end where the unlimited sequence of causes and effects can be linked together. The idea of historical causality is in fact modeled on the concept of causality in mechanical physics; both can function only on a homogeneous and continuous temporal axis, where the before directly determines the after.

In contrast to the present-footbridge, the *present-springboard* is a single moment of time when time is perceived in all its wealth and diversity. In the qualitative experience of time, as seen by subjectivity, every moment is unique; the present minute is not comparable to the one that precedes it or to the one that follows it. This is why moments cannot be summed up; time will then no longer appear as a river that flows toward its estuary but as a discontinuous sequence of states of quality and intensity that are each unique. The image of the horizontal will be contrasted here with that of the vertical: certain privileged moments will give the impression of suddenly breaking the litany of the days, or the anticipated chain of events, and opening a breach in time, through which the brand-new can break through. Such is the present-springboard that makes us escape the endless unfolding of historical time and projects us directly into a reality of a different essence.

To some extent, the present as springboard constitutes the permanent dimension of religious time. But it can also occur at the core of profane time: in our secularized societies, holidays still appear, even when their religious meaning has been lost, as enclaves of sacred time. Similarly, certain (personal or historical) moments of life appear made of a different cloth: favorable constellations suddenly bearing new promises and resembling authentic *messianic moments*. But on the other hand, each of these moments is also one point among others on the axis of time. Both different and identical, they indicate the fundamental ambiguity of historical time. The most banal moment can suddenly turn out to be a "springboard to eternity"; the most felicitous configuration can be only a pure illusion. In the chiaroscuro of history, everything remains to be deciphered: no historical situation promises beyond doubt the imminence of Redemption, but none excludes the possibility that, this time, it really is about to appear.

PART 2

WALTER BENJAMIN:
THE THREE MODELS OF HISTORY

Metaphors of Origin

IDEAS, NAMES, STARS

Reflection on the nature of history seems to have been a constant element in Benjamin's thought. From his youthful writings to his final texts, this preoccupation constitutes the guiding thread that grants that diverse work its secret unity, sometimes explicitly and sometimes implicitly. For Benjamin, the central question, the one on which all others depend, appears to have been, How can we talk about history? How can a chaos of events be made intelligible? It is a question less about the nature of historical processes than the manner of describing them, less about historiosophy than historiography. Or more precisely, even in its formulation, the question implies that history is constituted only through the very act of narrating, a problematic Benjamin summed up in *The Origin of German Tragic Drama*: "how is the question, 'What was it really like?' susceptible, not just of being scientifically answered, but of actually being put."[1]

Benjamin had discovered early on the idea that the transformation of the past into history is a function of the historian's own present, of the time and place where his discourse is created. Of the two classical aims of historiography—reconstituting the past and interpreting it—he always preferred the latter. Or, more precisely, he always denounced as illusory the pretension of reconstituting the past (and from the early 1930s, as a hoax), since, by definition, the image of the past becomes visible for us only through our account of it made from our own present. Hence, the crucial importance for writing history of the idea that the historian makes for himself of the present in which he lives.

For the young Benjamin, the "case of the present" of the historian orders not only his vision of the past but also, and for the same reasons, his vision of the future. Historians have always wanted, more or less explicitly, to be able to draw lessons for the future from the study of the past. The appearance of the ideology of progress in the eighteenth century gave these pedagogical ambitions a philosophical foundation, humanity's past progress allowing it to conclude its future progress with almost scientific certainty. It is remarkable that, in one of his very first texts, *The Life of Students*, dating from 1914, anticipating the final state of his thought, Benjamin criticized the idea of progress, challenging, in terms of the definition of the present as an original case in which historical time is generated, a conception of history that claims to reconstitute the past by accumulating "facts" and to predict the future by ignoring the role of radical novelty, that is, utopia, which constitutes its essence:

There is a vision of history which, based on trust in the infinitude of time, is satisfied to differentiate the fast or slow pace at which men and periods advance along the road of progress. With respect to the present, this vision corresponds with demands that are stripped of all coherence, all precision and all rigor. The following reflections, on the other hand, are aimed at defining a state of things in which the historical process is concentrated and immobilized in focus, like utopian images drawn for all time by philosophers. Here, the elements of the final state of history do not appear as works and ideas embedded in the heart of the present; but rather as the most dangerous, the most decried, the most ridiculed. The task of the historian consists of giving that still immanent state of completion an image, making it visible, making it prevail in the present. But that state of things could not be evoked by a pragmatic description of details (institutions, customs, etc.), since it challenges precisely these. It must be grasped in its metaphysical structure, like the idea of the messianic kingdom or of the French Revolution.[2]

The analogy of this youthful text with *On the Concept of History* of 1940 (Benjamin's last written text) is striking. A critique of the idea of progress based on a linear and continuous vision of historical time, a correlation of such a vision with a political attitude of resignation to the present, a definition of a new historical method no longer striving to follow the evolution of historical processes but to immobilize them, that is, to describe their privileged connections (in synchrony and not in diachrony), to identify the utopian elements in these connections and to evoke them in the form of images, to decipher that utopian moment precisely in everything that challenged the established order in the past, and finally to read the figure of utopia in the double theological and political model of messianism and Revolution—all these themes are exactly the same as those found twenty-five years later at the core of his final work. In the meantime, Benjamin went through a vast philosophical trajectory, leading him from a thought fed by theological intuitions to a vision of the world inspired by Marxism.

Yet, the term "trajectory" risks being deceptive if it means a continuous intellectual approach leading, in an even arc, from a point of departure to a culmination. What always remained constant in Benjamin was the permanence of certain preoccupations, the question of history being perhaps the most central of them. And this, precisely in the form we have just sketched: if it is true that a chaos of events becomes perceptible—and especially intelligible—only when it is interpreted, or in other words, if history is constituted only by being written, how should we read events; what grid should we apply to them to discern their significance? Formulated in these terms, the question implies the radical rejection of the historical method prevailing in those early years of the twentieth century, that is, historicism. This rejection applies first to its epistemological postulates but also, more profoundly, to the philosophy of history underlying it.

From Ranke and Treitschke to Meinecke, historicism had been the official doctrine of the German school of historiography. Its methodological axioms had been borrowed from the natural sciences, as understood in the nineteenth century: belief in the objectivity of "facts," the historical fact conceived on the model of "scientific facts"; use of a purely inductive method consisting of accumulating facts and abstracting general laws from them whose objectivity was held to be as certain as the facts themselves. This double belief defined the method of historicism as rigorously *positivist*. But that method also involved a certain vision of historical time and, more generally, a philosophy of history. Historicism conceived historical time in terms of the model of physical time, more precisely on that of the time of Newtonian mechanics, that is, as a medium both continuous and linear where an infinite series of causes and effects can unfold uninterrupted. This essential transposition of the principle of causality in the unfolding of historical time necessarily led to belief in a projection of historical knowledge into the future. For historicism, at least in principle, there had to be historical laws allowing predictions to be made—no doubt less precise than those of physics, but just as necessary. At the very least, by being based on the observation of progress realized by humanity thus far, the idea that this progress was destined to continue could be inferred from it.

On the other hand, the "scientific" nature of his method, which guaranteed the historian a knowledge of the past considered objective (or at least approximating objectivity), allowed him to strive for the ideal of a truthful reconstruction of the past, that is, encompassing the totality of conditions that explain its manifestations. For historicism, to understand a period historically is to reconstitute it "as it really was," that is, as its contemporaries understood themselves. In its belief in an approach seen a priori as unscientific, and entirely dependent on the point of view of the observer, historicism constitutes the historical object as the ideal focus of its search, as the locus of a truth before which the subject is annulled. In this sense, every historical object is "true" insofar as it is contained in the totality of its determinations. Hence historical relativism is the most profound characterization of the philosophy of history embraced by historicism.

It is against the background of historicism and his break with it that Benjamin's reflections on history must be viewed. By emphasizing the role of the historian in the constitution of history, by understanding this role not as a given but as the product of heuristic activity, itself a function of a specific "instance of present," Benjamin was necessarily led to raise the question of the *categories* of historical knowledge. Beyond its purely methodological aspect (how can history be known?) the question actually implies a more metaphysical choice: what kind of history do we want to formulate? In terms of what model shall we conceive it? This question in fact addresses the choice of a paradigm (in the sense of a model of intelligibility);[3] as Benjamin's thought evolved, he presented three very distinct responses. In an early stage, the two texts "On Language as Such and on the Language of Man" (1916) and "The Task of the Translator" (written in 1921, appeared in 1923) propose a *theological paradigm* of history. A little later, *The Origin of German Tragic Drama* (1923–1925, appeared in 1928) develops an *aesthetic paradigm* of history. Finally, beginning in 1925–1926, which marks Benjamin's Marxist turn, he gradually formulated a *political paradigm* of history most clearly presented in *The Arcades Project* and *On the Concept of History* of 1940.

Yet these three stages should not be imagined as being completely disconnected from one another. Developing a new paradigm does not mean that Benjamin abandoned the central categories of the preceding paradigm. Those categories are preserved, but in the new conceptual structure that emerges, they lose their dominant function and are subordinated to other new dominant categories. Thus, elements of the theological paradigm survive in the aesthetic paradigm of history, as developed in *The Origin of German Tragic Drama*. Similarly, the political paradigm that dominates the vision of history of *The Arcades Project* and *Theses* integrates several elements—now subordinate—of the aesthetic and theological paradigms.

If the relative importance of those three paradigms in Benjamin's thought is measured from the point of view of diachrony, the theological paradigm was the most stable, since, first manifest, then more or less implicitly, it remained present throughout his development. On the other hand, from the point of view of synchrony, the political paradigm appears the most complex since all the components of his vision of history are combined in it. But from the point of view of its function in the general economy of Benjamin's thought, the aesthetic paradigm certainly plays the most central role. And not only because in the evolution of that thought, it represents the median stage where the theological theses of the youthful writings are still the most overtly present, the one that is also extended most insistently to the core of the following stage, but especially because, in that last stage, aesthetics plays the mediating role between the theological and the political. When those two extreme poles of Benjamin's thought come together, it is almost always, as we shall see, because of the mediation of aesthetic categories. Note only the epistemological function of *images* in Benjamin's late thought, particularly in his philosophy of history. In the *Theses* of 1940, the vision of history, centered on the connection of the political paradigm and the theological paradigm, is crystallized in two images, that of the robot chess player and that of the Angel of History. These images do not serve to illustrate an idea that also exists outside of themselves. They are the form or the medium through which two conceptions of history are "telescoped" to give birth to a new vision.[4]

*

The two youthful works in which Benjamin spells out his theological paradigm of history complement one another perfectly so that both draw a perfect schema of human history, from its origins to its final fulfillment. At the same time, they are radically opposed by the tendency that animates them: "On Language as Such and on the Language of Man" presents human history as a process of decline, while "The Task of the Translator" describes it as a progress toward a utopian fulfillment. But those two contrary movements come together to trace the curve of the human adventure as conceived by the Judeo-Christian religious tradition: a glorious birth of humanity, original sin, and fall, followed by a process of purification and progress toward renewal. Decline and restoration, degradation and Redemption, those two phases of sacred History define the theological vision of history in Benjamin.

Yet, what gives this view of history its peculiar character is that it does not conceive man as an acting being, a producer of events, but as a speaking being, that is, a producer of signs. What gives meaning to the history of humanity is less, as in the Bible, the vicissitudes of its moral evolution than the various stages of its *relation to language.* The progress or decadence of humanity will no longer be measured by the distance separating it from an original Good but by its lapse from an original state of language. Confronting the values of Judeo-Christian historiography, that is a significant shift of emphasis. What interests Benjamin in the biblical view of history is not the relationship to God and the Law but the fact that it proposes a metaphysical model of knowledge based on the primordial function of language. Thus, according to Benjamin, the theological paradigm does not describe a providential history whose unfolding is inspired by divine wisdom but rather strives for a setting, for the scale of the absolute, of a history of man as a knowing being. A being, of course, as Benjamin will reveal in his 1918 essay "On the Program of Future Philosophy," whose knowledge is not exhausted in the field of experience as demarcated by the play of concepts, but that is also—and perhaps mainly—constituted through the symbolic functioning of language, as religious experience reproduces it for us.[5]

In "On Language as Such and on the Language of Man," based on an exegesis of the first chapters of Genesis, Benjamin evoked through a mystical process of the decadence of language the movement of decline that characterizes the history of humanity for him. If the Bible plays the role of a founding text here, it is because the narrative of Creation grants a central place to the birth of language, but also because as this narrative is reported, language is manifest closest to its original power. Benjamin distinguishes three stages in the biblical history of the genesis of language. The first, in which the divine word appears as creator (Genesis 1:1–31), indicates language in its original essence, where it coincides perfectly with the reality it designates. At that primordial level, to which man never has had and never will have access, the duality of the word and the thing does not yet exist; in it, language, in its very essence, is the creator of reality.

The second stage is that in which, according to the biblical narrative (Genesis 2:18–24), Adam names the animals. This act of naming establishes the original language of man, lost today, but whose echoes are still heard for us through the symbolic, that is, poetic, function of language. What characterizes it is the perfect accord of the word and the thing it designates. At this stage, language and reality are no longer identical, but there is a sort of preestablished harmony between them: reality is entirely transparent in language; with an almost miraculous accuracy, language joins the very essence of reality.

In the third stage, this "paradisiacal language," invested with a magic power of naming, has been lost and degraded into a simple instrument of communication. Benjamin, who interprets the narrative of the original sin (Genesis 2:25–3:24) in light of the episode of the Tower of Babel (Genesis 11:1–9), sees the communicative function of language as the sign of its decline. From the absolute precision of naming, language falls into the "abyss of prattle." Once the original agreement of word and thing is lost, language is condemned to a perpetual approximation, which Benjamin defines as "over-naming."[6] Communicative language is bankrupt not because it is too poor but because it is too rich. As a corollary, nature, because it is no longer understood by man, sinks into muteness and desolation. Only the presence of the symbolic or poetic dimension of language indicates that Adamic speech is not lost irremediably and that the original truth survives somehow in the depth of our decline.

In "The Task of the Translator," Benjamin starts from that present decline of language, in which the corruption of the human condition after the Fall is expressed, to sketch a return to lost perfection. Just as the descending stage of history is linked to the degradation of language, so its ascendant phase coincides with its gradual purification, or in other words, with the process of restoration of the Adamic language. Here, Benjamin reiterates the distinction between the communicative aspect and the symbolic aspect of language, but by combining it with another opposition, the act of signifying (*das Meinen*) and the way of signifying (*die Art des Meinens*). In communicative language, the speaker's intention is centered on the act of signifying, more precisely, on the content of the message he wants to convey. In the symbolic use of language, on the other hand, the emphasis is on the "way of signifying," that is, on what we now call the signifier. The more human discourse abstains from aiming at communicable contents, the more the way of signifying will be absorbed in attention, and the more language will reappear in its original purity.

Throughout history, this process of purification has been produced by the work of poets, but especially—Benjamin's central thesis—by that of translators. Real translation, which must strive much less to transmit content than to create a new system of signs, which is not mimetic with relation to that of the original but is complementary, contributes to advance language toward its utopian end, toward that "language of truth," which is simply the language of the origins. This process, which Benjamin defines as "messianic," and whose end simultaneously means a return to the origin, evokes the conception of history specific to Jewish mysticism, which has always conceived of the messianic end of history as the realization of the ideal plan implied in the Creation. In this sense, it means less a simple restoration of the origin than the realization, through the changes of human time, of all utopian potentials coded, so to speak, in the original program of the human adventure. This is a view of history that, although it is certainly not linear, is not cyclical either, since its end does not coincide purely and simply with its origin. On the other hand, if the presence at the origin of history of a system of invariable givens (in the case of the theological paradigm in Benjamin, it would be primordial "names" that constitute the Adamic language) confers a certain share of determinism on that history, those givens are still pure potential, whose realization depends either on chance or on human freedom. In "The Task of the Translator," the restoration of the paradisiacal language goes through the movement of verbal invention itself, so that the return to the original is in fact produced through the creation of the new.

*

In the preface to *The Origin of German Tragic Drama*, Benjamin developed a theory of knowledge that formed the background for the view of a primordial language of humanity as an original landscape of truth. In the beginning, the "names" that constitute the Adamic language seemed replaced here by platonic "ideas": truth is made of a multiplicity of fundamental intuitions, which represent so many categories of apprehension of the real. From the beginning, therefore, truth is presented as multiple and discontinuous, as opposed to the Hegelian theory of the Universal Spirit that, after being embodied in countless concrete forms, is identified again, at the end of its adventures, with its own essential unity. Benjamin constructs the model of a truth that has always been fragmented and that no synthesis will ever succeed in adding together. In this sense, the task of philosophy consists, as in Plato, of contemplating ideas in their plurality and diversity. Yet, if ideas are multiple, their number is not infinite; the history of philosophy proves that human knowledge obsessively revolves around a limited number of questions, always the same, and confronted by each generation. The totality of these questions, which are not so much to be resolved as put to rest again each time, outlines the original field of knowledge, the primordial background of all thought. Like Rosenzweig, Benjamin contrasted the metaphysical tradition of the Logos-One with the view of a truth originally *plural*, but appearing at the same time as a given, as the immutable background of knowledge. Each idea somehow defines a particular semantic space, the original place from which one of the fundamental questions humanity keeps returning to arises. In this sense, there is certainly an ontology of truth in Benjamin: the totality of ideas constitutes a system, a first landscape that is always present even when men have forgotten it and that is to be returned to.

The irreducible multiplicity of ideas, their coexistence within a system, and the fact that this system remains unchangeable even when it ceases to appear almost necessarily suggest the astronomical metaphor of the sky and its constellations. And that is indeed the image that will dominate the presentation of Benjamin's theory of knowledge, explicitly at first in *The Origin of German Tragic Drama*, then, until the very last works, in an increasingly coded way. In the book on baroque drama, it is through the cosmological metaphor that the primordial world of truth is described:

Just as the harmony of the spheres depends on the orbits of stars which do not come into contact with each other, so the existence of the *mundus intelligibilis* depends on the unbridgeable distance between pure essences. Every idea is a sun and is related to other ideas just as suns are related to each other. The harmonious relationship between such essences is what constitutes truth.[7]

But recourse to "ideas" seems to be only a first approximation in the theory of truth that Benjamin develops here. In reality, for Benjamin, the doctrine of ideas is only a veil behind which the theological view of his first writings on the philosophy of language stand out: "platonic ideas," he wrote, "are basically only deified words and verbal concepts. The idea is a given of the language, and in the essence of the word indicates what is symbol in it."[8] Thus, ideas truly refer to the primitive "names" that constitute the Adamic language. As we know, those indicate the symbolic aspect of words, their noncommunicative part, or their purely poetic part, through which they "magically" correspond to the very essence of reality. It is this miraculous coincidence of the word and the thing that has been lost, and this is what philosophy must try to rediscover. A case history, which, however, does not refer to "a palpable representation of images"; unlike platonic reminiscence, which is essentially visual, the anamnesis Benjamin alludes to is essentially *acoustic*. As in the biblical Revelation, it is not by sight ("a form of external sense," according to Kant) that truth is given to human perception but through hearing, as "a form of internal sense." *Hearing* must be understood here, in the physical sense of the word, as the faculty of perceiving through the ear the sonorous harmonies of the word. In this sense, knowing the original means rediscovering a first hearing, a new hearing—beyond the fading that repetition and habit have made it undergo—of the original signification of language.[9] "In this renewal," wrote Benjamin, "the original perception of words is reanimated"; a recurring movement of forgetting and re-remembering, the history of philosophy, far from forming a rising curve registering the regular progress of reason, "is nothing but an effort to describe a few rare words—always the same—that is, Ideas."[10] But "in philosophical contemplation the idea is detached from the deepest reality in the form of speech, which again demands the right to name things. From this point of view, it is not Plato but Adam, the father of humanity, who is the father of philosophy."[11]

In the first version of his introduction (not published in his lifetime), Benjamin underlined the theological connotations of this return to the origin more clearly than in the final text. In fact, there the original is defined as "an incomplete restoration of Revelation,"[12] meaning the order of the Adamic language. However, this does not mean a return to a beginning in time, but at each moment, a regeneration of the original meaning of the words. The original is in fact marked by a "double determination": "as such it gives up its secret only if both the restoration of the Revelation and the necessarily incomplete character of such a restoration are recognized in it." To hear anew the original meaning of a word means both to return to its initial truth and to discover it as if for the first time. The original is what is both absolutely primordial and radically new. Its appearance opens both toward what has always been there and toward what has never yet been known. This is certainly what distinguishes philosophical anamnesis, as Benjamin understands it, from simple repetition. Whenever reminiscence puts us in touch with original "names" again, we have a brand-new experience, and what is revealed to us in it is the order of the absolutely unknown. Certainly the void separating each of these experiences from the next one (which are those voids—or those ruptures—that, for Benjamin, constitute the history of philosophy) indicates a phase of forgetting the original truth.

But philosophical anamnesis—as a victory over forgetting—does not bring us back to the previous stage of reminiscence (or to any of those that preceded it); in the history of philosophy, there is no accumulation of acquired knowledge, which would, in effect, make the very idea of a radical innovation unthinkable. For Benjamin, to return to the origin means to start over from zero, to resume as for the first time the founding work of thought. But at the same time, this re-beginning is modeled every time on the immemorial presence of primordial "names." It is this contradiction that animates the act of reminiscence from inside and "confers [on it] its own mystery."[13] The original is both what is discovered as brand-new and what is re-known as having existed in all time: "Recognition of the extraordinary as something that comes from an immemorial order. Discovery of the present of a phenomenon as representing the forgotten order of Revelation."[14]

From this point of view, each great historical epoch will appear as an absolute re-beginning, as a new attempt to return to one of the primordial ideas or to one of the primitive names, whose totality forms the original landscape of truth. The phenomenon of origin will then be that through which a certain epoch aims a certain idea, or, conversely, a certain idea is embodied in historical reality (thus, for example, baroque drama is a phenomenon of origin). But a primordial idea, like that of the baroque, for example, can be embodied and reembodied several times in history until all the potentials it implies are realized. Hence, we understand how Benjamin can write that "origin, while being an absolutely historical category, yet has nothing in common with genesis."[15]

*

In the introduction to *The Origin of German Tragic Drama*, the two models of original truth—platonic and biblical—are then transposed into a language that may be even more essential, that of the metaphor of the stars. Ideas are names, but both shine like stars in the heaven of origin. The theory of knowledge Benjamin developed in his introduction is connected with the play of four notions: idea, concept, element, and phenomenon. Phenomena are source data of empirical reality; to be understood, they must be broken down into their elements, which is done by the analytical work of concepts. But those scattered elements would vanish into an unintelligible chaos if they were not reassembled into new figures; it is these figures that Benjamin calls "ideas."[16] But these figures are also called "configurations" or "constellations." "Ideas are timeless constellations, and by virtue of the elements' being seen as points in such constellations, phenomena are subdivided and at the same time redeemed."[17] It is because elements are, at the outset, parts of empirical realities that Benjamin could write: "Ideas are to objects as constellations are to stars."[18]

Two years before Benjamin wrote the book on baroque drama, the theme of the stars had already appeared in his study of *Elective Affinities*, not of course as an element of its apparent architecture but as a half-hidden figure of its secret text. At the end of his study, Benjamin evokes a stroll Goethe made through the German countryside, during which the poet, already quite elderly, admits to one of his companions how much the writing of *Elective Affinities* had upset him, and what passion he had felt for Ottilie, the heroine of the novel. "It was the hour," reports one of the witnesses of that conversation, "when the stars rose." For Benjamin, that detail is connected with the passage of the novel when the two lovers, Eduard and Ottilie, dare to take one another in their arms for the first and last time; the narrator then adds: "Hope soared away over their heads like a star falling from the sky." And Benjamin continued: "The most paradoxical, the most fleeting hope is born at the end of the novel in the guise of a reconciliation, in the way in which, when the sun has disappeared, twilight sees the rise of the Even Star which lasts longer than the night. . . . The symbol of the shooting star passing over the heads of the lovers expresses the mystery that inheres in this work better than anything. . . . That mystery promises much more than a reconciliation, it promises Redemption."[19]

In the context of the essay on *Elective Affinities*, the metaphor of the stars seems to refer to the idea of an intelligible world (perhaps a Kantian inspiration), which at very rare moments would stand out on the background of a novel dominated essentially by the Goethean belief in the omnipotence of nature. The presence of the stars, distant signs pointing toward the existence of an ethical sphere transcending the obscure inevitability of passions, would then be the only light of hope in the tragic world of the novel. But at the same time, the stars here clearly allude to astrology. Benjamin suggests that Goethe himself could have believed in astrology: in *Poetry and Truth*, Goethe begins the narrative of his life with a presentation—ironic or not?—of his horoscope, just as in his orphic poem "Original Words," he mentions the "decree of the stars"; the two passages, wrote Benjamin, "refer to astrology as a canon of mythical thought."[20]

Of course, in a certain sense, those two interpretations of the metaphor of the stars—the one Kantian and the other Goethean—contradict one another: ethical transcendence is opposed to mythical inevitability as freedom is to necessity. But this contradiction is also reminiscent of the tension that already characterized the Adamic language: each of the primordial "names" represents both an immutable given, an original invariant that somehow predetermines the history of thought, and the source of a permanent renewal of meaning. Empty forms bereft of all semantic content, the names that constitute the "language of truth" mean nothing, but sketch the inevitable background on which truth can unfold. Similarly, contemplation of the starry sky invites man to remember his vocation on the subject of ethics, but at the same time reminds him of the necessary laws that govern his fate. Names and stars, as metaphors of origin, open both toward the presence—always beyond ourselves—of an immemorial given and toward the constant emergence of the new. Two experiences of the original that, according to Benjamin, correspond to the two possible figures of happiness:

There is a twofold will to happiness, a dialectic of happiness. A hymnic figure and an elegiac figure. The One: the unheard-of that never was, the summit of bliss. The Other: the eternal once-again, the eternal restoration of the original, first happiness.[21]

The bond between the image of the shooting star and the idea of happiness is emphasized again, many years later, in the essay "Some Motifs in Baudelaire," one of the last texts Benjamin wrote: "in folk symbolism, distance in space can take the place of distance in time; that is why the shooting star, which plunges into the infinite distance of space, has become the symbol of a fulfilled wish. . . . The period of time encompassed by the instant in which the light of a shooting star flashes for a man is of the kind that Joubert has described with his customary assurance. 'Time,' he says 'is found even in eternity; but it is not earthly, worldly time. . . . [It] does not destroy; it merely completes.'"[22] The sight of a star that goes through thousands of light-years in a flash symbolizes the illumination in which the present suddenly joins the most distant past, or, vice versa, in which the most ancient hope is suddenly embodied in the present instant. This emergence of the immemorial in the midst of the present, this epiphany of the most distant under the closest spaces, is a precise description of the experience of the *aura*. Benjamin's definition of the aura in his 1936 essay "The Work of Art in the Age of Mechanical Reproduction": "the unique phenomenon of a distance however close it may be."[23] Here, the depths of space metaphorically translate the infinity of time, but those two dimensions of distance both refer to the incommensurability of the original. When the latter is embodied, as a flash, in the present second, we live an auratic experience. The aura is given to us as a beam of the original, just as the light of a star reveals to us the glow of a star that has long ago disappeared.

In the last text of the collection *One-Way Street*, titled "To the Planetarium," Benjamin links the perception of the starry sky with the "ecstatic contact with the cosmos" that, according to him, characterizes the view of the prescientific world; an experience that is essentially collective, comparable on an individual scale, to that of the drug "which we take possession of the nearest and the farthest, and never one without the other."[24] For Benjamin, in our secularized world, the auratic moments of life clearly represent the equivalent of the ancient "ecstatic experience of the cosmos."

On the other hand, the experience of the aura, as a manifestation of the original, is also seen through our relationship to the universe of names. In a brief aphoristic text dating from the same period, with the title "Platonic Love"—a text that is coded throughout and whose hidden meaning must be deciphered—Benjamin, playing with both meanings of the term "platonic," interprets the experience of love that remains chaste as desire for the name of the beloved, or for the idea embodied by that name, that is, as a return to the Adamic language equivalent to the original order of truth: "Platonic love [is that] which loves the beloved in her name itself." Unlike physical possession, love "in the name and by the name" is nostalgia for the distant, that is, auratic experience: "When [love] guards and protects the integrity and first name of the beloved, that is the only thing that expresses the tension, the attachment to distance that makes it a Platonic love. . . . For that love, the presence of the beloved comes from her name like the radiation of a hot fire. . . . So, *The Divine Comedy* is only the aura around the name of Beatrice."[25]

The idea that a person's being is revealed, from the origin, in the name he bears, appears very early in Benjamin's work and returns, as a secret theme, even his final texts. In the 1916 essay "On Language as Such and on the Language of Man," Benjamin stated that the name the parents give the child—a name that corresponds to no objective knowledge—is the only extant trace of the divine language within the language of man. In fact, that name, corresponding to no object, refers to a condition prior to that of the Adamic language, that is, to that first stage (mentioned in the first verses of Genesis) in which divine language is presented as a creator of reality. Similarly, man borrows from God the faculty of forming his own fate from the name he bears. The name of the person, as a mediate authority between the divine language and the human language, is both a given received at birth and the source of a permanent invention: by his name, "each man is guaranteed his creation by God, and in this sense he is himself created, as expressed by mythological wisdom in the idea (which doubtless not infrequently comes true) that a man's name is his fate."[26]

An empty form without defined semantic content, the name exists before the man, but from that pure structure, man engenders an infinity of new significations. Hence, in a pseudo-autobiographical text written in 1933, the fiction of a "secret name" his parents gave him at birth and that, ever since, governed his life. This name, Agesileus Santander, which Gershom Scholem has deciphered as an anagram of "Angelus Satanus," refers to Paul Klee's watercolor *Angelus Novus*, which Benjamin had acquired in 1921 and which would become for him the emblematic figure of his own fate.[27] The two metaphors of the angel and the name echo one another here as two representations of the manifestation, or rather the eruption, of the original in the heart of the present. "In the room where I lived in Berlin," wrote Benjamin, "that other name . . . had its portrait hanging on my wall: New Angel." But that angel also symbolizes the central intuition of Benjamin's philosophy of history: "The Kabala," he added, "tells that every second, God creates a host of new angels and that each of them has only one single function: to sing for a moment the praise of God before His throne before dissolving into nothingness. It was as one of them that the new Angel introduced himself to me before agreeing to reveal his name to me."

The meaning of history is not revealed, for Benjamin, in the process of its evolution but in the breaks in its apparent continuity, in its flaws and accidents, where the sudden emergence of the unpredictable interrupts its course and thus reveals, in a flash, a fragment of original truth. At the heart of the present, the most radically new experience thus transports us, at the same time, to the most immemorial origin. A dazzling experience in which time is disintegrated and realized at the same time: "What the Angel wants is happiness: a tension which contrasts the ecstasy of the uniqueness of the new, what had never been known, and that other bliss of beginning over, of rediscovery of the already experienced." This single rupture of the temporal fabric is seen both as an anamnesis, a recognition of the original harmonies of language, and as the vertiginous experience of an auratic love: "This is why the only novelty that [the Angel] can hope for goes through the road of return when it again involves a human being. Thus for me: as soon as I saw you the first time when I returned with you to the place where I came from."[28]

In the unfinished book on the arcades of Paris, the auratic connotations of the origin are again linked with the theme of the stars. But this time, the destruction of the aura during the Industrial Revolution, the triumph of technology and mass civilization, is symbolized by the absence of stars in the night sky of big cities: "the big city knows no true evening twilight. In any case, the artificial lighting does away with all transition to night. The same state of affairs is responsible for the fact that the stars disappear from the sky over the metropolis. Who ever notices when they come out? Kant's transcription of the sublime through 'the starry heavens above me and the moral law within me' could never have been conceived in these terms by an inhabitant of the big city."[29] Benjamin often noted that, in Baudelaire, who represents the archetype of the poet of modernity, the stars never appear. Certainly, he wrote at the end of his essay "Some Motifs in Baudelaire," the author of *Les Fleurs du mal* was fascinated by the magic of distances; but those take the ironic form of landscapes daubed on painted theatrical backdrops. For him, Baudelaire was "the melancholic whose star called him to the distance. But he didn't follow it."[30] For "renouncing the magic of distance is a crucial element of [his] lyricism."[31] Baudelaire heralds the sensibility of modern man, who knows sensation only at the price of "the disintegration of the aura in the experience of shock."[32] Baudelaire's sky, wrote Benjamin, is a "secularized space."[33]

But, ironically, is not obliterating the stars from the sky of big cities, provoked by the reflections of artificial urban lighting, compensated for by the very gleam of those artificial lights? A paradoxical reversal, with which the industrial civilization that destroys the aura produces as a result a "modern beauty," based precisely on the aesthetic of shock. In this sense, the "upheaval of tradition" (that is, forgetting the origin) would simply be the "obverse of the contemporary crises and renewal of mankind."[34] This thesis, which Benjamin develops in "The Work of Art in the Age of Mechanical Reproduction" and in his second essay on Brecht (1939), are both behind a note in *The Arcades Project*, in which Benjamin reinvests in the place-names of the streets of Paris—that is, an entirely secularized space—the lost powers of the Adamic language:

What was otherwise reserved for only a very few words, a privileged class of words, the city has made possible for all words, or at least a great many: to be elevated to the noble status of name. This revolution in language was carried out by what is most general: the street—Through its street names, the city is a linguistic cosmos.[35]

But Benjamin constantly contrasts the notion of a "modern beauty" peculiar to the forms of art produced by new techniques of reproduction with the ideal of the disappeared auratic beauty. In Baudelaire, the "Parisian Scenes," marked by an aesthetic of rupture and dissonance, contrasts violently with incantatory poems like "Former Life" or "Correspondences," which express nostalgia for a return to archaic forms of experiences, to magic modes of perception of the real. Of course, in "Some Motifs in Baudelaire," when Benjamin analyzed these "auratic" poems, he no longer mentioned, as least explicitly, the idea of a first origin of the language to be rediscovered. The lost origin is thought instead in terms of historical anthropology (as in "On the Mimetic Faculty" of 1933): as a very ancient state of civilization when man was able to decipher cosmic analogies and perceive the synesthetic unity of all sensations. This magic vision of the real continues, in Baudelaire, to stand out against the backdrop of our sensibility as modern men and, in contrast with it, as the already almost unconscious memory of a lost bliss. Auratic poetry, then, would be like the final trace, within our civilization of reading and writing, of an archaic cultural model (insofar as the experience of reading itself, lived as a "profane illumination" has kept something of its magical origin even today). Similarly, the philosopher who runs counter to the path of history or who reads the book of history "backwards," rediscovers in the heart of our most profane experiences a trace of the magic that inhered in them at the origin. This image of a ride backward on the road of time was inspired in Benjamin by Kafka's tale "The Next Village," of which he proposed the following interpretation (in his conversations with Brecht):

[T]he true measure of life is remembrance. Retrospectively, it traverses life with the speed of lightning. As quickly as one turns back a few pages, it has gone back from the next village to the point where the rider decided to set off. He whose life has turned into writing, like old people's, likes to read this writing only backward. Only so does he meet himself, and only so—in flight from the present— can this life be understood.[36]

Benjamin contrasted the young rider in Kafka's story, who will never reach the next village, with the point of view of the grandfather, whose retrospective look encompasses in the wink of an eye the whole length of a life. Unlike the essay on Proust, this is no longer only a rediscovery of the personal past, the restoration of a primordial happiness, that of childhood, but a return, within the present, to the origin of history itself.

These allusions—most often coded—to scattered traces of auratic experiences within modernity no doubt indicate the persistence in Benjamin of a theological model of history. Slivers of the original truth still exist today, hidden here and there in the depth of our profane world; the task of the "materialist historian," he said in *On the Concept of History*, consists precisely of gathering up these "sparks of hope" buried in the past and reviving them (as citations of ancient texts that recover their youth in the new context where they are integrated) in the very heart of the present.[37] But these "slivers of messianic time" are lost in a reality hopelessly emptied of all auratic magic.[38] In a world irrevocably deprived of the depth of distances, Baudelaire's poetry itself "shines in the sky of the Second Empire as a 'star without atmosphere.'"[39]

"The Next Village"

My grandfather used to say: "Life is astoundingly short." To me, looking back over it, life seems so foreshortened that I scarcely understand, for instance, how a young man can decide to ride over to the next village without being afraid that—not to mention accidents—even the span of a normal happy life may fall far short of the time needed for such a journey.

Translated by Willa and Edwin Muir, in *Franz Kafka, the Complete Stories*, ed. Nathan N. Glatzer (New York: Schocken Books, 1971), p. 404.

5

The Aesthetic Model

The first phase of human history, marked by the loss of the Adamic language and the fall into varied communicative idioms, is developed completely on the background of theology. Language, which forms the subject of that history, is conceived as an almost abstract medium not specified by any content. In the second phase, on the other hand, the one that somehow leads from the Fall to Redemption, the elements of language are crystallized and stabilized in the form of texts, whose sequence marks the development of history and measures the stages that bring it close to its messianic culmination. History continues to be controlled by a theological finality, but it is now embodied in the profane series of literary works. Thus, with the essay "The Task of the Translator," the aesthetic paradigm overtakes the theological paradigm, and at least to some extent, relegates it to the second level.

Two years later, the formulation of an aesthetic paradigm of history is one of the central subjects of the introduction to *The Origin of German Tragic Drama*. Benjamin was now concerned with defining, among the different elements of time, *a bond that is not a causal relationship*. By resorting to theology, Benjamin had wanted to establish his thought, well within positivism, on the philosophy of language and the view of history of German Romanticism. But the rejection of historicism also—and perhaps primarily—implied a critique of the idea of historical causality. A historical event does not engender another historical event as cause involves effect in Newtonian mechanics. Or, historical events do not follow one another with the same necessity as that which controls the different phases of the normal biological development of the living being. Thus, in a letter of 1923, when he was revising his book on baroque drama, Benjamin borrowed from aesthetics the model of a noncausal relationship between the various elements of historical time:

What preoccupies me is the question of the relationship of works of art to historical reality. In this respect, if there is one thing I'm sure of it is that there is no history of art. In the life of the human being, the unfolding of the temporal process implies an essential causality; moreover, life would be impossible without that causal sequence, as it appears in growth, maturity and death. It is quite different for the work of art; it is essentially a-historic. . . . In this sense, works of art are like philosophical systems. . . . The specific historicity of works of art is not manifested in the "history of art" but in their interpretations. This brings out correlations between the works which, while outside of time, are nevertheless not bereft of historical relevance.

What Benjamin means by the "a-historicity" of works of art is that they are not engendered by one another in a causal series. That is, the law of their sequence is unpredictable, that a work of art can never be deduced from those that precede it. Quite the contrary, every great work appears in the world as something radically new, so that no knowledge of the present, complete as it may be, allows the nature of tomorrow's great works of art to be predicted. Thus, the sequence of works of art defines a discontinuous temporality, escaping determinism, and even more, the illusion of progress. In a note on *The Arcades Project*, probably written between late 1937 and May 1940, that is, more than fifteen years after *The Origin of German Tragic Drama*, Benjamin cites a reflection of Baudelaire on this subject:

To the notion of progress in the history of art, Baudelaire opposes a monadological conception. "Transferred into the sphere of the imagination, the idea of progress . . . looms up with gigantic absurdity. . . . In the poetic and artistic order, inventors rarely have predecessors. Every flowering is spontaneous, individual. Was Signorelli really the begetter of Michelangelo? Did Perugino contain Raphael? The artist depends on himself alone. He can promise nothing to future centuries except his own works."[1]

The term "monadological," which appears for the first time in the introduction to the book on baroque drama, designates in Benjamin a discontinuous view of knowledge, defined by a multiplicity of points of view that cannot be summed up. Similarly, the monadological conception of historical temporality that Benjamin developed there stresses not the general laws of historical processes but, on the contrary, the individuality of each period, conceived as a specific phenomenon, which must be detached from the flow of becoming to be studied as an entity bearing in itself the law of its own functioning. A synchronic approach to history, inspired by Goethean morphology, but which must necessarily clash with the reality of change engraved in the very essence of time. Starting with the book on baroque drama, the question of articulating the synchronic and the diachronic is at the heart of Benjamin's reflection on history. Here, aesthetics provides him with the model of a specific historicity not governed by the principle of causality and based on the insertion of each work of art into a zone of autonomous temporality, engendering, so to speak, its own present, its own past, and its own future. These zones of temporality, as independent of one another as the works they surround, altogether, could neither add up to nor form a homogeneous evolution; but, on the contrary, they define a history made of a discontinuous series of discrete semantic units. In "The Task of the Translator," Benjamin had sketched the aesthetic model of history:

In the final analysis, the range of life must be determined by history rather than by nature, least of all by such tenuous factors as sensation and soul. The philosopher's task consists in comprehending all of natural life through the more encompassing life of history. And indeed, is not the continued life of works of art far easier to recognize than the continual life of animal species? The history of the great works of art tells us about their antecedents, their realization in the age of the artist, their potentially eternal afterlife in succeeding generations.[2]

In the first place, historical time is defined here not as an abstract category but as a lived reality, made of a diversity of concrete situations. This diversity is that of three modes of time, each presented as a specific experience, not reducible to the two others, so that, placed end to end, they would not form a homogeneous and continuous line. In fact, the past of a work of art, that is, its possible sources, could be reconstituted only after the fact and also completely hypothetically. The past could not be conceived here as the starting point of a causal series leading toward a determined future. Quite the contrary, the search for the sources of a work is always the effect of a work of interpretation of the work itself, and it is in terms of the "instance of the present" of the historian that its past is constituted. Similarly, the future of a work of art is not predictable in any way. Here, too, history is not endowed a priori with a decipherable meaning. It is after the fact that it can be determined if a work has survived and the meaning it implied can be discovered in the vicissitudes of its reception. Thus, the aesthetic model of history again questions the basic postulates of historicism: the continuity of historical time, the causality governing the sequence of events of the past toward the present and the present toward the future. For the aesthetic view of history, on the contrary, the past is not a given, any more than that the future can be predicted. It is in terms of the present as a case of interpretation that the dimension of the past is opened retrospectively; as for the experience of the future, for us, it is just as retrospective, since the only example we have of it is that of the metamorphoses of the past dictated by its various reinterpretations.

Moreover, the multiplicity of works of art, their irreducible uniqueness, shapes the model of a polycentric history in which each period, each style, each genre, and each mode of sensibility (and, *pace The Arcades Project*, each big category of social life) appear as the principle of a unity of historical intelligibility itself, with its specific present, past, and future. These entities, titled "ideas" in the introduction to *The Origin of German Tragic Drama*, function, we would say today, as *structures*, not only because they split time into discrete units but also because they put discontinuous elements of the historical process into relation. Thus, in *The Arcades Project*, Benjamin says that the idea of allegory takes account of the meaning of that figure of style in antiquity, the baroque, and Baudelaire.[3] Furthermore, the idea (or the structure) also combines the various levels of historical temporality into the same unity. Allegory, for example, designates both a figure of discourse, a literary genre, and in Benjamin, the principle of a certain mode of knowledge. Thus, the aesthetic model of history allows, above all, introducing parallelisms, breaks, stops, in short, synchrony into diachrony. Thus, history, split into signs, will appear as a *text* that can be deciphered.[4]

*

In *The Origin of German Tragic Drama*, the aesthetic paradigm of history is based on an aesthetic paradigm of knowledge. This produces a radical questioning of positivism, insofar as it states that the search for truth must be modeled not on natural sciences but on the philosophy of art. In a preparatory note to the book on baroque drama, Benjamin had already mentioned the "indissoluble correlation between fundamental metaphysical concepts and original phenomena of art."[5] The use of the Goethean term "original phenomenon" is not accidental. In his doctoral thesis on *The Concept of Art Criticism in German Romanticism* (1919), and especially in the last chapter devoted to "The Aesthetic Theory of Early Romanticism and Goethe," he had devoted a long analysis and discussion to the notion of "original phenomenon" in Goethe. This discussion, resumed in the 1922 essay on *Elective Affinities*, led him to denounce, in Goethe's use of that term, a confusion between two meanings, one physical and empirical, the other aesthetic and ideal. In the book on baroque drama, Benjamin, refusing the organicist connotations of that notion in Goethe (biological evolution, natural continuity), kept of the "original phenomenon" only the signification—dominant in his view—of an ideal principle of organization and structuring.

Indeed, it does seem that around the 1920s, Goethean morphology, understood as a theory of forms, inspired a whole current of research that, at the same time as the works of the Prague linguistic circle and apparently without any connection with them, tried to go beyond historicism by replacing the reconstruction of an evolution with the description of structures. Carlo Ginzburg, who called attention to this phenomenon, cited Propp's *Morphology of the Tale*, Jolles's *Simple Forms* (written in 1923 and published in 1930), Wittgenstein's 1931 note on Frazer's *Golden Bough*, Walter Benjamin's book on baroque drama (and we could also add to the list Oswald Spengler's *Decline of the West*, subtitled *Sketch for a Morphology of Universal History*).[6] *The Origin of German Tragic Drama* uses an extract of Goethe's writings on morphology as an epigraph:

Neither in knowledge nor in reflection can anything whole be put together, since in the former the internal is missing and in the latter the external; and so we must necessarily think of science as art if we expect to derive any kind of wholeness from it. Nor should we look for this in the general, the excessive, but, since art is always wholly represented in every individual work of art, so science ought to reveal itself completely in every individual object treated.[7]

This passage contains two of the central ideas of Goethean morphology, on which Benjamin based his theory of knowledge, as revealed in the introduction to the book on baroque drama. First, there is the idea (perhaps

inspired by the *Critique of Judgment*) that the contradiction between objectivity ("knowing") and subjectivity ("reflection") could be resolved only
in the aesthetic experience. For Goethe, the objective knowledge aimed at
by natural sciences, by definition, does not take account of the depths of
human subjectivity. But when the latter is defined, as in the young Romantics, his contemporaries, above all in Friedrich von Schlegel, by the infinite
play of mirrors of a reflection that keeps reflecting itself, it is condemned
to lack the objectivity of the real. Beyond those two partial approaches to
truth, art, defined as the model of a knowledge rooted in subjectivity but
that at the same time reveals unchanging—that is objective—forms, in the
complexity of nature, achieves for him "some form of totality." As for Benjamin, he denounces the methodological easiness of positivism, which, to
justify its claims to scientific objectivity, makes do with copying from mechanical physics the model of a linear sequence of causes and effects; but it
still rejects "the naively realist point of view that claims to avoid questions
of method," and that in fact "is not the view of the object, resolved in the
idea, but that of subjective states of the recipient projected into the work."[8]
Goethean morphology then supplied him with the model of a knowledge
conceived according to an aesthetic paradigm in which a combination of
forms, which function as so many semantic units, constitute a kind of al-
phabet that allows the text of the world to be deciphered.

On the other hand, these semantic units ("ideas" or "monads" corresponding to the Goethean "original phenomena") are not revealed in
the abstract, as general categories that might be spoken of outside their
embodiment in the particular. No, the totality attained by the Goethean
Urphänomen or by the idea in Benjamin is never given except in and
through particular phenomena. In this sense, aesthetic knowledge as
Goethe intended it and as Benjamin also defined it is the exact opposite
of taxonomy, all systems of genres. For Benjamin as for Goethe, aesthetic
knowledge does not deal with the relations between the individual and the
general but with the relations of the particular and the universal. If the aesthetic experience can serve as a model for knowledge, it is precisely insofar
as, through it, the universal is revealed in the particular. In the introduction to the book on baroque drama, Benjamin wrote: "[T]he more significant works . . . fall outside the limits of genre. A major work will either
establish the genre or abolish it."[9] This is the same paradigm of knowledge
that Benjamin applied again, this time to social history, in *The Arcades*

Project, when he defined his method: "To discover in the analysis of the smallest particular element the crystal of becoming in its totality."[10]

Thus, the aesthetic paradigm of knowledge in the introduction to the book on baroque drama can be summed up in two points: on the one hand, Benjamin maintained, against positivism and its cult of "facts," the reality of "original" (i.e., universal) phenomena; on the other hand, against idealism and its method of abstract generalization, he highlighted the primacy of the concrete. Thus, the archetype of truth will be the work of art, where the totality is embodied in the particular. This is why the analysis of the work of art (what Benjamin called its "interpretation") is contrasted both with the inductive method of positivism and the deductive method of idealism. "To accumulate facts to induce general characters from them," wrote Benjamin in the first version of his introduction, "is to mask the diversity of facts under the uniformity of stereotyped psychological reactions which only reflect the subjectivity of the historian. [Those] are unable to take account of the essence of an esthetic domain whose structure could be described by formal concepts."[11]

But conversely, Benjamin criticized the deductive method for "projecting [ideas] into a pseudo-logical continuum."[12] One of the central theses of his theory of knowledge is that this continuum does not exist. Knowledge cannot be gathered "in an encyclopedic accumulation of items of knowledge . . . divested of their false unity so that . . . they might partake of the genuine unity of truth."[13] Like Rosenzweig, whose *Star of Redemption* had impressed him a great deal, Benjamin conceived truth on the background of the plurality of experiences we have of it, experiences that are irreducible each time and cannot be totalized. But while for Rosenzweig, this plural character of truth is engraved, so to speak, in the most basic structure of our presence in the world, Benjamin revealed its model, in a less spontaneous and more mediated way, in the multiplicity of our aesthetic experiences. For Benjamin, there was a discontinuity of Being that is revealed to us through the irreducible diversity of works of art. An idea that seems to echo the one developed by Proust, almost at the same time, in *Remembrance of Things Past* (which, however, appeared only in 1927, that is, three years later):

Thanks to art, instead of seeing one world, our own, we see it multiplied and as many original artists as there are, so many worlds are at our disposal, differing more widely from each other than those which roll round the infinite and which, whether their name be Rembrandt or Ver Meer, send us their unique rays many centuries after the hearth from which they emanate is extinguished.

In Benjamin, the multiplicity of works of art provides the model of an ontology, or of a view of the truth, characterized by the plurality of Ideas. Just like aesthetic experiences, Ideas add up to form a homogeneous system. At the most, it might be said that they maintain an ideal relationship of coexistence comparable to that of sounds in music: "Each idea is a sun," he wrote. "The sonorous harmony of those entities is called truth." Like Rosenzweig, Benjamin here opposed Hegel's logic. Truth is not constituted in a continuous dialectical movement in which each new element preserves the preceding one while going beyond it, but is given from the outset as an original discontinuity.

For Benjamin, who relied here on the analyses of Émile Meyerson, which seem to herald, to some extent, the theses of Popper and Kuhn about scientific revolutions, natural sciences do not progress on a linear trajectory either, but by breaks and leaps: each new system of postulates claims to resolve problems left hanging by the preceding system, while maintaining that these same problems cannot be resolved in an absolutely satisfactory way, and that they will have to be taken up anew each time. Moreover, this discontinuous progress does not develop at the same pace in the different disciplines: each has its own special history, so that science doubly confirms—both in the nature of its evolution and in the independence of its different areas—the discontinuous structure of truth.[14]

These multiple signs under which truth appears to us are what Benjamin called Ideas. Units of primordial intelligibility, Ideas are original semantic entities that cannot be reduced to one another and that outline the ultimate horizon of truth. The platonic reference of the term "Idea," or the Leibnizian reference of the term "monad," which Benjamin used synonymously, must not be taken literally. Benjamin's theory of knowledge does not adopt the theories of Ideas or monadology in all their technical complexity. What it retains of those two systems is the equivalence of Being, truth and multiplicity. As in Plato and Leibniz, Ideas or monads are ontological realities; yet, even if the philosopher, in the impetus of his metaphysical desire, aspires to grasp them as such, they are revealed to him only within concrete reality. Ideas, wrote Benjamin, are represented "through the medium of empirical reality."[15] It is here that Benjamin is probably closest to an authentic aesthetic theory of knowledge. This is located in fact at the confluence of two movements of absolutely opposite directions. On the one hand, Benjamin conceived the aspiration for truth as a form of metaphysical desire, like nostalgia for an Absolute that absolutely transcends all possible objects of knowledge. Knowledge and truth are radically contrasted here as a mode of objectivation, striving for the synthesis of the data and its representation, and a form of revelation. A contrast that seems to herald some of the central themes of Levinas's philosophy, between the intentionality of knowledge and the fundamentally nonintentional nature of the relationship to truth: "Truth does not enter into relationships, particularly intentional ones," wrote Benjamin. "Truth is an intentionless state of being, made up of ideas."[16] This is why "[t]he being of ideas simply cannot be conceived of as the object of vision, even intellectual vision."[17] And, in a formula that highlights the exteriority of ideas in relation to all possible subjects of knowledge, Benjamin specified: "truth is not a process of exposure which destroys a secret, but a revelation which does justice to it."[18]

For Benjamin, the revelation of truth is given in philosophical contemplation. But—and this is the second movement of his theory of knowledge—this contemplation is accompanied by a "return to phenomena."[19] In fact, truth appears to us only in the contemplation of particular phenomena. Hence, the perception of truth conceived by Benjamin is on the exact model of the aesthetic experience: totality is manifest in it as species of the particular. From this perspective, the aesthetic experience seems to be a faithful reflection of the structure of the work of art; both are epiphanies, appearances of a totality through a unique phenomenon. But in reality, the work of art could not be dissociated from the experience in which it is perceived: its beauty does not exist in itself; it is constituted as a beautiful work in the eye of the beholder. Similarly, if truth as such, that is, in its absolute transcendence, evades all grasp (at the risk of deteriorating into one of the subjects of intentional consciousness), it can, on the other hand, appear or rather, *be exposed*, to the metaphysical desire that aspires to it. This exposition, this appearance of truth, as it is given in Plato's *Symposium* to the quest for Eros, is fulfilled in the form of *beauty*. For Benjamin, there is a beauty specific to philosophical discourse, a beauty that veils truth without obscuring it, and through which it can be revealed. "Truth is beautiful, not in itself but for Eros," wrote Benjamin in the first version of the introduction to the book on baroque drama. And a little later: "The exposition of itself implied by truth is the last refuge of beauty."[20] It is in philosophical writing that truth takes shape. This is not a simple matter of "style"; it is because language originally knew a perfect equivalence between words and things, that philosophical discourse—like poetry—can hope to recover the "language of truth."

Thus, philosophical discourse is far from being a simple form. In itself, it is Eros, an aspiration to truth; to the same extent that ideas are nothing else, in reality, than the profane expression of the original "names" composing the Adamic language. Benjamin insisted on the fact that, for him, Ideas are not images but words. As in the biblical tradition, the revelation of truth is not visual but auditory.[21] Thus, beyond the "prattle" we have fallen into, it is the original and utopian persistence of the paradisiacal language that guarantees philosophical discourse—insofar as it appears as a form of poetic discourse—the possibility of achieving truth. And this is because, in our secularized world, "philosophy may not presume to speak in the tones of revelation."[22] That "reminiscence," that "return to original comprehension," must necessarily be done through the poetic exercise of language.

*

In the introduction to the book on baroque drama, the transition from an aesthetic paradigm of knowledge to an aesthetic paradigm of history is performed through the analysis of the *original*. This notion, central in *The Origin of German Tragic Drama*, indicates the feature that, in certain privileged phenomena, identifies them as embodiments of an idea. In fact, if ideas are given to knowledge only through the medium of phenomena, that does not mean, vice versa, that all phenomena are the manifestation of an Idea. Quite the contrary, in the disorder of phenomena of all nature that makes reality, rare are those that seem invested from the outset with the sign of the original: a quality specific to the phenomenon that does not convey compliance with some objective criterion, but that is obvious to us, said Benjamin, as the evidence of an authenticity. A phenomenon is given to us as original when it evokes in us the echo or memory of an idea—or rather a word—in its original meaning. The discovery of the original is an experience that bears in itself its own truth, comparable in that to aesthetic judgment according to Kant, while, by revealing sensibility and subjectivity, implies the universal validity of its assertions. In this sense, the identification of a phenomenon as original certainly depends on an aesthetic type of intuition; to recognize that a phenomenon is original is to apply the same sort of judgment as that which consists of asserting that a certain work of art is beautiful.

As in Goethe, original phenomena in Benjamin occupy an intermediary place between the world of ideas and the empirical world. They allow the abstract idea of unity or invariance to be recovered within the multiplicity of the perceptible. In the book on baroque drama, the perceptible is defined above all as the world of change and temporality. The original thus appears there as an epiphany of the idea under the species of temporality. In other words, *original phenomena of knowledge are given to us as original phenomena of history. Those, in turn, will appear to us as original phenomena of art.* That means, first, that each great historical period (antiquity, the Renaissance, the baroque) has the same specificity, the same irreducible nature as great works of art, each of which defines its own system of norms, so that no causal bond can make them proceed from one another. Thus, the various historical periods will have to be conceived not as links of a chain but as independent semantic units, that is, as Benjamin himself put it, as "structures." Benjamin contrasted a Hegelian view of history, defined as the projection on a linear and continuous temporal axis of a dialectic immanent in the human spirit, with the idea of a discontinuous series of "original phenomena," able to appear on a multitude of temporal lines independent of one another. Yet—and here the survival of an underlying theological paradigm is indicated—the great moments of history still outline a process (that is certainly not linear) of teleological inspiration: just as (in "The Task of the Translator") the sequence of great literary texts and their translations mark stages of the restoration of the Adamic language in its original integrity, so the emergence of historical "structures" accentuates the process through which different ideas (that is, primordial names) are gradually embodied in historical reality.[23]

But what mainly characterizes aesthetic knowledge, as manifest in the intuition of the original, is that it gives access to a specific form of the experience of time. To recognize a work as original is to discover something in it that is both absolutely first and radically new. The original is what seems to have existed in all times and that yet happens to us for the first time. In the experience of beauty, time opens to us in the double dimension of the brand-new and the immemorial. This paradox translates the duality inherent in every idea into the medium of temporal experience: it certainly belongs to the world of truth, but it is only a fragment of it; as an elementary sign of the Adamic language, it is part of Revelation, but it presents precisely only one part of it. Similarly, the original phenomenon refers to the primordial order of truth but at the same time indicates the fact that, in the reality of the world, this truth is still incomplete. "The original," wrote Benjamin, "is always presented as a discovery that would, at the same time, be a rebirth. A rebirth of the unprecedented as something that would come from an immemorial medium. Discovery of the reality of a phenomenon as represented the forgotten medium of Revelation."[24] What is fundamental in the perception of the origin is in fact its "double determination": "The original as such reveals its secret only if both the restoration of Revelation and the necessarily unfinished nature of such a restoration are recognized in it."[25]

Thus, the experience of the original, as given par excellence in aesthetic perception, opens onto a completely specific apprehension of temporality. Temporality is presented to us simultaneously, so to speak, in the dimension of the past and of the future. This means that neither exists outside of the present experience that we are in the process of making. In the perception of the original, we do not discover the past as a fact that, at any rate, would exist outside of us but as the immemorial background of our present experience. Similarly, the future does not appear there (as in the idea of progress) as a linear extension of the past but as a utopian promise engraved in our intuition of the original phenomenon. Here, the theological schema of the youthful writings is rediscovered, that the final stage of history will be that in which all potentials engraved in the original order will have been realized. But at present, the concrete model of such a teleology is provided by the temporal structure of the work of art, which also returns for Benjamin through the structure of the aesthetic experience that constitutes this temporality.

The perception of the original is the proceeding of the present in relation to which the two dimensions of the past and the future are constituted. On the one hand, insofar as the primordial reality of the idea is reflected through it, the original phenomenon is absolutely specific, bearing, like all past, the mark of *uniqueness*. But on the other hand, precisely because it is part of empirical reality, there is in it a share of limitation and incompleteness: it never represents anything but one of the possible embodiments of the idea, and as a result, it has a future in store, other recurrences, different from the ones we know; in this sense, it is essentially *repetitive*. This is the paradox of historical time according to Benjamin: the primordial data that constitute it (events, periods, works, or structures) are unique and archetypal, irreversible and recurrent, at the same time.

This view of history, which is at the core of the book on baroque drama, will be developed again in *The Arcades Project*, where allegory, for example, will be presented as an "original phenomenon" embodied successively in the literature of antiquity, the Middle Ages, the baroque, and finally in Baudelaire. Similarly, in *On the Concept of History*, the various revolutionary attempts humanity has known, from Spartacus to 1917, represent so many reincarnations of the original phenomenon of Revolution.[26] Hence, we can better understand Benjamin's formulation to define the function of the original phenomenon in the constitution of historical time, in the introduction to the book on baroque drama: "There takes place in every original phenomenon a determination of the form in which an idea will constantly confront the historical world, until it is revealed fulfilled in the totality of its history."[27]

Thus, each original phenomenon becomes the center of a unit of historical intelligibility, with its own present, past, and future. To go back to an example Benjamin gave at the end of *The Origin of German Tragic Drama*, the baroque can be understood as the past of an original phenomenon of which expressionism is the present; as for its future, as unpredictable as that of every work of art, it will be constituted according to the various reinterpretations of that same primordial "idea" embodied also by the baroque and expressionism. Thus, separate, autonomous, and nontotalizable histories are formed, like so many galaxies, around the multiplicity of original phenomena. Is there not a contradiction between that idea of a fragmented history resistant to every synthesis, and the teleological conception of history as a progressive realization of all potentials inherent, as it were, in its original plan? And in fact this tension, still implicit in the book on baroque drama, is discussed only later in *The Arcades Project*, then especially in *On the Concept of History*, where utopia (or Redemption) is conceived precisely as the final gathering, at the end of each of the "monadological" processes that make up history, of all messianic attempts undertaken thus far by humanity. But this model—inspired implicitly by Jewish messianism, then rethought in aesthetic terms—was already present in "The Task of the Translator" and in the introduction to *The Origin of German Tragic Drama*.

In each of the units of historical intelligibility of which the original phenomenon is the center, a history comes to a halt and becomes structure; diachrony is absorbed in it by synchrony:

> Virtually, because that which is comprehended in the idea of origin still has history, in the sense of content, but not in the sense of a set of occurrences which have befallen it. Its history is inward in character and is not to be understood as something boundless, but as something related to essential being, and it can therefore be described as the past and subsequent history of this being. . . . It is no longer pragmatically real, but as natural history, is to be inferred from the state of completion and rest, from the essence. The tendency of all philosophical conceptualization is thus redefined in the old sense: to establish the becoming of phenomena in their being. For in the science of philosophy the concept of being is not satisfied by the phenomenon until it has absorbed all its history.[28]

*

Remarkably, at the same time, *The Origin of German Tragic Drama* presents another conception of history that is also inspired by an aesthetic model and whose significance seems strictly opposed to the one we have just outlined: this is the baroque view of history as Benjamin revealed it through his theory of *allegory*. In fact, if in the introduction to the book, Benjamin presented his own doctrine of historical knowledge, the chapter on allegory analyzes the view of history specific to baroque literature. But this is not a simple objective presentation; the baroque concept of history reflects a culture that marks, for Benjamin, the beginning of modernity. The idea of a world deserted by divine grace, abandoned entirely to secular powers, which was at the heart of Counter-Reformation theology, and as a result, at the heart of baroque art, inaugurates to a certain extent the great movement of the secularization of the world and history that still characterizes European culture. But the baroque had also interpreted this fall into the secular in a profoundly theological way, as the sanction of original sin, that is, as a misfortune and the sign of our damnation. In these two aspects of the view of the baroque world, Benjamin rediscovered the bases of his own philosophical tradition: both his membership in a culture that is irremediably secularized and the painful awareness of the fact that this secularization represents an essential break, as the loss of an ideal state he would never have mourned. In this sense, for Benjamin, the melancholy of the baroque artists clearly represents the model of his own melancholy.

For baroque art, as Benjamin understood it, history after the original Fall is nothing but an irreversible process of decline: "This is the heart of the allegorical way of seeing, of the baroque, secular explanation of history as the Passion of the world; its importance resides solely in the stations of its decline."[29] It is as if, for Benjamin, the baroque view of history coincided with the tragic schema he had devised in his youthful text "On Language as Such and on the Language of Man"; in the historical trajectory drawn by biblical theology, only the downward part had been adopted by baroque art, while the idea of an upward movement, a return to lost integrity, no longer corresponded to the pessimism of the Counter-Reformation. In his 1916 text, Benjamin had indicated that the original fall out of the paradisiacal language had hurled humanity not only into the "abyss of prattle," but also into the endless disorder of "significations." Outside the primordial harmony of the word and the thing, the gulf of arbitrary denominations opens up, of random attempts to subject the real to abstract categories. In contrast to the concreteness of the Adamic language, the language of fallen humanity, marked by the forgetting of original "names," bears in it the rift of the sign and the object it claims to designate; it is in this rift that significations are always reengendered. Just as death, as a sign of the Fall, represents the split of man from his original nature, so the arbitrary multitude of significations manifests his split from the order of the *physis*.

Death and signification on the one hand, original nature on the other: between these two irremediably separate orders, the baroque, according to Benjamin, tries to rebuild bridges by creating a profusion of images that are supposed to give meaning to reality, but that, in fact, only deepen the gulf separating us from it. By the profusion and arbitrariness that constitute it, the baroque allegory indicates precisely the inability of a fallen humanity to recover the original meaning of the world:

The greater the significance, the greater the subjection to death, because death digs most deeply the jagged line of demarcation between physical nature and significance. But if nature has always been subject to the power of death, it is also true that it has always been allegorical. Significance and death both come to fruition in historical development, just as they are closely linked as seeds in the creature's graceless state of sin.[30]

Thus, for Benjamin, allegory is not a simple rhetorical figure. It is a privileged signifier that refers, well beyond its aesthetic signification, to a whole view of history. A radically pessimistic view, not only because humanity appears cut off from truth in it (not by a lack but by an excess of signification), but especially because it is condemned to remain forever a prisoner of its finitude: the fall is definitive; it is what seals our fate; nothing will ever allow us here on earth to recover the Adamic perfection:

[I]n allegory the observer is confronted with the *facies hippocratica* of history as a petrified, primordial landscape. Everything about history that, from the very beginning, has been untimely, sorrowful, unsuccessful, is expressed in a face— or rather in a death's head.[31]

Baroque emblems freeze the development of history into static allegories, into funereal images, like fetishes, given to the morose contemplation of a melancholy spectator. Benjamin interpreted the various forms of baroque aesthetic—ornament, scroll, fragment—as so many projections into space of a petrified temporal dynamic. In this sense, baroque forms express nothing; they are pure variations, arbitrary signs that refer to nothing, like a play of hieroglyphs hiding no meaning. Hence, the importance of theater, where history, stylized and stopped, is projected onto the stage:

When, as is the case in the *Trauerspiel*, history becomes part of the setting, it does so as script. The word "history" stands written on the countenance of nature in the characters of transience. The allegorical physiognomy of the nature-history, which is put on stage in the *Trauerspiel*, is present in reality in the form of the ruin. In the ruin history has physically merged into the setting. And in this guise history does not assume the form of the process of an eternal life so much as that of irresistible decay.[32]

In *The Origin of German Tragic Drama*, this baroque model of a catastrophic history is contrasted with the theological model of a history oriented toward a messianic completion. Between the two, a "formalist" theory of historical knowledge, inspired by Goethean morphology, ultimately grants the historian himself the freedom to interpret historical structures, in their multiplicity and their autonomy, as so many "original phenomena," that is, as so many stages in the process of reconstitution of the primordial landscape of truth, or as fragments bereft of meaning, whose accumulation sketches nothing but a field of ruins.

The Angel of History

History as messianic process, history as catastrophic process; at the horizon of those two paradoxical visions is a single conception of the work of the historian: what we call history is generated in the writing of history; writing history is not rediscovering the past; it is creating it from our own present; or rather, it is interpreting the traces left by the past, transforming them into signs; it is, ultimately, "reading the real as a text."[1] It is remarkable that all these themes, already underlying the book on baroque drama, reappear as central categories in the final period of Benjamin's work, the one initiated around 1926, when his thought began to be oriented toward historical materialism. There is not one element of the aesthetic paradigm of history that is not found either under a more or less modified form or in a strictly identical way in the philosophy of history of his "Marxist" period. In Benjamin's thought, there is an exceptional continuity: nothing is ever abandoned, everything is preserved, the appearance of a new paradigm does not abolish the former paradigm; more than evolution, we must talk here of stratification.

The emergence of the political model of history does not involve the cancellation of the aesthetic model or, a fortiori, that of the theological model. The turn or, if you like, the revolution in Benjamin's thought, is not expressed by a break with the preceding stage but by a reordering of the elements that constitute it; the appearance of a new category (here, politics) implies the loss of primacy or, if you like, its reinterpretation in light of politics for the previously dominant category (aesthetics). As for the theological categories, predominant in his youthful writings, subordinated to the aesthetic categories in the book on baroque drama, they function henceforth as almost esoteric references (for example, in the essay "The Work of Art in the Age of Mechanical Reproduction," or in the text "The Narrator"), to resurface only with *On the Concept of History.*

The transition from the aesthetic to the political paradigm of history turns on a very precise point: it concerns a reinterpretation of the present moment of the historian, conceived in *The Origin of German Tragic Drama* as an aesthetic condition, and beginning with the preliminary notes for *The Arcades Project*, as a political condition. In the book on baroque drama, the historian had been presented as an artist, impelled by his desire to contemplate ideas, and who, through the exercise of a quasi-poetic writing, achieved comprehension of the original phenomena of history. In this sense, the proceeding of the historian's act of speech coincided with contemplating the present moment. There, the immemorial past and the utopian future of the original phenomenon flowing from the source to the sea are open to him.

Benjamin's "Marxist" turn is manifested, among other things, by a new distrust of the abstract, speculative, and irresponsible character of a purely aesthetic vision of history. "To understand actuality as the reverse side of eternity, the side lodged in history and to take the imprint of that hidden side of the seal"[2]—this became Benjamin's aspiration. We see eternity; it is not absent; it remains in the background of this concept as the theological horizon from which facts, works, and events free themselves; furthermore, as in the book on baroque drama, the historical is nothing but the trace eternity prints on time. Novelty is elsewhere: in the new emphasis on *actuality.* If eternity is engraved in time, it is no longer through the *nunc stans* of aesthetic contemplation but through the actuality of the historical moment, both in its transience and in all the weight of its political reality. Moreover, as in the case of the original phenomenon, it is no longer the crystallization of a presence "in miniature" of eternity in time but of a reverse trace left by the other side of a medal: in an entirely secular world, historic structures never draw anything but the intaglio of an invisible eternity. The historian's present moment, where other dimensions of historical time are opened to him, comes to signify the concrete historical situation—an intersection of antagonistic forces—where his discourse is generated.

In a first attempt (not subsequently followed up) to realize this new political constitution of historical time, Benjamin had conveyed the abstract opposition of the present and the past by the concrete tension of *sensation* and *tradition*. Concerning his project on the Parisian arcades, he had written in 1928 or 1929: "One of the tendencies of the present work: to purge history radically of all 'evolution,' and represent becoming as a constellation of Being, dividing it dialectically into sensation and tradition."[3] Later on, the present condition of historical knowledge is conveyed by another metaphor, central in the economy of *The Arcades Project*, that of *awakening*. "Just as Proust begins the story of his life with an awakening, so must every presentation of history begin with awakening; in fact, it should treat of nothing else," Benjamin wrote. "This one, accordingly, deals with awakening from the nineteenth century."[4] The image of awakening does not mark a transition between sleep and the state of waking but a dialectic overturn, a qualitative metamorphosis of awareness: at the extreme edge of sleep, what still seemed to us to be the medium of dream is transformed into reality, while what we had taken for reality is revealed in retrospect as having been a dream.

A founding element of consciousness, in which what was lived as reality sheds its mask and is revealed as illusion, awakening is the metaphor par excellence of sobering up, demystification, the cathartic moment when the veil is ripped off; an illumination that makes us achieve a superior stage of consciousness, and that, in Benjamin, also refers both to the Freudian anamnesis and to the dialectical reversal of Hegel or Marx. It is this sudden clarity, this exposure of illusion, which now defines the historian's present condition: "The new, dialectical method of doing history presents itself as the art of experiencing the present as waking world, a world to which that dream we name the past refers in truth," wrote Benjamin. "Awakening is namely the dialectical, Copernican turn of remembrance."[5] An essentially political revolution, since it is now writing history *in reverse*, from the historian's present, understood as the very place of truth. Whether this new conception of history is presented theoretically but through a metaphor, and whether that metaphor is itself borrowed from a literary work, is what indicates the permanence of the aesthetic paradigm. But this is now restored to a pure function of signifier; in other words, the signified, the philosophy of history to which it refers, is political.

Yet, it is certainly these metaphors, these "dialectical images," that form the language the historian uses to decipher the past. The historical object is not given; it is constructed by the writing of history, that is, by dialectical images. Those, of which Benjamin says that they are the "original phenomena of history,"[6] allow the various elements of the past to "achieve a higher degree of actuality than in the time when they existed."[7] Thus, each dialectical image is the expression of a certain form of "awakening"; in the past's perception of itself, it highlights a part of illusion, of self-mystification, but in the process, it also reveals the truth that past bears for us today. One example, among many others: the invention of the Chinese puzzle at the beginning of the nineteenth century meant only the appearance of a new parlor game for contemporaries; for the historian of today, it "reveals the century's awakening sense for construction, . . . and [is] a first presentiment of the cubist principle in the plastic arts."[8] It is the encounter between the Chinese puzzle and cubism that is engendered by the dialectical image. "A lightning conjunction between past and present" from which a "constellation arises," such is the dialectical image; there is no causal relation between the Chinese puzzle and cubism: "it is not a process, but an image, there is a leap."[9] Thus, dialectical images mark a "caesura in the movement of thought," but insofar as history is structured, that is, becomes legible, only through writing history, they also define the historical object itself as a "caesura in the unfolding of time."[10]

Thus, we see that the dialectical image, an aesthetic category, ultimately determines the political perception of history: to provoke the "telescoping" of the past and the present to give birth to a dialectical image is precisely to decipher the past through our present, that is, to read it politically. Aesthetics, a privileged signifier, provides the language through which the fundamentally political nature of history is revealed. The metaphor of awakening and that of the dialectical image internally transform the idea of the present as a simple transition between past and future. The case of the historian's discourse is no longer perceived as a neutral place, an observation point located anywhere, somewhere in the intermediate zone separating past from future, but as a specific moment, a lived instant, loaded with all the tensions and contradictions that produce a precise historical intersection. This, then, is the revolution Benjamin called for: transposing the experience of lived time from the personal sphere to the historical sphere, deformalizing historical time as Saint Augustine or Bergson deformalized physical time, replacing the idea of objective linear time with the subjective experience of a qualitative time, each instant of which is lived in its incomparable uniqueness.

As in Saint Augustine, it is the present, the only indisputable reality, that polarizes the past and the future in Benjamin, but this present is no longer that of internal life, nor can it be limited any longer to the lightning flash of aesthetic experience. The "present of knowledge," that "time of now" from which all apprehension of the past and future emerges, is defined increasingly clearly, since 1936–1937, as a moment of history, and more precisely, of politics: it is in terms of a concrete experience of collective crises and conflicts in which he himself is involved that the historian lives his double relationship to the past and the future. Like Saint Augustine, Benjamin might say: "there be three times; a present of things past, a present of things present, and a present of things future";[11] but this both unchanging and always new present is not a spiritual state for him; it is an inscription in history.

Hence, the fundamentally historical nature of his perception of both the past and the future; Benjamin could have adopted the formula of the *Confessions* for himself: "present of things past, memory; present of things present, sight; present of things future, expectation";[12] but all those notions represent historical categories for him: memory is what evokes the recollection of past generations; expectation is the collective salvation of humanity; as for vision, Benjamin understood it as the *prophetic* quality involved in the *political* intuition of the present: "It is no accident that Turgot defines the notion of a present, the intentional object of a prophecy, as a fundamentally political reality: 'Even before we could have found out about a certain state of things,' says Turgot, 'this state had already changed numerous times. Thus we always apprehend too late what has happened. One could thus say that politics is destined, as it were, to anticipate the present.' The actuality of an authentic writing of history is founded on just such a conception of the present."[13]

Thus, to understand the present politically requires anticipating the future somehow; yet, this anticipation is not prediction, as if the future were inevitably shaped in the present; rather it is deciphering the future as a chess player reads the arrangement of the pieces on the chessboard, that is, by realizing in advance the possible developments it implies. Contrary to naïve, that is, nonpolitical, perception of the present, which never discovers more than the repetition or trace of a situation that has already occurred, the political reading of a given constellation will be the one that shifts it toward the future. If we can talk here of prophecy, Benjamin wrote, "It does not predict the future. It suffices but to indicate the hour which is about to toll."[14] For Benjamin, this is also true of authentic historical knowledge. This knowledge can apprehend the past, that is, grasp the meaning it can have for us, only by starting from very sharp awareness of the present moment and its significance for the future.

Yet, conversely, the present assumes its meaning only in relation to the past, or rather to some specific moment of the past, which it extends or, more precisely, which is *reincarnated* in it. Just as genuine (that is, political) awareness of the present involves a certain anticipation of the future, it also manifests a certain *tropism* toward the past. This does not mean leaving the present to think back and identify (as in Fustel de Coulanges's theory of historical empathy) with some special moment of the past but, on the contrary, of reading in our present the trace of a forgotten or repressed past. The political vision of the present highlights the kinship of the situation we are living with the struggles and suffering of preceding generations. But this historical memory has nothing cumulative; it is not designed to load the present with a burden of events it is fated to preserve. It is, rather, as if the political awareness of the present leaped over centuries to grasp a moment of the past in which it recognizes itself; not to commemorate it but to reanimate it, give it a new life, and try to achieve today what once failed. The Proustian experience of resurrecting the past in the illumination of recollection is raised to the status of a historical category. In Proust, it is less a matter of recovering the past than of *saving* it. No doubt, in a certain sense, saving it from oblivion. But if memory is content to restore events of the past to the collective heritage and celebrate them as a cult, they would forever remain prisoners of the conformity of tradition. For Benjamin, saving the past means especially "to wrest it from conformity, which at every moment threatens to harm it,"[15] to give it a new relevance in the heart of our present. For "the way [the past] is honored as 'heritage' is more disastrous than its simple disappearance could ever be."[16]

Thus, the three dimensions of historical time are connected to a fundamentally political experience of the present. This is the home where past and present meet. Here the always individual Proustian experience of resurrecting the past in the present is replaced by the historical awareness of a *today* where the memory of past generations converges. At the same time, it appears as a radical innovation, a manifestation of what had never happened before. If this *actualization* of the past and the future is necessarily political, it is because, for Benjamin, it depends on a choice. The historian who saves some moment of the past from the conformity that threatens to engulf it by granting it a new significance, in light of his own present, does so because he feels *responsible* for the past. The past is transmitted to us through a hermeneutic *tradition*, which selects events, keeps some, rejects others, and which, sometimes, decides on their interpretation. This is the image of the past constructed by that tradition Benjamin called "the history of the victors." What characterizes it is the continuity with which it is handed down from generation to generation; this is, in fact, the indispensable condition for its endurance. To be challenged, the continuity of historiographical tradition must be broken at a certain point: even when the "materialist" historian intervenes to cast a new look at the past and save the "history of the vanquished" from oblivion. The construction of history, as he understands it, will then be "dedicated to the memory of the nameless."[17] This radical change of historical perspective, this desire to take on the memory of the forgotten, is certainly the result of a decision that can be called political, in the broadest sense of the term, but that, for Benjamin, is also presented as an ethical decision.

From this point of view, the specifically political dimension of the "present of knowledge" is inseparable from a moral vision, from a sense of responsibility of the historian toward a past and a future he must answer for somehow. It is right here that Benjamin splits radically from the Marxist philosophy of history (either in its orthodox form or in its social-democratic variant): for him, the historical dialectic (that is, class struggle) is not a *necessary* process leading inevitably to the victory of the oppressed, and as a result, the task of the materialist historian does not consist solely of recording the stages of that dialectic. Quite the contrary: far from indicating an irreversible movement of progress, history is the site *at each moment of time* of an ever-renewed struggle between an obsessive tendency (illustrated by Blanqui's *Eternity Through the Stars*) to the incessant return of the Same and the appearance, amid the infinity of possibles, of the brand-new that Benjamin called Redemption. It is in this uncertain struggle that the revolutionary historian intervenes trying to liberate the element of radical novelty contained in each moment of the past. Thus, the fate of history is played out in the present of the historian; it is this present that is the genuine site of the Last Judgment. "The apocryphal saying of one of the Gospels: 'On whatever I meet a man, so shall he be judged,' sheds remarkable light on the Last Judgment. It is reminiscent of Kafka's aphorism in which the Last Judgment is a martial court always assembled. But the Gospel says more: according to it, the Day of Judgment is no different from any other day. In any case, this saying supplies the notion of the present the historian must adopt as his own. Each moment of time bears judgment on moments that precede it."[18]

The connection between politics and theology in Benjamin's final philosophy of history is at the heart of this conception of the present. Compared with the claim of historicism to attain objective knowledge of the past, "now-time" defines a vision of history governed by the demands of the present situation; but this essentially political vision of history also reveals the conflict that constantly contrasts the two principles of repetition and revolution, continuity and rupture, the unchanging and the new. But these two forces are not equal: it is the status quo that is handed down from generation to generation by those in power, that is, by all those who were once victorious. The inertia that perpetuated past injustices can be broken only by the eruption of something radically new, which could not be deduced from the sum of past events. It is this break of historical temporality, this appearance of the unpredictable, that Benjamin called Redemption. But this is not located anywhere at the end of time; on the contrary, it happens (or it can happen) at any moment, precisely as each moment of time—grasped as absolutely unique —brings a new state of the world into being. The qualitative difference of each of the fragments of time always brings a new possibility of an unforeseen change, a brand-new arrangement of the order of things. In contrast to the Marxist idea of the "end of history," based on a quantitative and cumulative vision of historical time, what is drawn here is the idea, borrowed from Jewish messianism, of a *utopia appearing in the very heart of the present*, of a hope lived in the mode of today.

In this sense, the Last Judgment takes place every day. But despite appearances, Benjamin here is farthest away from Hegel's formula that "universal history is a universal judgment." For Hegel, it is history that ultimately determines the meaning of events; through the success or failure of human enterprises, it decides which of them participates in the adventure of Reason. The very essence of this history, whose sentences constantly sanction the triumph of the strongest and the disappearance of the weakest, represents the history of the winners. On the contrary, Judgment, in the sense that Benjamin understood it, indicates the ever-renewed fight of the living—including the historian—to try to save the heritage of the losers. For Hegel, the Judgment of history is that by which history judges man; for Benjamin, it is the one by which man judges history.

It is in this questioning of the omnipotence of historical reality in the name of an ethical exigency that we must seek the "theological meaning" of Benjamin's final philosophy of history. The concepts derived from Jewish mysticism subvert historical Reason by giving a new opportunity to everything that has been erased, forgotten, or not accounted for in the past. It is thus that the Benjaminian notion of "recollection" (*Eingedenken*) continues the Jewish category of "re-remembering" (*Zekher*), which does not denote the preservation in memory of events of the past but their reactualization in the present experience. The task of recollection, wrote Benjamin, is to "save what has failed," just as Redemption for him does not mean a tangential relationship to the future but the ever-present possibility of "achieving what we were refused." As for the messianic hope, it must not be conceived as aiming for a utopia destined to be realized at the end of time but as an extreme vigilance, a capacity to detect what at each moment shows the "revolutionary energy" of the new.[19]

*

The theological-political model developed by Benjamin in the last phase of his reflections on history is based on a rigorous critique of the positivist vision of historical temporality. Point by point, this critique addresses ideas developed a decade earlier in the introduction to the book on baroque drama, but by shifting the emphasis from the aesthetic to the political experience, or more precisely, to that extreme limit where politics must be told in theological terms if it is to be thought to the end. *A critique of temporal continuity, a critique of historical causality, a critique of the ideology of progress*—these are the three themes the work of theological politics uses to undermine the very foundations of the positivist vision of history.

In *The Arcades Project*, there are entries contrasting the false continuity postulated by historicism with the reality of discontinuity manifest in the always unpredictable appearance of new works of art. But much more fundamentally, the idea of historical continuity is exposed once and for all as an illusion maintained by the mythology of the winners to wipe out all trace of the history of the losers. For these are the ruptures of the historical fabric, the spasms and revolts of the oppressed, or even more essentially, the underground tradition of the excluded and the forgotten, who bear witness for all the victims of history. "The history of the oppressed," wrote Benjamin, "is a discontinuous history,"[20] while "continuity is that of the oppressors."[21] However, this does not mean that continuity and discontinuity confront each other as two equally polemical—that is, equally biased—conceptions of the historical process. If it is true that each represents a weapon in the always renewed confrontation of the victors and the vanquished, it is the memory of the defeated alone that reveals the truth of history, since it is doomed to forget nothing, neither the rule of the powerful that victimizes them nor the tradition of victims that it must perpetuate.

Here, Benjamin's thought encounters a paradox (which, as we shall see, has sustained Jewish messianism from its origin) but does manage to avoid and perhaps even overcome it. If it is in fact true that the history of the oppressed is essentially discontinuous, how can they *tell* it, that is, unfold it in a sequence of events without unwittingly imposing the schema of temporal continuity on it? This objection is addressed primarily to Marxist historiography, which, for Benjamin, had always threatened to transform the tragic history of the oppressed proletariat and its vain revolutionary attempts into a victorious epic. But, more generally, it is also aimed at the apologetic temptation in the name of which the victims of history risk freezing their own past into a "heritage" destined not to be reactualized in the struggles of the present but to become a simple object of commemoration. In other words, if, vis-à-vis the *history* of the winners, there really is a secret *tradition* of the losers, is this not always threatened to be co-opted in turn by another form of conformism?

In a preparatory note for the *Theses*, Benjamin wrote that there is a "fundamental *aporia*"; if one wants to contrast "tradition as the discontinuity of the past" with "history as the continuity of events," how can it be maintained at the same time that "the task of history is to lay hold of the tradition of the oppressed?"[22] If we admit that if the tradition of the oppressed can, in turn, become the object of a history, this will be a radically *different* form of history; this *other history*, which Benjamin had initially defined in theological terms, then in reference to the aesthetic experience, and now grasped in terms of the theological-political angle, maintains a completely different relationship with the past from the one that historic Reason cites in the constant process of its evolution. When history takes account of the memory of the losers, it borrows from tradition its most specific traits: its nonlinearity, its breaks and irregularities, in short, the presence of a radical *negativity* in it. In contrast to historical rationality, based on the fiction of a homogeneous temporal flow connecting successive instants, tradition—the transmission from one generation to another of a collective memory—involves as its very condition the rupture of time, the break between periods, the hollow void between fathers and sons.

If, for Benjamin, tradition conveys the authentic historical awareness, it is because it is based on the reality of death. Unlike Bergsonian *durée*, a flow of pure positivity producing a private psyche removed from history, tradition owes its real creativity to the fact that it incessantly collides with death—that is, its own interruption—but that, above that abyss, it does not cease to reassert itself.[23] "While the idea of continuity crushes and levels everything in its path," wrote Benjamin, "the idea of discontinuity is the foundation of authentic tradition."[24] It is not from the endless flow of instants that the new can reappear, but from stopping time, a break, beyond which life begins again in a form that constantly eludes all prediction. Hence, the essential relationship that, in Benjamin, binds tradition and Redemption; it is the break of time, that is, meaning, that reappears. "The Messiah interrupts history," he wrote; "the Messiah does not appear at the end of an evolution."[25]

In *On the Philosophy of History*, those privileged moments that break the course of time and initiate a new era are defined as the junctures where revolutions burst: "The awareness that they are about to make the continuum of history explode is characteristic of the revolutionary classes at the moment of their action. The great revolution introduced a new calendar. The initial day of a calendar serves as a historical time-lapse camera."[26] But for Benjamin, that essentially political experience, when time stops to produce the new, itself appears as the secularized form of a very ancient religious experience, that of the interruption of profane time and the eruption of a qualitatively different time, that of festival and rite, a moment of death and rebirth, where the old duration is abolished to produce the new: "it is the same day that keeps recurring in the guise of holidays, which are days of remembrance. Thus the calendars do not measure time as clocks do; they are monuments of a historical consciousness of which not the slightest trace has been apparent in Europe in the past hundred years."[27]

The theological-political criticism of historical causality is expressed in the light of this idea of discontinuous time. For two events to be connected by a bond of cause and effect, they must be located on a continuous temporal axis. Here, too, the always unforeseen appearance of new works of art had provided the model of nonlinear history, independent of the principle of causality. But henceforth, it is the instability of history itself that forbids seeing it as a succession of cause and effect: the duality of a visible history, as depicted by the history of the winners, and a secret history, passed on from one age to another by the tradition of the losers; fractures of historical time, revolutions, mutations, and especially, the change of generations, relentless death, separating sons from their fathers, force the post-positivist historian to resort to another model of interpretation. The penultimate paragraph of *On the Concept of History*, devoted to the criticism of historical causality, indicates the nature of this new model:

Historicism contents itself with establishing a causal connection between various moments in history. But no fact that is a cause is for that very reason historical. It became historical posthumously, as it were, through events that may be separated from it by thousands of years. A historian who takes this as his point of departure stops telling the sequence of events like the beads of a rosary. Instead, he grasps the constellation which his own era has formed with a definite earlier one. Thus he establishes a conception of the present as the "time of the now" which is shot through with chips of Messianic time.[28]

Benjamin's criticism clearly does not relate to the principle of causality in general but to its application to history. Benjamin accused historicism of imposing on history the model of mechanical causality in which the cause of an effect must immediately precede it (or at least be very close) on the temporal chain. For him, the establishment of a causal link between two successive events does not, in itself, create historical intelligibility. This can stem only from the encounter between a past and a present moment, the one where the historian is located. The historian's interest in any particular period or event translates a kind of elective affinity between two moments of history, but an affinity that is experienced less as a harmonious agreement than as a shock, as the sudden collision of two temporal entities that can, as Benjamin says, be separated by millennia. From this encounter, a new type of historical intelligibility is born, based not on a *scientific* model of knowledge, designed to reveal the *laws* of historical process, but on a *hermeneutic* model, tending to the *interpretation* of events, that is, toward illuminating their *meaning*. The "telescoping" of these noncontiguous events engenders a new form of thought, in which the present fertilizes the past and awakens the forgotten or repressed meaning it bears, while the past, in the heart of the present, discovers a new vitality.

For Benjamin, this encounter of the present and the past functions in terms of the model of *metaphor* in which the encounter of two signifiers in different semantic fields engenders a third brand-new signifier. In fact, it is not a matter of subsuming the present and the past within a common category but, on the contrary, of generating a new reality from their conjunction. This idea appears elsewhere in Benjamin's writings in the form of a (dialectical) *image*, which confirms the central role the aesthetic model of history continued to play in his thought at the core of a theological-political critique of historical Reason. This distinction between the two models can be perceived clearly in the fifth thesis on the philosophy of history, devoted precisely to the critique of historicist epistemology:

The true picture of the past flits by. The past can be seized only as an image which flashes up at the instant when it can be recognized and is never seen again. "The truth will not run away from us": in the historical outlook of historicism these words of Gottfried Keller mark the exact point where historical materialism cuts through historicism. For every image of the past that is not recognized by the present as one of its own concerns threatens to disappear irretrievably.[29]

But what is new here, and is emphasized strongly in the next thesis, is that the present in terms of which the past is grasped as in a flash is a fundamentally political moment. It is, wrote Benjamin, "to seize hold of a memory as it flashes up at a moment of danger."[30] This danger, he explained, is that which "affects both the content of the tradition and its receivers. The same threat hangs over both: that of becoming a tool of the ruling class."[31] Note that, for Benjamin, this term denotes the heirs of all winners; the moment in question is the one in which the losers of history, in a sudden illumination, grasp that they are going to be robbed of the meaning of their past, or in other words, their tradition is going to die. It is an extremely paradoxical moment, since it is precisely the revelation of that mortal threat that allows wrenching from the control of official history the "spark of hope" imprisoned in a moment of the past. It is this ambivalence that defines the place of the historian, that "now-time" that magnetizes and revives aspects of the past that had been sacrificed to the past; it is a case of a present that is both political—since it is in the name of today's struggle that it takes up the heritage of the losers of history— and theological insofar as those sparks of hope hidden deep in the past are also "bursts of the messianic age."

Questioning a conception of history based on the idea of temporal continuity and governed by the principle of causality leads to a radical critique of the ideology of progress:

It may be considered one of the methodological objectives of this work [*The Arcades Project*] to demonstrate a historical materialism which has annihilated within itself the idea of progress. Just here, historical materialism has every reason to distinguish itself sharply from bourgeois habits of thought. Its founding concept is not progress but actualization.[32]

In fact, in the lightning flash engendered by the dialectical image, "blasting a specific life out of the era or a specific work out of the lifework,"[33] the historian will necessarily be led to read history as a series of breaks and re-beginnings. This does not mean only that significant historical moments are revealed less in evolutions than in revolutions, but also and perhaps especially, that even in evolutionary processes, in the "long run," the historian will reveal the absolute novelty borne by each moment: "for every stage in the dialectical process (like every stage in the process of history itself), conditioned as it always is by every stage preceding, brings into play a fundamentally new tendency, which necessitates a fundamentally new treatment."[34] Thus, the critique of the ideology of progress (and not, of course, of progress itself) refers both to the perception of the past as a linear continuum and to the idea of a future determined entirely by the past and thus predictable. In an early age, the fundamentally indeterminate nature of the future was still affirmed in the name of an aesthetic model of history. In *The Arcades Project*, he wrote:

In every true work of art there is a place where, for one who removes there, it blows cool like the wind of a coming dawn. From this it follows that art, which has often been considered refractory to every relation with progress, can provide its true definition. Progress has its seat not in the continuity of elapsing time but in its interferences—where the truly new makes itself felt for the first time, with the sobriety of dawn.[35]

However, this clearly refers to the historical idea of Progress as conceived by Enlightenment philosophy before dominating liberal thought in the nineteenth century, on the one hand, and the Marxist dialectic on the other. But above all, it is the *political* use of the idea of Progress by the left against fascism and Nazism, first in Weimar Germany, then after 1933, in the Western democracies, which Benjamin denounced as tragically inappropriate. *On the Concept of History*, written in 1940, stated clearly that the naïve belief in the inevitable nature of historical Progress indicates an absolute ignorance of the real nature of history (of which fascism and Nazism are much more conscious): "The current amazement that the things we are experiencing are 'still' possible in the twentieth century, is *not* philosophical."[36] It is precisely this nonphilosophical vision of history that, according to Benjamin, underlies the naïve political practice of the social-democrats (and perhaps also that of Stalinist communism at the time of the German-Soviet pact, as the reference of the tenth thesis that the "politicians in whom the opponents of Fascism had placed their hopes are prostrate and confirm their defeat by betraying their own cause"[37] seems to suggest); it is faith in an irreversible process that, despite all appearances, necessarily leads humanity to the final triumph of the Good.

This quasi-religious belief in historical Progress is inherited directly from the ideal of scientism as conceived in the nineteenth century; what in fact characterizes the ideology of Progress is that it is based on the model of technical progress, and thus it "recognizes only the progress in the mastery of nature, not the retrogression of society."[38] More precisely, it involves three fundamental postulates that are cruelly refuted by the reality of history: Progress is *that of humanity itself* (and not only of its capacities and its knowledge); progress is *infinite* (corresponding to an endless perfectibility of humanity); it is *irresistible* (automatically following a linear or spiral trajectory).[39] Clearly, each of these points is refuted by the spectacle taking place in Europe as Benjamin was writing *On the Concept of History*. But what is questioned here even more originally is the providential nature of history, as the Enlightenment inherited it from Christian theology, or more precisely from its *theodicy*: as if it were possible at any moment in time to "measure the span between a legendary inception and a legendary end of history."[40]

In fact, in its theological basis, the idea of Progress does imply being able to locate each moment of time not only in relation to an absolute origin but especially in relation to a culmination at the extreme end of the historical process. This conception of time as a measurable entity is essentially *quantitative* and thus contradicts the mainly *qualitative* character of religious time. What Benjamin, for his part, borrowed from the religious experience is precisely the extreme attention to the qualitative difference of time, to the incomparable uniqueness of each moment. If there is one point where political vigilance almost connects with religious sensibility, it is here, at the very core of the perception of time. Hence, the central importance of that entry in *The Arcades Project*, probably dating from 1937 to 1940, in which Benjamin quoted from the philosopher Hermann Lotze (who inspired his critique of the ideology of Progress):

Denial of the notion of progress in the religious view of history: "History, however it may more forward or fluctuate hither and thither, could not by any of its movements attain a goal lying out of its own plane. And we may spare ourselves the trouble of seeking to find, in mere onward movement upon this plane, a progress which history is destined to make not there but by an upward movement at each individual point of its course forward."[41]

For Benjamin, this formulation applied in the same way to the political vision of history: by definition, the radical change aspired to by all utopias could not be the result of an evolution in which facts, events, or historical situations accumulate, which despite their apparent diversity, always repeat a limited number of figures. The eternal return of the Same produces an unfathomable melancholy in the observer who forever abandoned the consoling belief in a happy end of history. As Benjamin wrote in *The Arcades Project*: "The concept of progress must be grounded in the idea of catastrophe. That things are 'status quo' *is* the catastrophe. It is not an ever-present possibility but what in each case is given. Thus Strindberg (in *To Damascus*): hell is not something that awaits us, but this life here and now."[42]

At the same time, however, the awareness of the qualitative uniqueness of each instant opens, in the present itself, infinite possibilities of renewal. To wrench from the passing second the explosive charge it contains, to interrupt the course of things, to realize all the hope of the world—the one past generations believed in vain, the one whose fulfillment utopia postpones to the mythical end of time—in the instantaneous invention of the new, such is the "weak messianic power" that is reserved for us.[43]

*

Benjamin's critique of the positivist conception of history has its counterargument in Benjamin in the elaboration of another form of historic temporality. "The concept of the historical progress of mankind cannot be sundered from the concept of its progression through a homogeneous empty time. A critique of the concept of such a progression must be the basis of any criticism of the concept of progress itself."[44] The perception of time as an empty form in which events of mental life are lodged had been questioned at the beginning of the century by Bergson, and on different premises, by Husserl, then by Heidegger in *Being and Time*. A deformalization of time that Franz Rosenzweig had also undertaken in *The Star of Redemption*, whose meaning was summarized a few years later in the following formula: "Events do not come to pass in time; it is time itself that comes to pass."[45] Benjamin applies the principle of this deformalization to the analysis of historical time by showing that the past, present, and future are not successive segments on a continuous line but that they represent three specific states of historic consciousness. Hence, one can no longer speak—as historicism does—of a "universal history"; such a "universal history," wrote Benjamin, "proceeds by addition. It mobilizes the inestimable mass of facts of the past in order to fill homogeneous and empty time with them."[46]

But in reality, the "historical fact" does not exist as such, since it is constructed by the writing of history, no more than the continuous temporal relation postulated by historicism exists, for "the relationship of what-has-been to the now is dialectical: is not progression but image, suddenly emergent."[47] In fact, historic time is born neither in the consciousness of the historian nor in that of the actors of history, because "image is that wherein what has been comes together in a flash with the now to form a constellation."[48] In other words, physical time that we perceive spontaneously as continuous and irreversible does not have a historical character in itself; *for time to appear as history, its development, on the contrary, must be interrupted*. The historicism of time is revealed whenever a new dialectical image emerges; yet, those images do not belong to the continuous order of time but, on the contrary, they break it and thus escape it.

In this sense, it is not precise to say that dialectical images are constituted in the consciousness (of the historian or the actors of history), which would imply that they are the result of a voluntary effort to rediscover the past, and tend to be organized in meaningful sequences that gradually weave the narrative fabric of memory. Insofar as they interrupt the continuity of internal time, they must originate elsewhere, in that invisible domain Benjamin called, pace Proust, involuntary memory. At the same time, in "Some Motifs in Baudelaire," he compared that memory with the Freudian unconscious. It was a matter of understanding the themes of "previous life" and "correspondences," as the condensation of images expressing nostalgia for an original state of "auratic" happiness, whose memory is preserved in the depths of the psyche, sheltered from the trauma of modern life. But at the same time, those images—"original phenomena" of historical consciousness—are born of a shock, a trauma, the lightning flash of an encounter, like that with the stranger of the sonnet "To a Passerby," in which the experience of the most irrevocable ephemera—two looks crossing—wrenches the poet out of the order of time and transports him, as in a flash, to a sort of eternity.[49] This paradoxical experience accurately represents the emergence of the authentic historical consciousness from the break of temporal continuity. What appeared, in that disjunction of time, is, as in Baudelaire's poem, like a revelation: a discovery both of an elective affinity between the present and the past, and of their irreducible otherness. As in the encounter with the unknown passerby, the eternity glimpsed fades just as quickly; the image of the past flees like a wind and is given only in the flash of an image.

In the lightning flash of such an image, historical time emerges just as physical time is abolished. This, for Benjamin, is the secret of the *actualization* of time. The dialectical image, born in the illumination of the present instant, gathers a moment of the past and a moment of the future. The *nunc stans* of "now-time" breaks up chronology, not by canceling the temporal difference but by making past and future coexistent in the present. The experience of historical time in Benjamin is very close to what Rosenzweig mentioned in *The Star of Redemption*; there, too, it is a past that does not stop passing, a present that is renewed at each moment, and a future always in the process of becoming. *On the Concept of History* is largely devoted to the description of the various historical configurations of "now-time." But note that, in *On the Concept of History*, the form of discourse itself rests entirely on the grammatical mode of *actualization*, in particular on the systematic use of verbal forms of the continuous present, and all sorts of indicators of permanence and contemporaneity; the third thesis, for example, mentions Redemption in the present tense: "only for a redeemed mankind has its past become citable in all its moments . . . and that day *is* Judgment Day." The questioning of the power of the winners takes place "each time anew"; similarly, Redemption as daily as "that sun which *is rising* in the sky of history" (Thesis IV). Similarly, each epoch must tackle that harsh task *anew*: to liberate tradition from the conformism *about to violate* it; for "The Messiah *comes* not only as the Redeemer, he comes as the subduer of the Antichrist." Obversely, since the present is the place where the fate of history is played out, the threat of the eternal return of the Same is also permanent: "The victorious enemy *is not even impeded* by the dead; . . . And this enemy *has not ceased* to be victorious" (Thesis VI).

But the most striking example is no doubt that of the Angel of History mentioned in the ninth thesis. For the systematic resort to all the modalities of the continuous present are intended not only, as in the previous examples, to translate the theme of the actualization of time into the form of discourse itself. What structures the text, on the other hand, is a permanent tension between the described scene (the *uttered*) and the linguistic implementation of the description (*the utterance*). The Paul Klee watercolor that inspired the text represents, said Benjamin, an angel with wings spread, swept away by such a violent storm that he cannot close them; this wind "irresistibly propels him into the future to which his back is turned, while the pile of debris before him grows skyward." This scene, which Benjamin interpreted allegorically, means that it is the Angel of History dragged to the future against his will (his face turned to the past); as for the storm, "it is what we call progress." Thus, the scene represents a violent, irresistible movement that Benjamin interpreted as the image of humanity reluctantly carried toward a future that horrifies it. Benjamin clearly expressed here (and for the last time) his radical refusal of the ideology of Progress. The Angel "would like to awaken the dead, and make whole what has been smashed": a figure of the messianic interruption of history in the present moment that, each time, might produce the new.

But it is precisely this hope of renewal that the vision of the Angel intends to refute. While the text denounces the idea of Progress as an illusion, the utterance, that is, the subjective implementation of the linguistic forms of description, destroys from inside the very idea of the present as a permanent source of re-creation. For the only object of grammatical present found everywhere here is to freeze movement, to immobilize the Angel not in the perfection of a moment removed from the vicissitudes of time but, on the contrary, in the fossilization of an ineluctable horror. As in the book on baroque drama, allegory appears here as mortification of appearances; an emblem of terror, the Angel is gripped for eternity in a gesture of horror: "His eyes *are* staring, his mouth *is* open, his wings *are* spread." This present is the opposite of that of renewal and invention; it is the present of repetition, course, inescapable glaciation. An allegorical embodiment of the other aspect of the present, of that ever-repeating catastrophe in which time is plunged when it stops producing anything new, the Angel is the dark side of all representation: "a single catastrophe *without modulation or respite*, piles wreckage upon wreckage and hurls it eternally at his feet."

If it is true that the evil tempest blowing since the origins of time drives the Angel toward a future that terrifies him, this is not a long-past episode of the mythic history of mankind; as in Kafka's aphorism that Adam and Eve continue to be driven out of Paradise every single day,[50] the Angel of History is the prisoner of an eternal catastrophe, an irremediable perversion of time, condemned to the endless repetition of the same tragedy: "But a storm *blows* from Paradise. This storm *drives him* irresistibly toward the future, against which the Angel *never ceases* to turn his back while the rubble before him *grows* skyward" (Thesis IX).

A melancholy with no way out of the historical view that Benjamin rediscovered in Nietzsche's nihilism, for whom "nothing new occurs any more,"[51] or in Blanqui's formula in *Eternity via the Stars*, "The new is always old, and the old always new,"[52] but perhaps mainly in Baudelairean spleen: "It is one and the same historical night at the onset of which the owl of Minerva (with Hegel) begins its flight and Eros (with Baudelaire) lingers before the empty pallet, torch extinguished, dreaming of bygone embraces."[53] The present as a synchronic gathering of a same "intrigue of being" (to adopt a notion of Emmanuel Lévinas), in which the same original synthesis is played again ceaselessly, or a present as an always new acceptance of responsibility of the pains and hopes of men who have gone before? Between these two modes of actualizing time—both included in the experience of the present—the difference, for Benjamin, is *ethical*. Like an actor in history, the historian can extract from the moment the messianic spark it contains only if he is inspired by some other concern than that of pure knowledge (which is, of course, indispensable): that of his responsibility for the past and for the future in his charge.

*

"Now-time" polarizes a double relationship of the present to the past and to the future. However, in Benjamin, these two relationships are not symmetrical: the "secret rendezvous between past generations and our own," mentioned in the second thesis, refers to the most fundamental aspect of "now-time," when the present is lived as a permanent reactualization of the past, as the constant attempt to restore life to what was once unrecognized or sacrificed. This primary movement of historical consciousness involves, not as its consequence, but as its fulfillment, the utopian tension toward the future, or more precisely, the anticipation of utopia in the heart of the present. In reality, the thwarted hopes of past generations are the soil on which we build our own dreams. In Benjamin, utopia is a function of memory. "The seer," reads a note to *The Arcades Project*, "turns his back on the future: it is through the twilight of the past, slowly vanishing before him into the night of time, that he glimpses her face."[54]

It is this utopian relationship to the past that, in his final philosophy of history, he called *remembrance (Eingedenken)*. A central category of "now-time," remembrance is distinguished from involuntary memory in that it is a conscious act; this difference that, along with the sudden appearance of memories according to Bergson and Proust, marks the transition in Benjamin's theory of historic time from an aesthetic model to a political and theological one. But in contrast to voluntary memory, remembrance does not make do with *evoking* a moment from the past but aims to *transform* it: "What science has 'determined,' remembrance can modify. Such mindfulness can make the incomplete (happiness) into something complete, and the complete (suffering) into something incomplete";[55] it is the instrument of the retroactive effect of the present on the past; because of it, historical time no longer appears irreversible.

When the law of historical time is contrasted with that of physical time, said Benjamin, "it is theology."[56] Hence, it can be understood that the term "theology" denotes for Benjamin the specificity of historic time itself as "now-time," that is, as a time in which human activity can intervene to change its meaning retroactively. The "theological" dimension of historical temporality, therefore, does not refer to the presence in it of some modality of the irrational; it simply manifests the fact that historical time was henceforth conceived by Benjamin as an internal event, an event of the psyche. This is why Benjamin could write that "in remembrance we have an experience that forbids us to conceive of history as fundamentally atheological, little as it may be granted us to try to write it with immediately theological concepts."[57] This conception of historical time that, on the one hand, is opposed to the ("immediately theological") belief in a history progressing inevitably toward final salvation, but that, on the other, borrows from Jewish theology the idea that historical time is not irreversible and that what came after can modify what came before, is precisely the one that Benjamin revealed in the last thesis of *On the Concept of History*:

The soothsayers who found out from time what it had in store certainly did not experience time as either homogeneous or empty. Anyone who keeps this in mind will perhaps get an idea of how past times were experienced in remembrance—namely, in just the same way. We know that the Jews were prohibited from investigating the future. The Torah and the prayers instruct them in remembrance, however. This stripped the future of its magic, to which all those succumb who turn to the soothsayers for enlightenment. This does not imply, however, that for the Jews the future turned into homogeneous, empty time. For every second of time was the strait gate through which the Messiah might enter.[58]

When this quasi-aphoristic text is returned to its essential point of origin, it may be said that Benjamin contrasted three visions of historical time: from the epistemological point of view, it is a question of determinism, the belief in destiny, and the conception of "open" time. From the perspective of the history of cultures, these three visions serve (in the logic of Benjamin's text) as the vehicle for modern rationalism, the religions of pagan antiquity and Jewish messianism. The neutral and cumulative time of modern philosophies of history, conceived according to the model of physical time as the vector of a series of predictable phenomena (since knowledge of the conditions prevailing at any moment in the temporal chain allows the advance calculation of the nature of conditions that will prevail at a given future moment), contrasts with the magical customs of archaic religions, as well as with Jewish religious life; both are informed, instead, by the experience of an infinitely modulated time, in which the seasons and the months, the days of the week and hours of the day, even the particular constellation of each passing moment, have their own essence and distinct meaning.

The perception of time in Jewish tradition is thus much closer to that of so-called archaic cultures than that which underlies the modern vision of history since the Enlightenment. From this point of view, the Jewish practice of recollection relates to the past in the same way as that by which ancient arts of divination consulted the future: in both cases it is a matter of an *actualization* of distant time within the experience of the present. In his 1923 essay "On Mimetic Powers" (*Über das mimetische Vermögen*), Benjamin explained magical practices as the application of a symbolic view of the cosmos, perceived as a *text* whose secret analogies must be decoded. In the case of divination, it was most important to use a highly specific code to decipher the signs that, in a given situation, herald a future situation. Similarly, remembrance deciphers the tracks left in the present by the past; for "history is like a text in which the past has deposited images, as if on a light-sensitive plate. The future alone has reactants powerful enough to make this image appear in all its detail."[59]

But beyond this common reference to the experience of the actualization of time, there is a fundamental difference separating divination and recollection. The first postulates, in effect, the existence of a *necessary* link between past and future; not the necessity of causality, which would be determinism, but of analogy, that is, of *fate*. If the present contains the true image of the future in itself, this is not because today is cause and tomorrow effect, but because the forces secretly mustered in the present constellation are the virtual prefiguration of those that will manifest themselves in some future constellation. What unites present and future is a process of passing from power to act, based on the principle of structural similarity between various moments of time. What will be tomorrow is only the explanation of what already exists, invisible to the profane, in the order of things today. Hence, the inevitable character of what *must* happen; not external necessity, as expressed by causality, but *internal*, which explains that nothing can stand in the way of fate.

As for the relationship created by remembrance between the present and the past, no aspect of it is necessary; on the contrary, remembrance establishes a link between two moments of time that would not appear or exist without it. Between the two instants brought together by remembrance, there is neither a causal nor an analogical relationship; the affinity between the two is not given but chosen, or rather freely created. The present chooses its own past, composes its own history. What guides the relation to the past in this case is the will to save it, to deliver it from forgetfulness or ossification. Inversely, it is also the desire to attach the present to a tradition, to revive in it the aborted hopes of past generations. For Benjamin, this ever-renewed encounter between memory and utopia characterized the Jewish religious experience as it is formed and expressed in study of the Torah and the practice of prayer. The true visionary, wrote Benjamin, is one who "turns his back toward the future." In a preliminary note to *On the Concept of History*, he emphasized "the importance of the notion of return (*Umkehr*) for the philosophy of history and for politics"; and added that "the Last Judgment is a present turning backward."[60] Because it is guided by the concern to "linger at the disaster, to dress the wounds and awaken the dead,"[61] remembrance, "in which we must see the quintessence of the theological conception of history of the Jews,"[62] can only be understood as a category of ethics.

Within such a differentiating and qualitative perception of time, completely foreign to the idea of time conceived by historicist rationality, Jewish tradition and magical thought are opposed to one another as freedom is opposed to fatality, responsibility to fate. Yet, relative to the modern conception of historical time, the vision of the future that informs ancient fatalism seems less paradoxical than the vision of the past sustaining the idea of recollection. Whether the future is predetermined by the law of fate or by the necessity immanent in the historical process, it appears, in both cases, as essentially *predictable*. The Marxist theory of the "meaning of history" is no more (or less) irrational than the ancient belief in the ineluctable nature of events to come. But to claim that the past can be modified by the present is what most undermines modern man's trust in the irreversible nature of historical time. The idea that remembrance calls into question is at the very basis of modern historical consciousness, that is, that the judgments of history cannot be appealed as in the biological process of natural selection; the evolution of humanity is measured, from one generation to the next, by the disappearance of the losers and the survival of the winners.

As for Benjamin, he proposed the vision of a history in which nothing is sacrificed, nothing is lost forever. If each moment of the past can be reactualized, replayed under other conditions on a new stage, nothing in human history is irreparable. By the same token, nothing in the future is inevitable. Such a temporality, fundamentally *uncertain*, that is, sufficiently independent of the principles of continuity and causality, can allow, at every moment, the *correction of the errors* of the past, and at the same time, the always unexpected emergence of an incalculable, if not unlimited number of new *possibilities*. It is a case, then, of two forms closely bound up with the same phenomenon of actualizing time: the return to life of the past in the light of the present is just as charged with utopian potential as the hope in the emergence of the new. Even more, it is in this upheaval, this revolutionary transformation of the past, that the appearance of the new is manifested. In this sense, as Gershom Scholem emphasized, we find in Benjamin, as in Jewish mysticism, a projection of utopia into the present. Messianism is no longer conceived as waiting for an apotheosis that will materialize at the end of linear and continuous time, but rather as the possibility offered at each moment of time of the advent of the new: for the Jews, "For every second of time was the strait gate through which the Messiah might enter."

Benjamin therefore proposed a double resolution of utopia as a function of the experience of the present—what is called Redemption in *On the Concept of History*. This term signifies, on the one hand, the idea of a humanity that has completely won back its past: each moment of the past thus becomes a "citation à l'ordre du jour" in each instant of the present (Thesis III). In a preparatory note to *On the Concept of History*, Benjamin uses another metaphor, this one drawn from the cult of the Hebrews described in the Bible: "The eternal light is an image of authentic historical existence. It calls up the past—the flame that was once lit—and this perpetually, feeding it with ever-new fuel."[63] In this sense, "the messianic world is a world of total and integral actuality."[64] But in another sense, Redemption also points to a way the future can be lived in the heart of the present: "Our image of happiness," says the second thesis, "is indissolubly bound up with that of Redemption." In effect, the idea of future happiness is, by contrast, guided by the experience of our present failures. If, for Benjamin, the idea of happiness reflects that of Redemption, it may be said to be precisely as the term (*Er-lösung*) must be understood as the *un-knotting* of the paradoxes of the present.

PART 3

GERSHOM SCHOLEM:
THE SECRET HISTORY

The Paradoxes of Messianism

For Gershom Scholem, World War I represented a founding event that determined the future orientation of his life to a large extent. In particular, the twenty months he spent with Benjamin in Bern were decisive for his intellectual orientation. From early adolescence, Scholem had known that he was going to devote his life to the study of Judaism,[1] and from that point of view, it was he who played the role of initiator for Benjamin. But it was Benjamin who provided Scholem with the conceptual references that were to form the philosophical background of his historical research: their discussions on Kant and Goethe, Hölderin and the German Romantics; their critical reading of Hermann Cohen's *Logic of Pure Knowledge*; their conversations about Nietzsche, Rilke, and expressionist painting; Benjamin's interest in dreams, fantasies, as well as the premythic origins of consciousness, indicate a radical questioning of nineteenth-century rationalism. Similarly, Benjamin's philosophical use of theological notions like Creation, Revelation, and Redemption; his reading of biblical texts as bearers of a specific form of intelligibility; the importance he granted to the concepts of doctrine (*Lehre*) and tradition marked Scholem's intellectual progress forever.

In an autobiographical text dating from 1937, Scholem tells how, in about 1918, he decided to give up mathematics to devote himself to the study of Jewish mysticism.[2] What had fascinated him from the beginning in Kabbalah was not diving into an irrational universe but the intuitive discovery of *another type of rationality*. Reading the work of Franz Joseph

Molitor, *Philosophie der Geschichte oder Ueber die Tradition* (1857), had revealed to him the presence of a body of specific doctrine, a vision of the world that was both systematic and absolutely original behind the Aristotelian cloak of Judaism in Maimonides or behind its neo-Kantian facade in Hermann Cohen. The goal he then set for himself (in terms of the situation then prevailing in Jewish studies, that juvenile ambition was both naïve and excessive) was to reconstitute the metaphysics of Judaism. Molitor's book had shown him that, in the vision of the Kabbalistic world, this was not reduced to the abstract idea of monotheism, but it also revealed profound affinities with the world of myth and pantheism. As Molitor presented Kabbalah, it could not simply be reduced to a reemergence of myth or pantheism. But what the young Scholem sensed was that the authentic metaphysics of Judaism, as expressed in its mystical tradition, had to be located beyond the opposition of pantheism and monotheism, myth and Reason. "I was particularly incensed by three authors . . . who conceived as their main task to construct antitheses to myth and pantheism, to refute them, although they should have concerned themselves with raising them to a higher level." And he added: "I sensed such a higher level in the Kabbalah, regardless of how distorted it might have been in philosophical discussion."[3]

Yet, from then on, Scholem understood that the metaphysics of the Kabbalah could not be approached directly, for its basic texts present it through the mediation of a network of symbols that obscure it as much as they reveal it, and those must first be deciphered. After he discovered the texts, he had to reconstitute them scientifically, a hermeneutic task, but first of all, a philological labor. Thus, said Scholem, before discovering the philosophy of the Kabbalah, it is a matter of "the wall of history." For "the mountain, the corpus of facts, needs no key at all; only the misty wall of history, which hangs around it, must be penetrated."[4] But at the same time, Scholem was aware of the paradox immanent in every historical study of a mystical tradition: the one that claims to provide direct access to the absolute can be revealed only by historical explanation that, by displaying it in time, relativizes it. The whole originality (and no doubt the greatness) of Scholem's position comes from his refusal to dissolve the paradox by denying one of its terms: he never thought (as did Jewish Orthodoxy) that the historical dimension of mystical texts could be abstracted to aim at their metaphysical meaning from the start; but nor did he accept the postulates of the positivist school, for which there is no "truth" of mysticism beyond its registration in history. "Today, as at the very beginning, my work lives in this paradox," concluded Scholem in his 1937 text.[5]

However, this same text shows how this epistemological paradox—without annulling the tension that constitutes it—can open a space where the truth of mystical phenomena would be revealed. That requires that the two poles of the act of thinking—historical thought and its object—shift imperceptibly until the lightning moment when they somehow come into the same wavelength. On the one hand, the meaning hidden in the depth of the mystical text must somehow signal to the historian, even before he has properly deciphered it. The historian himself responds to this "true communication from the mountain," as Scholem put it, not with the study of continuous historical sequences that would create the illusion of an evolution but, on the contrary, of flaws, breaks of the historical process. It is by glimpsing "that most invisible, smallest fluctuation of history" that the historian will be able to "penetrate the misty wall of history" and bring out the truth borne by mystical discourse.[6]

Among the many aspects of Jewish mysticism studied by Scholem, messianism is one that appeared latest in his work. His first studies on the Sabbatarian movement appeared in Hebrew in 1944 and 1946, his monumental work on Sabbatai Zevi in 1957. The first version of the essay "The Idea of Redemption in Kabbalah" did appear in 1941. But his major synthesis, "Understanding Jewish Messianism," was not published until 1958. Yet, the problem of messianism had certainly begun to concern him very early, in any case, since 1923, when he arrived in Palestine. To understand the relatively late appearance of this central theme in his work, beyond purely biographical contingencies, we might refer to a more essential hypothesis: *for Scholem, the messianic idea is closely connected with the experience of failure*. This must be understood in a double sense, referring both to the genesis of the messianic idea and to its structure. For Scholem, messianism is always born of a historical frustration, it appears, in the collective consciousness, as compensation for a loss, as a utopian promise designed to make up for current misfortune.

From the beginning, the eschatological visions of the prophets of Israel emerge against the background of a series of national catastrophes: Isaiah prophesies on the background of the destruction of the kingdom of Israel by the Assyrians; Jeremiah and Ezekiel, in terms of the collapse of the kingdom of Judah and the Babylonian Exile. Later, talmudic eschatology will respond to the destruction of the Second Temple by the Romans and to the dispersion of the Jews. Similarly, according to Scholem, the Kabbalah of Safed and, particularly, the great Lurianic myth of Exile and Redemption appear in the sixteenth century as a response to the historical catastrophe of the expulsion of the Jews from Spain in 1492.[7] This is the same schema that Scholem applies to account for the birth and lightning-fast spread of Sabbatarianism in the seventeenth century. It can be asked if Scholem's intellectual passion after 1944–1945 for the systematic study of Jewish messianism was not a secret response to a historical constellation perceived by him as doubly desperate: the trauma of the extermination of the Jews during World War II combined in him with the sense that Zionism, in its political realization, had betrayed the utopian hopes in whose name it had appeared.

But for him, this decline of a mystique into a politics was the sign of a contradiction inherent in messianism itself, which, in its most profound depths, is the *aspiration for the impossible.* In Jewish messianism, there is a demand for the absolute that no historical reality will ever be able to satisfy. Yet, at the same time, the final Redemption it strives for is authentic only on condition of taking place in the light, on the stage of history, by radically transforming the reality of the world itself. That is, the Jewish idea of messianism is essentially a *paradox*: messianism can be asserted only in realizing itself, but as soon as it realizes itself, it denies itself. Hence its tragic nature: the messianic tension of the Jewish people has always made them live in the expectation of a radical upheaval of life on earth, which, whenever it seemed to be heralded, quickly appeared illusory. In Jewish mysticism, therefore, the permanent warning against the temptation of impatience, of premature intervention in the progress of history. And hence, in Jewish religious consciousness, a very strange experience of time: it is lived, in its very nature, in the mode of *expectation*; neither the pagan joy of the present moment, nor a spiritual escape beyond time, but an always renewed aspiration for the emergence, in the very heart of time, of the brand-new. This is conceived as able to emerge at any moment: Redemption is always imminent, but if it emerged, it would immediately be challenged, in the name of the demand for the absolute it claims to fulfill.

Scholem has called this permanent expectation of an end that is always hoped for and always postponed, "life in suspension."[8] This, he wrote, "is the grandeur of messianism as well as its constitutive weakness. What is called Jewish 'life' implies a tension that is never really relaxed, never resolved."[9] It is this demand for the absolute itself that has prevented the Jewish people from putting itself into history to work in it directly for the realization of the utopia it bears within itself. But, on the other hand—and this is the heart of the paradox of messianism—it is, perhaps, that distance from history that guarantees the Jewish people its permanence. The question Scholem then asks is whether the price of that permanence—historic impotence, absolute vulnerability to persecution—is not itself excessive. This question, which concludes the study of Jewish messianism that appeared in 1957, of course refers to the annihilation of European Jewry during World War II. In fact, it can be asked whether the massive extermination of the Jews is not an absolute condemnation of the vision of history that prevailed for almost two thousand years in religious Judaism, which maintains that loyalty to divine promises forced the Jews to wait passively for the coming of the messianic age, even at the price of martyrdom. That is the question posed by Zionism, which Scholem seems to echo here.

Breaking with the resignation preached by the religious tradition, Zionism had called on the Jewish masses to take their fate into their own hands and act in history to win their collective liberation by themselves. Yet, from the start, Scholem emphasized that Zionism itself is the heir of Jewish messianism, since—in a secularized form—it has adopted one of its most central aspects, that is, the utopia formulated by the biblical prophets of the "return of the exiles" and the restoration of national sovereignty. In this sense, according to Scholem, Zionism is authentically loyal to the spirit of messianism. For "the precept of the necessary historical passiveness that translates a very ancient tendency of orthodox Judaism . . . is hardly compatible with the deepest impulses of messianism and in fact [represents] its perversion."[10]

But, by the same token, Zionism cannot escape the constitutive paradox of messianism either. Scholem distinguished between the "messianic harmonies" of Zionism that works in the reality of secular history and the metahistoric messianism invoked by the religious tradition.[11] But these harmonies themselves are sufficiently present in Zionism to expose it, too, to the dilemma inherent in the very nature of messianism: either participate, like all the "nations of the earth," in the big game of history to realize in it the national aspirations of the Jewish people, at the risk of sacrificing its religious vocation of "keeper of the absolute," and also at the risk of involving it in the cycle of life and death common to all nations, or—since recent horrors have revealed the retreat into metahistory as illusory—to take the risk of an uncontrolled explosion of eschatological rage, to translate the religious utopia into messianic activism, and live as if the end of time had already come. For Scholem, those two risks seemed complementary; the Zionist process of secularizing Judaism—a process that is inevitable as soon as the Jewish people actively enter history—involves both the danger of total assimilation to the logic of politics, in which the Jews risk an irrevocable loss of the sense of their religious, that is, ethical and universal, vocation, and in reaction to that spiritual impoverishment, the reverse temptation, that of a compensatory outburst of anarchic messianic aspirations.

This fundamentally paradoxical nature of messianism, for which Redemption must be visibly manifest in the concreteness of history, but for which, at the same time, no real messianic attempt will ever be up to its aspirations, is found, always in different forms, in each of the three great themes underlying the history of Jewish messianism. We shall call them the paradox of absolute utopia, the paradox of radical Revolution, and the paradox of internal perfection.

As one of the essential features of Jewish messianism, Scholem stressed the distinction between two great tendencies, one *restorative* and the other *utopian*. The first of those two projects, already revealed in the biblical prophets, strives for the return of the exiles, the reunification of the two kingdoms of Judah and Israel, the restoration of national independence and Davidian royalty, and finally the reconstruction of the Temple of Jerusalem and the reinstitution of the cult. It is a return to an ancient order, an original state of abundance that was lost but destined to be recovered. This "elegiac" attitude, to use Walter Benjamin's term (who saw it as one of the two forms of universal aspiration for happiness),[12] understands the fulfillment of history as a return to origins, as the reestablishment of a primordial harmony temporarily destroyed. This restorative element is found in some form in all Jewish messianic conceptions, because in a history stemming from an initial divine plan, there is no possible innovation that does not refer in some way to that original landscape of truth.

In contrast to that restorative tendency, the utopian current feeds on the dream of a radical upheaval of all reality, of the appearance of a brand-new world: "a hymnic figure of happiness," to quote Walter Benjamin again, evoking "the extraordinary, what never was, the summit of bliss."[13] Several passages in the Talmud are devoted to evoking the miracles of the messianic age, from the political utopia of the end of all persecution and the establishment of an era of universal peace, to the vision of a redeemed Jerusalem, with walls of diamonds and streets paved with precious stones, or the dream of a new cosmic order in which the moon would become a new sun. But Scholem noted that neither of those two currents ever exists in a pure state; even the most fantastic utopias contain restorative elements, just as the restorative plan always includes a share of utopia. Thus, for example, in the biblical prophets, the ideal of the reestablishment of the Davidian royalty is always accompanied by the vision of a spiritually regenerated Jewish people; conversely, the talmudic passage announcing that, at the end of time, the moon will become like the sun bases that cosmic revolution on the fact that, in the original order of Creation, the two stars were in fact designed to be of equal size.

This ambivalence of the elements of preservation and innovation in the messianic idea reflects a more fundamental tension, unique to the religious historiosophy of Judaism, between the two principles of the given and the new, structure and history, being and becoming. But, even more originally, this duality is rooted in the very idea of the Creation. In fact, it refers both to the establishment of a given, an order, an invariance, and to the reemergence of the brand-new and unforeseen. A completed Creation and a continuous Creation, from the beginning, those two aspects have determined the Jewish idea of historic time, which is then marked by an apparently insoluble contradiction. Two models of messianism seem to compete within it. The first model is *archaeological*: the world is the expression of a divine plan, and from the beginning of things, this is inherent in the secret structure of Being. The harmony of this plan was destroyed by a primordial catastrophe (which can be reproduced in some form, throughout history). The human adventure, then, will consist of repairing what was broken, that is, always recovering anew the original landscape of truth. For this truth exists, it was set from the beginning, and it remains unmoving even when it seems to evade us. The other model is *eschatological*: truth is in becoming; it is constituted day after day, as the invention of the new goes along. Even in this eschatological model, there is certainly an original structure of truth; but it is only a purely abstract form, without an identifiable semantic content. Symbolized by the Tetragrammaton, this may be said to resemble a mathematical formula; to be filled with a meaning accessible to man, it must be embodied in our empirical world, that is, unfolding in time, a source of infinite renewal, in which it reassumes ever-changing forms. It is at the ideal end of this process, when it will have known all its possible incarnations, that truth will appear in all its universality but also in all its concrete abundance.

But because each of these two models has its own legitimacy, messianism constantly hurls from one demand to another, unable to satisfy either. For the return to the origin, the integral restitution of all things is just as impossible as the final emergence (or eruption) of a radically new order. On the one hand, in fact, the inevitable reality of time and change prevents the End from being identical to the Beginning; but on the other hand, the presence of an immutable given at the origin of history always limits the arbitrariness of innovation. Even the most unbridled eschatological visions must be compatible with the initial plan of Creation. In this sense, the most exact formulation of the philosophy of history underlying Jewish messianism might be the following: *there are too many constraints (or meanings) at the origin of history for it to be absolutely unpredictable; but there are not enough for it to be entirely determined.* From this point of view, the constant aspiration of Jewish messianism for the establishment of a brand-new order, mixed with the awareness that such a revolution would be incompatible with the presence of a structure within Creation, must have been lived as a paradox. The appearance of the Lurianic Kabbalah in the sixteenth century was necessary to resolve this paradox, as we shall see.

The second paradox of messianism, that of radical Revolution, concerns the nature of historical temporality in the Jewish eschatological tradition. Does progress toward messianic time unfold in historical time or in metahistorical time? And is it really a progress, a process? Is the history of the coming of Redemption made of a series of stages each bringing us closer to the end of time? In other words, can messianic temporality be identified with a form of historical progress? Or is it a completely different type of temporality? Will the Messiah come at the end of history, or will he emerge unexpectedly in the heart of time? Is messianic Redemption the product of an evolution or the sudden burst of a revolution? Can its coming be hastened, or must we be satisfied with waiting until it emerges? Here, too, all these questions refer to a fundamental opposition between continuity and discontinuity, between a logic of evolution and a nostalgia for the break.

In this respect, Scholem's central thesis consists of radically dissociating the idea of Redemption from the notion of historical progress in Jewish messianism. Although, as we shall see, Scholem does not deny that there are also elements of evolution in the traditional concept of Redemption, he nevertheless considers them marginal in terms of the central importance of the idea of tearing apart the historical fabric. Note, however, that this thesis is applied primarily to classical forms of the messianic idea, as expressed in the biblical prophets and in rabbinic literature (Talmud and Midrash); as for the Kabbalah of the sixteenth century, it reintroduced the idea of evolution into the great Lurianic myth of Exile and Redemption. Yet, at the start, according to Scholem, the Jewish conception of history has nothing in common with the idea of progress: "In the ancient classical sources, there is no connection between messianism and progress. . . . Redemption [there is conceived] as a new state of the world without any connection with what had preceded it. Redemption [is not] the consequence of a constant evolution of the previous state of the world. . . . It must be produced as the result of a general upheaval, a universal revolution, catastrophes, unheard-of calamities, by virtue of which history must collapse and be wiped out."[14]

Note that that critique of the idea of progress in the analysis of messianism brought Scholem very close to the vision of history of Walter Benjamin and Franz Rosenzweig. This is the heart of the constellation formed by those three thinkers. The critique of historic Reason, the questioning of belief in a history that bears, in itself, a teleological meaning, the definition of another model of history, open to the unpredictable eruption of the new, all these subjects are common to *The Star of Redemption, On the Concept of History*, and Scholem's writings on Jewish messianism. This affinity appears even more clearly when Scholem traces the interpretation of messianism as a form of historic progress to Enlightenment philosophers: "The idea that Redemption would be the result of an immanent development of history is a modern idea, born of Enlightenment philosophy. . . . Redemption is the emergence of a transcendence beyond history, an intervention that makes history fade and collapse."[15] In the first place, this means that the time of messianism does not know causality; Redemption is not the necessary consequence of a preceding state; it does not result from the play of some historic determinism. Hence, it is fundamentally unpredictable. This is also why man cannot induce its coming. The Bible certainly often makes the fulfillment of divine promises depend on the loyalty of the Jewish people to the revealed Law. But the bond it institutes here is not a relation of causality, since following the Law does not *necessarily* involve the realization of the promises; it only creates the conditions for it, in other words, it makes that realization *possible*. Beyond that possibility, nothing is acquired; whether the divine promise is fulfilled or not no longer depends on men but on totally unpredictable factors.

This distinction of a determination by causes and an indetermination on the horizon of conditions, in other words, of a logic of necessity and a logic of possibilities, underlies Scholem's argumentation, without ever being clarified in it. In any case, this is what allows him to highlight two other central aspects of that vision of history peculiar to Jewish messianism: on the one hand, Redemption does not depend on men, and on the other hand, it can emerge at any moment. According to the rabbinic tradition, "certain acts contribute to the advent of Redemption and help give birth to it, so to speak. . . . But that is not genuine causality. . . . In fact, there is never a question of preparing for the coming of the Messiah. . . . He must emerge suddenly, without being announced, at the very moment where he is least expected and when hope in his coming has been abandoned a long time ago."[16]

The idea that Redemption is not the end of a process, that it does not represent—as Hermann Cohen and other theoreticians of Jewish liberalism thought—an ideal toward which humanity tends asymptotically, but that, at any moment, it can break the fabric of time, is a center common to the work of Scholem, Benjamin, and Rosenzweig. It marks the precise point of the break with the Hegelian model of history, and even more essential, with the model of a theodicy inherited both from the Enlightenment and from the Christian theology of Salvation. Scholem's insistence on the idea of the always possible imminence of Redemption recalls both the notion of anticipation and Redemption in Rosenzweig and Benjamin's concept of "now-time." Surely, it is no accident that both Scholem and Rosenzweig cite the same rabbinic teaching on the permanent relevance of Redemption: "If Israel repented, if even for a single day, it would be redeemed instantaneously, and the Son of David would come on the spot, as it is written: 'Today if ye will hear his voice.'"[17]

According to talmudic sources, the suddenness with which the Messiah will erupt into history will be expressed by a series of catastrophes, by the brutal collapse of the old world before a new reality emerges. In the Talmud terrible images of a world gripped by the convulsions of famine, war, and moral decay are contrasted with the utopian visions of the marvels of the messianic age. The age that will precede the coming of the Messiah, says the Talmud, will be that of a "generation with the face of a dog."[18] As for the return of the Jews to their ancestral land, it can be done only at the price of a morally insoluble conflict between the old and the new occupants of the land, so that even God Himself will be torn by it.[19] This explains why one of the most prestigious sages of the Talmud summed up his personal attitude toward the coming of the Messiah thus: "Let him come, but let me not see him."[20] Scholem who had always granted major importance to the destructive factors at work in history, was so fascinated by that apocalyptic aspect of Redemption that he made it the essential characteristic of Jewish messianism. Once more, like Walter Benjamin, he clearly ran counter to the historical optimism that had characterized belief in the continuous progress of humanity in the nineteenth century.

Yet, Scholem did emphasize the existence in rabbinic Judaism of an opposite thesis, that Redemption will not emerge unexpectedly but will be manifested in stages. A text from the Zohar, quoted by Scholem, compares the coming of Redemption to sunrise and the slow victory of light over night.[21] Thus, historical temporality is conceived here as a continuous but not a causal process. From this point of view, Scholem is very interested in a mystical treatise written in Spain in the early thirteenth century, the *Sefer ha-Temunah* (Book of the Picture), which develops a theory of cosmic eons that correspond to the different ages of humanity. The sequence of these eons marks the progressive revelation of Redemption in the world. This mystical historiosophy forms the background of eschatological calculations of several Kabbalists to try to predict the date of Redemption. But, if the Messiah can come at any moment, such calculations clearly make no sense. And thus Orthodox Jewry has always forbidden them, not so much to ban the premature revelation of the moment Redemption will come, as to emphasize its fundamentally unpredictable nature.

The contrast between those two visions of Redemption—the one in which it is constructed gradually through the medium of time, the other in which it breaks temporal progression—is connected with another discrepancy of visible Redemption and invisible Redemption. While in the biblical prophets and then in the talmudic tradition, Redemption was clearly presented as a public event, progressing in full view of everyone on the stage of universal history, the reflection of the Kabbalists increasingly tended to emphasize the personal, internal, and invisible aspect of Redemption. Without entirely wiping out its collective and historic dimension, they nevertheless foregrounded the internal work of individual consciousnesses, the spiritual development of each soul to purify itself and recover its original integrity. From this perspective, there is a special affinity between the historical vision of Redemption and the idea of its progressive development through the various stages of time on the one hand, and on the other hand, between the internal conception of Redemption and the idea that the moment of its visible emergence is totally unpredictable. While, in the first case, messianic utopia must necessarily pass through historic time to be realized, the other thesis separates those two logics, the internal adventure of souls then being played on a level that is completely different from that on which historic events unfold.

The contrast between those two schemas then leads to another paradox: how is it possible to think the historical nature of Redemption and its apocalyptic character at the same time? The radical upheavals heralded for the end of time in fact intend to reverse the laws of nature and history and not to fulfill them. Precisely because of their excesses, apocalyptic visions are denounced as pure creations of the imagination, as metaphorical constructions whose meaning must be deciphered, as figures referring to the end of the spiritual adventure of humanity. Conversely, if Redemption is considered as a historic process, actually unfolding in the natural world, it can no longer be imagined as a radical revolution that would explode the laws of reality. History could no more produce metahistory than metahistory could be dissolved in the laws of history. In other words, to conceive of Redemption as the eruption of transcendence into the world is to give up its historical reality, but to consider it as historic is to limit its radical nature and make do with seeing it, like some sages of the Talmud and Maimonides later on, as the solution of the political and social conflicts of humanity.

These different visions of messianism, which Scholem contrasted by underlining their incompatibility in principle (even if, in the practice of the texts, some of their elements can coexist), are not necessarily at odds.

Beyond the binary categories Scholem worked with, both of them might refer to a more complex perception of history that would integrate both the model of continuity and that of discontinuity, the logic of processes and the unpredictability of breaks. If it is true that the Jewish tradition has never thought of history in terms of mechanical causality, it has nevertheless discerned processes in it, sequences of events that might be defined as *random sequences*, or *open series*. On the ideal line of historic time, each moment would then create a system of constraints that, without determining the next moment, would, however, limit the number of its possible figures. Which of these figures will in fact come into existence? That is a matter of chance, or perhaps, of human freedom. Each moment of historical time might then be conceived as a bifurcation opening several paths; the choice between those different paths would be fundamentally random; but once the path is established, it would then create a combination of constraints acting as a system of conditioning of the next moment, which would appear as a new bifurcation opening a limited number of paths. It is this *stochastic* conception of history that is offered by biblical narratives, examined carefully.

The most striking example is perhaps that of the history of the patriarchs Abraham, Isaac, and Jacob, whose line is established through a series of unpredictable bifurcations, but where events once occur, they irreversibly determine the following temporal sequence. What is at stake in this narrative is, through a process of selection, the progressive formation of a genealogy, the elaboration of a collective identity. At each stage of this history, the father confronts several sons, without knowing which one will continue the line. The narrative, told from the point of view of the actors, thus progresses from one bifurcation to another, always unpredictable, punctuated by a series of accidents, errors, or contingencies that end, in retrospect, by giving the impression of a necessity.

From this point of view, the case of Abraham may be most symptomatic. Since his wife, Sarah, remains sterile for a long time, it is Hagar, his Egyptian servant, who gives him the son that will assure his posterity. The context of this episode demonstrates clearly that this son, Ishmael, has been designated by the Divine Will to perpetuate the line (Genesis 15:1–4), the promise made to him (Genesis 16:10–15), and the covenant with him (Genesis 17:1; 17:27). Yet, a few years later, God announces to Abraham that Sarah is also going to give him a son. Everything in the biblical narrative contributes to show that this promise is unlikely, that such a birth, given the ages of Abraham and Sarah, would contradict the laws of nature. A radical break with the laws of time and with the logic of history, this promise bursts the order established by the sequence of past events and makes him fear the death of Ishmael: "And Abraham said unto God, O that Ishmael might live before thee!" (Genesis 17:18). But this unpredictable bifurcation does not cancel what, in past sequences, has already been established in history; those sequences simply become secondary, marginal, in relation to what now appears as the central temporal line: "And God said, Sarah thy wife shall bear thee a son indeed; and thou shalt call his name Isaac; and I will establish my covenant with him for an everlasting covenant, and with his seed after him. And as for Ishmael, I have heard thee: Behold I have blessed him and will make him fruitful, and will multiply him exceedingly; twelve princes shall he beget, and I will make him a great nation. But my covenant will I establish with Isaac, which Sarah shall bear unto thee at this set time in the next year" (Genesis 17:19–21).

This vision of history as a series of random sequences is illustrated by a very ancient Jewish liturgical text that has subsequently become part of the Passover Seder. This text, denoted in Jewish folklore by its refrain, "Dayenu" (That would have been enough for us), is made of a series of tercets, all structured in the same way: the first verse is a positive conditional proposition, the second a negative conditional proposition, the third verse representing the refrain. The sequence of strophes is based on the following principle: the second verse of each tercet (the conditional negative) is taken up again, but in a positive form in the next tercet. The transformation of the negative hypothesis ("If He had not . . .") into a positive hypothesis ("If He had . . .") creates an effect of both temporal continuity and logical discontinuity, since an event posed as only possible but not necessary (if it hadn't happened, the sequence would have reached its end all the same) at a certain stage of the temporal series becomes real at the next stage. This transformation of the possible into the real does not represent a logical passage from power to act (and even less, of course, a causal sequence) but, on the contrary, the unexpected emergence of the new: the events of sacred history do not occur as consequences of the previous event but as the unforeseen eruption of a new reality, that is, on the theological background of that liturgical text, as gratuitous interventions of God into history. It is as if the biblical narrative of the Exodus from Egypt had been fragmented into a discontinuous series of disjunctive sequences, each of which could have been the last, but each of which leaves open the possibility of a continuation of history.

However, the idea of the absolute unpredictability of Redemption does not take account one of the most central theses of traditional Jewish historiosophy, that is, that the history of humanity is the result of an original plan inherent in the very structures of Creation. Even admitting that man can glimpse the nature of this plan only in its most abstract and general form (for Jewish mysticism, this formula is revealed, as we have seen, in the four letters of the Divine Name), and that, on the human scale, this extreme generality leaves a vast empty space for the random play of historical contingency, it is still true that human history must be guided, in its depths, by the invisible law of this original plan. Moreover, the idea of historical discontinuity, which no doubt allows the freedom of each individual to interrupt the progression of time at any moment, does contradict the conception, so fundamental in Judaism, of a collective effort of humanity, of a transmission from generation to generation of the same redemptive plan.

It is precisely these paradoxes of rabbinic messianism that the Kabbalist system elaborated in Safed in the Galilee at the end of the sixteenth century, by Isaac Luria, attempted to resolve. This system, since considered the canonic expression of the Kabbalist vision of the world, develops a brand-new concept of history with respect to the one that underlies the messianic teachings of the Talmud. The historiography of Lurianic Kabbalism is closely tied to its cosmogony. For Luria, the divine plan that ruled at Creation can be imagined as a total plan in which the many faces of a single truth were inherent from the start. This truth, which evades us in its primordial unity, is revealed at first in a fragmented form. Thus, the original landscape of truth is already that of the dispersion of meaning, its dissemination into so many primordial sememes, which, in Lurianic symbolism, are called *souls*. This term indicates that the original horizon of meaning is given to us at the start, prior to knowing everything, under the species of the *human*. The adventure of meaning is played out through countless personal fates, since each human being is assigned somehow to realize in the world the part of truth he embodies.

This task entrusted to men is especially difficult since, in a second moment of the mythical history of the Beginning, an original catastrophe (the "breaking of the vessels") shatters the primordial world of truth: the many units of meanings (the "souls") wrenched out of their common landscape, are projected into the material world, where they are swallowed up. Even worse: the souls themselves explode, break into countless fragments scattered in the depths of the material world. From the midst of that exile, the exploded souls, scattered to the four corners of the universe, try from then on to pull themselves out of their alienation, each to set off on the search for the scattered splinters whose sum formed their original unity, to reconstitute that original form and thus to contribute, each for itself, to the realization in the concrete world of the initial plan of Creation.

According to Luria, this cosmic myth of Exile and Redemption is the key to the secret history of humanity. For what characterizes this doctrine is that it radically separates the visible history of events from the invisible history of souls. Visible history in fact remains marked here, as in the talmudic tradition, by discontinuity, unpredictability, and contingency; but invisible history, which secretly rules the fate of humanity, unfolds as a continuous process, which can know moments of stopping or regression, but which, in the end, tends irresistibly toward Redemption. In fact, the history of souls is a cumulative process; from generation to generation, the accomplished work of purification is preserved and transmitted, through a mythical process of transmigration of souls, which might be interpreted as a metaphor of the idea of a spiritual progress of humanity.

This progress is certainly invisible, and thus that idea must not be confused with the modern Enlightenment thesis of a constant progress of morals and civilization. In the Lurianic myth, the sequence of events on the stage of history tells us nothing about the secret rhythm of the history of souls. Situations can be imagined when the apparent progress of civilization would indeed contrast with the extreme slowness of the invisible history of Redemption, and others when catastrophic phases of human history would hide its imminent emergence. This is precisely the discrepancy between those two rhythms that take account both of the absolutely unpredictable nature of Redemption and the legalism that guides its secret progress. In this sense, the Lurianic myth may succeed in resolving the central paradox of Jewish messianism: from the point of view of visible history, Redemption can emerge at any moment of time, even if, from the point of view of the secret history of souls, that moment will mark the final end of an age-old process.

Kafka, Freud, and the Crisis of Tradition

Scholem was always fascinated by Kafka's work, seeing it as a paradigmatic image of the spirit of our time, the minute representation of a world deserted by the idea of the divine, but whose immanence must be deciphered as the other side of a lost transcendence. A "theological" reading of Kafka? Not, in any case, in the sense intended by Max Brod, for whom it meant understanding Kafka through positive religious categories, with *The Trial* and *The Castle* symbolizing two different approaches of the same "quest for God." For Scholem, it was precisely these kinds of notions that were radically challenged by Kafka's work, which reflected, on the contrary, the spirit of a time for which the very idea of a presence of divinity in the world has lost all meaning. Yet, if Kafka's characters seem to stray in a reality that has become indecipherable for them, according to Scholem, the reader who is sensitive to the latent metaphysical dimension of that work cannot help discerning the deeply engraved trace of an escaped transcendence in the obsessive repetition of the themes of doubt, uncertainty, and forgetting, as in the proliferation of linguistic forms of negation or ambiguity. If this interpretation can still be defined as theological, it is only as a fundamentally negative theology, for which all we can assert of God is the very fact of his absence.

Scholem saw Kafka's work as the reflection of the crisis of tradition that he considered characteristic of our age. It presented not only the challenge to the contents of religious belief, dating from the Enlightenment, but also the deterioration of the procedures of its transmission. The study of Jewish mysticism had taught him the vital importance of oral transmission for the perpetuation of a culture. In the Jewish tradition—indeed in all civilizations—the texts themselves assume their meaning only through the teaching that reinterprets and updates them from one generation to the next. The institutions responsible for this transmission in Christian Europe (churches and universities) did not exist in Diaspora Judaism. Its tradition was passed down in the private space of the study and prayer house, through the face-to-face relationship of master and disciple, and especially in the intimacy of the family, through the personal relation of father and son. If the crisis of religious belief in Christian Europe since the Renaissance was engendered mainly by a questioning of the contents of faith in the name of the critical spirit, since the Emancipation, European Judaism has suffered from an explosion of traditional social structures, primarily from a shock to magisterial and paternal authority threatening the principle of transmitting revealed texts. Thus, what is compromised here is not so much the validity of the contents of belief as the process of their transmission. For most Western Jews, entering the modern age certainly coincided with the abandonment of traditional Jewry; but if this abandonment often meant a conscious rejection of ancient norms and values, it was more frequently the result of an apparently irreversible attack on collective memory.

In the Judaism of the nineteenth and twentieth centuries, this dislocation of the processes of transmission was inseparable from the intellectual confusion of the generation of the sons. Long before Kafka's "Letter to His Father," the classical revolt of sons against fathers was experienced in Jewish families as a fundamental ideological quarrel about the validity of the traditional norms of life and thought. In the microcosm of the Jewish family, the rebellion of the sons, a banal theme in literature at the beginning of the century, assumed the dimension of a genuine overthrow of values. It may not be accidental that the invention of Oedipus and his founding role in the constitution of the psyche dates from the early years of the twentieth century and appears precisely in Vienna, where the process of assimilation of the Jews of Central Europe peaked at that time. The history of Freud's discoveries shows clearly all that the development of his theory owed to his clinical experience, nourished by narratives of the psychological conflicts so characteristic of a Jewish bourgeoisie on the path to absorption in the surrounding society.

Furthermore, the biography of the Freud family itself provides an exemplary illustration of the historical process in which the Jews of Central Europe gradually liberated themselves from traditional lifestyles and beliefs and adopted the social and intellectual norms of the Western world. In the case of the Freud family, this evolution strictly parallels a geographical shift from east to west:[1] Sigmund's grandfather was still a pious Jew from Galicia; his son, now semi-emancipated, immigrated to Moravia, where Sigmund was born and spent his first years; finally, Freud's father settled with his family in Vienna. Like Franz Kafka thirty years later, the young Sigmund Freud clashed with the contradictions of a father who was already detached from most of the traditional norms and behaviors but still preserved a sentimental loyalty to the disparate residues of rituals and beliefs. In *The Interpretation of Dreams* (1900), conceived, among other things, as an autobiography of his own unconscious, Freud confided, through the narration and analysis of some of his dreams, the semicoded narrative of his secret conflicts with his father and the central role the question of his Jewish identity could have played in this antagonism.[2]

In Freud, as in Kafka, it is the father's ambiguities about his own Judaism, the inconsistencies of a demand in whose name the son is induced to remain loyal to values the father has not succeeded in handing down to him (or, even more, legitimating), that deprives the paternal discourse of its credibility. This is a double bind that reflects the uncertainties of a transition generation, torn between its attachment to the past and the attraction of assimilation, and where paternal authority is irremediably depreciated. The permanence of tradition in Judaism rests precisely on the intangible power of that authority; for it is the authority of the father that guarantees the authenticity and ever-current validity of Divine Law. So, it is no accident that the Freudian critique of religion is based on the demystification of the idea of God, conceived as a projection of the image of the father, and on the conception of the Law as paternal injunction.

For Scholem, this is the background for understanding the theme of Law in Kafka. In "Letter to His Father," a pitiless settling of accounts with the almost mythical image of the father-tyrant, Kafka expatiates at length on the question of Judaism. His attitude toward Judaism, he writes, knew three phases, all closely bound up with his relations with his father.

In childhood, religion seemed to him the direct emanation of paternal authority, and his indifference to practice had given him a permanent bad conscience that merged with his feeling of guilt about his father. Later, as an adolescent, he couldn't understand how his father, "with the insignificant scrap of Judaism you yourself possessed . . . could reproach me for not making an effort . . . to cling to a similar insignificant scrap." For his father's Judaism, wrote Kafka, was "a mere nothing, a joke—not even a joke."[3] The sarcastic description of the father's religious practices, in which the child, and then the adolescent, was forced to participate, reconstructs with a minute cruelty the state of spiritual dilapidation of the bourgeois Jewish communities in the big cities of Central Europe, like Vienna, Prague, and Berlin, where social assimilation had already led to forgetting the Hebrew language, ignorance of the traditional texts, and total disregard of the metaphysical meanings of Judaism. In "Letter to His Father," the narrator identifies in retrospect with the demystifying look of the child who, beyond indifference and boredom, exposes the grotesque aspect of a ritual deprived of meaning. "This was the religious material that was handed on to me," wrote Kafka. "How could one do anything better with that material than get rid of it as fast as possible."[4]

But the central idea of that indictment is not that the father imposed on the son a Law he himself refused. What Kafka accused his father of, on the contrary, was not knowing how to hand down the Law to him, or, more precisely, for handing down to him only absurd residues. "It was also impossible to make a child . . . understand that the few flimsy gestures you performed in the name of Judaism, and with an indifference in keeping with their flimsiness, could have any higher meaning. . . . Had your Judaism been stronger, your example would have been more compelling too."[5] The last point of this excerpt is perhaps the most revealing. In it, Kafka mentioned his stirring interest for Jewish things after 1912.

It is precisely at that moment that a paradoxical reversal occurred in his father. For the father, the Judaism his son rediscovered suddenly became (and Kafka here seemed to quote his father's own expressions) "abhorrent to you, Jewish writings unreadable; they 'nauseated' you."[6] What Kafka did not say here is that the father's rage aimed precisely at that pre-Emancipation Judaism the son boasted of recovering, that Judaism of the East whence he himself had come and that he had tried, at the cost of an almost superhuman effort of assimilation, to forget forever. The "abhorrence," the sense of nausea, tells the horror inspired in the generation of the fathers by the Judaism of their own parents, that form of life they had seen as miserable and backward, with its "primitive" rites and its sacred texts that, for that generation of the Emancipation, had in fact become really "unreadable." That the son—that Dr. Franz Kafka, a symbol for the father of a finally successful integration into the Western world—could be fascinated by the backward world he himself had escaped, that he would make a symbolic alliance with the father's father, against the tide of progress, was a genealogical scandal, *the negation of the direction of history*. It is for this ambivalence about the tradition that Kafka reproached his father. For the father, the Law no longer represents anything but an empty frame, deprived of meaning. Yet, he did not question its validity, and he expected his son would also preserve that same formal loyalty. For that generation of fathers, the Law had no other content than its legality itself; it expressed nothing but its own authority, but signified nothing, established no symbolic order: its only function was that of a sign, the sign of an identity.

Scholem was also part of the generation of sons who were both lost and rebellious, who received from their father only the injunction to remain loyal to an identity emptied of all content.[7] Perhaps this was the source of his fascination with Kafka's work. At the core of this work, Scholem detected, as an ever-present interrogation, the *question of the Law.* A question that bears less on its nature or its meaning than on its place or nonplace, on that flight, that endless retreat of a principle presented as absolute without ever revealing where its authority comes from. Yet, there is no systematic study devoted to Kafka in Scholem's work. His reflections on the author of *The Trial* are scattered in the margins of his work, especially in his correspondence with Walter Benjamin and later in certain writings on the Kabbalah.

Yet, in this lifelong dialogue with the work of Kafka, three stages can be distinguished. The first two are linked with his epistolary discussion with Benjamin and deal with the possibility of a "theological" interpretation of Kafka's novels. This discussion, beginning in 1931, culminated in the summer of 1934, as Benjamin was writing the final version of his study of Kafka. It essentially revolves around the exegesis of a "didactic poem" by Scholem in which he develops his own interpretation of *The Trial* and the metaphysics that, according to him, are implied in that novel. The second stage took place four years later, in November 1938, when Scholem took a position with regard to a long correspondence in which Benjamin had revealed the final state of his theories on Kafka's work. Twenty years of intense labor on Jewish mysticism follow, from which Kafka is totally absent (as if, after Benjamin's death, it was impossible for Scholem to return to that subject). It is only at the end of the 1950s that Kafka's name reappears in several studies on the Kabbalah, always in particularly strategic places.

Those three stages correspond to Scholem's successive highlighting of three major themes of his interpretation: the correspondence of 1934 bears essentially on the *theme of the Law*; in November 1938, the letter to Benjamin deals with *the problem of truth*; the texts of the 1950s mainly emphasize the two closely linked motifs of *religious nihilism* and the *dialectic of tradition*. The whole of that interpretation, as developed over the years, can be summed up in a few central theses:

1. Kafka lived at a time of a general crisis of traditional values, more particularly, Jewish religious values. It is this crisis which is portrayed most profoundly in his work.

2. Through this metaphorical representation of the crisis of the modern world, paradoxes and contradictions that were always inherent in Jewish mysticism are exposed, especially in the most radical forms, bordering on nihilism and even heresy.

3. These concern historical parallels that go beyond the author's intentions and which he was probably never aware of.

4. According to Scholem, the resemblances between Kafka's fictional world and that of certain Jewish mystical heresies are the following:
   a. obsession with the Law;
   b. and this, in a world from which God is absent;
   c. the fact that the Law is open to an infinity of interpretations;
   d. the fact that it is unworkable;
   e. the idea that truth is inaccessible.

As Scholem saw it, these ancient motifs are found in Kafka's novels in a new form, not as ideas explicitly presented in the text but rather as thematic constants that permanently underlie the edifice of fiction. This is how we must understand the formula Scholem liked to repeat to his students: "To understand the Kabala today, we must read the works of Kafka, mainly *The Trial*."[8] All this revolves around the term "today": for us mod-

erns, who live in a time of radical secularization, the inevitable deterioration of religious belief, Kafka's work offers the image of a world bereft of
meaning, empty of all divine presence, but where hollow traces still exist
of the escaped transcendence: unanswered questions, unsolved enigmas,
whose negativity indicates the power exerted over us by "the shadow of the
dead God." According to Scholem, to discover these traces in Kafka's work
requires recourse to the categories of Jewish mysticism. Conversely, to grasp
all the negativity, the tragic awareness of the immanence of the world implied by the Kabbalah requires deciphering through the sensibility unique
to Kafka's work. A play of mirrors? An epistemological circle? Instead, that
constant coming-and-going between Kafka and Jewish mysticism recalls
those "dialectical images," which, at the same time, Walter Benjamin discussed in his book on the arcades of Paris, those images "when the past res-
onates for a flash with the present to form a constellation with it."[9]

*

The first time Scholem stated the central theme of his interpretation
of Kafka is in a letter to Walter Benjamin dated August 1, 1931: Kafka constantly contrasted the concrete reality of human life with the ideal of an
absolute justice (an ideal symbolized by Jewish tradition in the image of divine judgment). Basically, Kafka kept questioning himself about the possibility of such a judgment. Here, Scholem started from the chapter in *The
Trial* ("In the Cathedral") where K. and the priest discuss the possible different interpretations of the legend of the keeper of the gate and showed
how much the method of exegesis used by these two characters resembles
that of talmudic discussions. Such discussions never follow a linear argumentation but develop in an apparent disorder, according to an essentially
dialogical logic in which each speaker proposes in turn his own hypothesis,
which never functions as anything but a temporary stage of reasoning. This
is also the movement of Kafkaesque speculations, which seem to get lost in
infinite labyrinths, where every conclusion is immediately questioned, as if
to prove that, concerning the Law (hence, truth), the last word can never be
uttered: "I suppose this is what the moral reflection—if it were possible (and
this is the hypothesis of presumptuousness!)—of a halakhist who attempted
a *linguistic* paraphrase of a divine judgment would have to be like."[10]

Jacques Derrida has devoted to these pages of *The Trial*, and to the
legend that forms the heart of them, a study in which he showed that

the inaccessible nature of the Law in Kafka comes not from the fact that it is too complex or too demanding but from the fact that the very concept of the Law is deprived of its own foundation. Freud showed that the idea that the Law is the emanation of a transcendental principle is only an illusion of the Ego; according to Derrida, the same is true of Kafka's text, whose topography makes the idea of an origin, of a primary Law of Law that would guarantee its authority inconceivable.[11] On this point, Scholem's position is quite different. In a passage of his journal of April 18, 1934, the Jerusalem philosopher Schmuel Hugo Bergman quoted a manuscript note of Scholem on the biblical notion of the "God who turns away His face."[12] "It would be too easy," wrote Scholem, "to understand this passage with the help of moral categories. In reality this is the idea that God goes away *without leaving any traces*. It is not enough to say, as in Kafka, that the master in this house had withdrawn to the upper floor: No, he has left the house and cannot be found. It is a condition of unfathomable despair. Now, religion teaches us that there God is discovered."[13]

Unlike the extreme radicalness of Derrida's interpretation, Scholem's text still clearly bears the mark of a negative theology, or more precisely, of a negative mystique, since the irremediable absence of God would be the surest means of finding him. As for Kafka, according to Scholem, he would still be located far beyond that moment of "unfathomable desperation," since for him God would not have "left the house" and would not have "be found": no, he would simply have "withdrawn to the upper floor." Hence, we can better understand why Scholem ended his letter to Walter Benjamin with the following statement: "Never did the light of Revelation burn more implacably than [in Kafka's work]."[14] For Scholem, this represents another moment—certainly, a moment-limit—of the history of Revelation. God is obviously absent from Kafka's world; but his traces are still so visible there that it is enough to decipher them to discover the place where he has withdrawn: into the wings of a Law that has become incomprehensible but that still continues to rule the conscience of modern man.

It is in his "Didactic Poem" of 1934 that Scholem develops his most detailed interpretation of Kafka:

> Are we totally separated from you?
> Is there not a breath of your peace,
> Lord, or your message
> Intended for us in such a night?

Can the sound of your word
Have so faded in Zion's emptiness,
Or has it not even entered
This magic realm of appearance?

The great deceit of the world
Is now consummated.
Give then, Lord, that he may wake
Who was struck through by your nothingness.

Only so does revelation
Shine in the time that rejected you.
Only your nothingness is the experience
It is entitled to have of you.

Thus alone teaching that breaks through semblance
Enters the memory:
The truest bequest
Of hidden judgment.

Our position has been measured
On Job's scales with great precision.
We are known through and through
As despairing as on the youngest day.

What we are is reflected
In endless instances.
Nobody know the way completely
And each part of it makes us blind.

No one can benefit from redemption.
That star stands far too high.
And if you had arrived there too,
You would still stand in your way.

Abandoned to powers,
Exorcism is no longer binding.
No life can unfold
That doesn't sink into itself.

From the center of destruction
A ray breaks through at times,
But none shows the direction
The Law ordered us to take.

Since this sad knowledge
Stands before us, unassailable,
A veil has suddenly been torn,
Lord, before your majesty.

Your trial began on earth.
Does it end before your throne?
You cannot be defended,
As no illusion holds true here.

Who is the accused here?
The creature or yourself?
If anyone should ask you,
You would sink into silence.

Can such a question be raised?
Is the answer indefinite?
Oh, we must live all the same
Until your court examines us.[15]

This poem does not claim to offer a strict literary interpretation of *The Trial* but rather is presented as a personal meditation, an orchestration of echoes that can be evoked by Kafka's novel in a mind nourished by the texts of Jewish mysticism. As in Benjamin's epistemology, two universes, Kafka's and the Kabbalah's, meet in a flash and—outside every causal connection—create a new configuration. This reflection on Kafka comes from Scholem's concrete situation at that moment of his life: living in Jerusalem for more than ten years, he soon saw his ideal of a "spiritual" Zionism devoted to the internal regeneration of the Jewish people collapse in the contact with the political reality of the country. In Scholem, this disillusion assumes the proportions of an authentic metaphysical crisis. His increasingly pronounced interest in heretical mystic doctrines combines with his political disenchantment to lead him close to a radical nihilism. In contrast with the naïve optimism of his youthful years in Germany, he now (a bit like the allegorist mentioned by Benjamin ten years before in his book on German baroque drama) abandoned himself to the unfathomable melancholy of the scholar-philosopher who has penetrated the inconsistency of a world delivered to pure immanence. Yet, at the same time, the idea of God, as a guarantee of an ultimate sense of the real, keeps all its validity for Scholem; not, certainly, as a substantial presence but as a horizon on which the empty forms of things stand out. Hence, the paradoxical discursive status of that poem that deals with the absence of God yet incessantly invokes him.

This is the same paradox that Scholem thinks he has found in the novels of Kafka, whose characters manifest a stubborn will to find a meaning in a world that is visibly (i.e., from the perspective of the author) deprived of one. In other words, if Kafka's work presents no answers, it is still obsessed with one and the same question, that of knowing what is the nature of a world manifestly abandoned to arbitrariness and disorder, and yet still haunted by the idea of the Law. This appears in *The Process* as a parody of itself: it is not a question only of courts that sit in dark attics, penal codes that hide pornographic pamphlets, judges who don't judge, lawyers who no longer believe in the Law, policemen and executioners who look like pathetic provincial actors. That justice of ungraspable mysteries does not convey any rational order, nor does it express the slightest real will. In truth, it is content to reflect the restless wanderings of the accused himself: "The Court wants nothing from you. It receives you when you come and it dismisses you when you go."[16]

For Scholem, the Law in Kafka represents a metaphor of the idea of meaning. Its rule equals the presence of the divine in the world; its corruption or negation equals its absence. In "Didactic Poem," that withdrawal of meaning results in the deletion of the three modalities—Creation, Revelation, Redemption—by which the divine is manifested in the world according to Jewish tradition. But should it not be said rather that it is manifested by the traces left by that deletion? It is those traces, inverted marks of an escaped transcendence, that Scholem's poem deciphers one by one. The first three strophes expose the idea of Creation, that is, the belief that the world has a meaning, as a simple illusion: "The great deceit of the world / Is now consummated."

Is Scholem alluding here to the dreamlike atmosphere that so often characterizes descriptions of the real in Kafka? Obviously he is also referring to certain a-cosmic tendencies of Jewish mysticism in which the material world is reduced, in relation to the infinity of the divine Being filling all conceivable space, to a pure game of appearances. In both cases, the world is no longer conceived as an objective reality but as a fortuitous collection of shadows and reflections. For Scholem, this derealization of the world conveys the spirit of contemporary nihilism but also refers to his personal discouragement. At the time when the triumph of Nazism in Germany and the duty to receive the victims of persecution in Palestine seemed to confer a new legitimacy on the Zionist enterprise, the latter, confronted with the nationalist demands of the Arabs, went through the most serious moral crisis of its history. For Scholem, convinced that Zionism was above all a spiritual project and that, to remain faithful to itself, it had to recognize the historical aspirations of the Arabs of Palestine, the choice of the official leaders of the movement of a shortsighted realpolitik signified the failure of the utopian vision in which he had always wanted to believe. Thus, in Scholem, political circumstances, religious nihilism, and Kafka's work seem to refer incessantly to one another.

The second part of "Didactic Poem" (from strophe 4 to strophe 7) deals with the fate of Revelation in a period that no longer believes in God:

> Only so does revelation
> Shine in the time that rejected you.
> Only your nothingness is the experience
> It is entitled to have of you.

The notion of the "nothingness of Revelation" constitutes the core of Scholem's interpretation of Kafka. Scholem tried to explain the meaning of it in two letters to Walter Benjamin during the summer of 1934. Adopting the formula of "Didactic Poem," he had first written: "Kafka's world is the world of revelation, but of revelation seen of course from the perspective in which it is returned to its own nothingness."[17] Two months later, he went into more detail:

You ask what I understand by the "nothingness of revelation"? I understand by it a state in which revelation appears to be without meaning, in which it still asserts itself, in which it has *validity* but *no significance*. A state in which the wealth of meaning is lost and what is in the process of appearing (for revelation is such a process) still does not disappear, even though it is reduced to the zero point of its own content, so to speak. This is obviously a borderline case in the religious sense, and whether it can really come to pass is a very dubious point.[18]

In Scholem's work, the term "Revelation" translates the Hebrew notion of "Torah," and, in accordance with the polysemy of that term, this also involves the notions of Law and Doctrine. Thus, the "nothingness of Revelation" denotes a paradoxical moment in the history of tradition, that of a decisive (but not definitive) break in which the Law has already lost the principle of its authority, but in which its shadow continues to stand out on the horizon of our culture. That historical moment is certainly only an imperfect embodiment of all the possible connotations of the "nothingness of Revelation," since it is a "limited case of religion," always threatening to swing below or beyond its own axis, either in pure and simple atheism or in more or less radical forms of doubt or religious anguish. But it is precisely this instability, this wandering back and forth on a frontier, that is itself volatile, that prevents understanding the "nothingness of Revelation" in terms of the logic of opposites and that allows us to glimpse its meaning only through the maze of fiction.

The thesis that Revelation "preserves its validity" even when it is "emptied of all meaning," and that it can thus be elevated to an interpretative category, clearly distinguishes Scholem's position from Benjamin's. Their discussion had started with a passage of Benjamin's essay on Kafka concerning the meaning of the *student*, one of the typical characters of Kafka's novels. Trying to explain the symbolic function of that character in the universe of the novel, Benjamin spoke of "disciples who have lost the Scripture."[19] Scholem disputed this interpretation, whose meaning seemed only too clear to him: for Benjamin, it means asserting that, in our irremediably secularized world, religious tradition can no longer provide a convincing model of explanation of the real. Scholem on the other hand, understood Kafka's students as symbolic representatives of a period when "they can't decipher [it]."[20] This formula is just as coded as Benjamin's and means that, even if Revelation (that is, for Scholem the texts of the Jewish tradition) seem incomprehensible to us today, it is not necessarily obsolete forever, and a time may come when it will speak again to men. When Benjamin replied that, basically, the two interpretations amount to the same thing, at least concerning the judgment of the modern age we live in, Scholem strongly emphasized that the entire difference is located precisely in the judgment on the future of the tradition. Is it dead forever, or has it simply been interrupted? In other words, is the tradition capable of being radically renewed, of someday assuming forms that are unforeseeable today, which would restore its lost relevance? It is precisely on this belief in an infinite malleability of the tradition that Scholem's "negative theology" is based, and this is what distinguishes it from a pure and simple nihilism.

Yet, belief in a possible awakening of the tradition finds its counterpart in the disenchanted observation of its deep sleep today. That the text
of the Revelation is no longer decipherable for us is manifested in Kafka's
work by the metaphor of the unintelligible Law. Yet, although it seems
to have lost all meaning, it continues to persecute the Kafkaesque hero
with an obsessive violence. In *The Trial*, that Law from the father appears in the symbolic form of a court sitting in shadow, whose sentences
are never uttered, but that preserves the power to condemn the accused
to death. In "Letter to His Father," Kafka talks of the "sense of unlimited
guilt" provoked in him by paternal tyranny and quotes the last phrase
of *The Trial*: "it was as if the shame of it must outlive him."[21] It is this
sense of unlimited guilt that, for Scholem, makes Kafka's hero the symbolic representative of modern man who still lives in the shadow of an
obsolete law:

> Thus alone teaching that breaks through semblance
> Enters the memory:
> The truest bequest
> Of hidden judgment.
>
> Our position has been measured
> On Job's scales with great precision.
> We are known through and through
> As despairing as on the youngest day.

The experience of the contradictory demands we confront contrasts with
the uniqueness of the Law; the inevitable dispersal of our practice makes
the idea of a coherent ethics unthinkable:

> Nobody knows the way completely
> And each part of it makes us blind.

The same image appears in Kafka, in a completely different context. In
his tale "The New Advocate," the traditional metaphor of the road is also
broken up in the labyrinthine progression of the narration. Moreover, the
fact that today the idea of a path leading to truth has become unthinkable
is linked, in Kafka's text, to the revolt against paternal authority:

Nowadays—it cannot be denied—there is no Alexander the Great. There are
plenty of men who know how to murder people; the skill needed to reach over

a banqueting table and pink a friend with a lance is not lacking; and for many Macedonia is too confining, so that they curse Philip, the father—but no one, no one at all, can blaze a trail to India. Even in his day the gates of India were beyond reach, yet the King's sword pointed the way to them. Today the gates have receded to remoter and loftier places; no one points the way; many carry swords, but only to brandish them, and the eye that tries to follow them is confused.[22]

Drawing inspiration from one of the fundamental themes of Lurianic cosmogony, the beam of divine light that, the result of the primordial Infinite, goes through nothingness and thus links the created world to its transcendent source, Scholem reversed the traditional meaning of that mythic image and, instead of seeing it as a metaphor of the revelation of meaning beyond the abyss that separates us from the Infinite, read it, on the contrary, as the symbol of subversion itself:

> From the center of destruction
> A ray breaks through at times,
> But none shows the direction
> The Law ordered us to take.

For Scholem this withdrawal from the Law, which somehow reflects modern man's distance from it, does not mean that the idea of Law itself has become foreign to us, but rather that, in its very essence, it is exposed as *impracticable*. First, because we no longer know what that Law we no longer understand really demands of us. And second, because, since it is presented as the translation into practice of an absolute truth, it confronts us with an insoluble contradiction of perfection and reality. The practical injunction to realize the Absolute clashes with an impossibility as fundamental as the theoretical ambition to think Infinity. In 1932, Scholem wrote that "the absolutely concrete is absolutely impracticable."[23] Clearly, this was directed not at the formalism of Kantian Law but rather Jewish religious Law, defined by its extreme concreteness, the minute precision with which it codifies the slightest aspects of daily conduct. The endless deliberations of Kafka's characters, their hesitations at the slightest concrete decision, reminded Scholem of the perfectionist obsession of Jewish religious practice.

It is remarkable that that same formula recurred almost literally twenty-five years later in one of the statements in *Ten Non-historical Statements about the Kabbalah*, a crucial text in which Scholem revealed some of his most personal views on understanding Jewish mysticism. "The true language," he wrote, "could not be spoken any more than the absolutely concrete could not be realized."[24] The notion of a "real language" refers to a classical notion of traditional Judaism, that of an ideal language reflecting the very essence of the real, and that alone makes the utopia of a universal communication at the end of time conceivable. At the same time, Scholem referred here to the concept of "real language" developed by Walter Benjamin in "The Task of the Translator," that "language of truth that tensionless and even silent depository of the ultimate truth which all thought strives for."[25] However, in Benjamin (and no doubt also for Jewish mysticism), that ideal language could not be a verbal language, since no individual idiom can realize a perfect coincidence with the totality of the real: "Only insofar as it is fragmentary can the language be spoken," wrote Scholem.[26] Thus, if the "true language" must be understood as an abstract totality, the truth of the Law, then, appears as a concrete totality, that is, as a general principle that governs all individual behaviors. This excessive claim (which precisely defines Jewish law) clashes with the unlimited multiplicity of the real or, in other words, with its essential unpredictability. This is why the Law, whose totality (that is, true meaning) can be conveyed only through the esotericism of its mystical interpretation, is accessible to us, in practice, only in an infinitely divided form, of an endless collection of detailed precepts; as a signified totality, it is fundamentally unworkable.

On the other hand, Kafka's world seems to be seen through an extraordinary microscope, so that it seems endowed with an almost supernatural concreteness. Everything in it is unstable, stumbling, and precarious, but at the same time desperately immutable and ossified. This decline, with no way out that Scholem detected in it and that is reminiscent of the description of the baroque world in Walter Benjamin, is that of an irremediably corrupt universe that can no longer be saved. The Law is no longer any help here, even if the world evoked by Kafka seems to expect its own redemption at any moment. But things are so heavy that nothing can move them anymore; in Kafka, the slightest change, the slightest decision assumes the dimension of superhuman effort, doomed in advance to failure: "it seems to me utterly compelling that a world in which things are so cannily concrete and in which not a step can be fulfilled will present an *abject* and by no means idyllic sight."[27]

In such a universe, all hope of redemption is clearly illusory. Here, too, Kafka's work appears to Scholem as a metaphoric representation of our modern world "from which God has withdrawn":

> No one can benefit from redemption.
> That star stands far too high.
> And if you had arrived there too,
> You would still stand in your way.

Three years earlier, Scholem had written to Benjamin that, in Kafka, "the anticipation of redemption isn't possible."[28] This formula, like the strophe of the "Didactic Poem," alludes to *The Star of Redemption*, one of whose central ideas is precisely that of the anticipation of Redemption. We know that, for Rosenzweig, the Jewish people lives in advance of the final fulfillment of history through the symbolism of rituals. The symbolic anticipation of the future is the only way of living as a current experience the essentially imaginary nature of Redemption. Scholem, who had a profound admiration for *The Star of Redemption* ("it is rare to see such a big star appear on the horizon," he wrote in 1931),[29] nevertheless judged that the idea of a symbolic anticipation of Redemption deprived Jewish messianism of its historic dynamism, reducing it to the exercise of a pure piety. The Lurianic Kabbalah had no doubt also insisted on the redemptive function of ritual observances; but, for Scholem, modern man, having lost belief in the absolute authority of the Law, can no longer activate the utopian forces that, according to the Kabbalah, it conceals.

Similarly, Kafka's characters are no longer defined by their degree of proximity or distance with regard to the Law, since they are ignorant of its exact demands. On the contrary, they are abandoned to the arbitrariness of a play of forces whose mechanism eludes them. If the shadow of the ancient Law continues to hover over them, making them experience the torments of an endless trial, the final judgment, however, can never be given; for the infinite complexity of a reality no longer explained by religious categories involves prosecutors, attorneys, and judges in a labyrinth of arguments and counterarguments that is impossible to get out of. This is why Kafka's world is that of a perpetual *questioning*: are we really the victims of an indecipherable Law, or is the idea that a trial is carried out against us only an illusion we ourselves have forged? Scholem answered this question with another question that challenges the legitimacy of the first. For how could we know if the universe of the Law exists outside our mind, since the border that is supposed to separate consciousness and what is outside it, the inside and the outside, is itself only an element of our subjectivity, an imaginary line that can be shifted infinitely?

> Can such a question be raised?
> Is the answer indefinite?

These questions that refer incessantly to other questions, this permanent undermining of each query, so characteristic of Kafka's logic, seem to echo in the most original principle of Kabbalist epistemology, as Scholem defined it in *Ten Non-historical Statements*:

> The nature of knowledge in the Kabbalah: the Torah is the medium inside which all knowledge is fulfilled. The symbol of the "mirror that enlightens," which the Kabbalists applied to the Torah is instructive in that respect. The Torah is the medium in which knowledge is reflected. . . . Knowledge is the beam of light through which the creature tries to get out of that medium to join its own source; but it is ineluctably condemned to remain within the medium, for God Himself is Torah, and knowledge itself could not make us get out of it. There is something infinitely desperate in the idea developed in the first page of the Zohar, that the ultimate knowledge is without object. The mediate nature of knowledge is revealed in the classic form of the question: knowledge is a question based in God and no answer corresponds to it.[30]

This is why, in the endless spiral of questions without answers, our abandonment is such that only death can put an end to the trial:

> Oh, we must live all the same
> Until your court examines us.

*

In 1937–1938, Scholem often asked Benjamin to tell him the condition of his most recent ideas on Kafka. Hence, the long letter of June 12, 1938, in which, shifting the emphases, Benjamin started (implicitly at least) from a reflection on *The Castle*. Although the name of the novel is not mentioned explicitly, Benjamin was clearly referring to K.'s adventures in the village where he is temporarily living. First, Benjamin asserted that K.'s efforts are not directed so much at reaching the castle (as Max Brod maintained) as at learning the truth about it. But he soon understands that such a truth is unattainable and that it may not even exist. In fact, each of the villagers has formed his own opinion about the nature of the castle, and these different points of view are so contradictory that K. comes to ask himself if, behind that multiplicity of divergent narratives, there is a single truth. In other words, the different narratives— which are so many oral traditions—cannot be added together to form a homogeneous corpus.

In a 1936 essay dedicated to Lesskov, Benjamin had defined the narrative as the transmission of a piece of wisdom; this wisdom, in turn, would represent the "epic side of truth,"[31] the organization of the narrative reflecting, on the narrative mode, the internal coherence of a certain vision of the world. It is precisely this epic coherence of truth that, for Benjamin, no longer exists in Kafka. Thus, *The Castle* would be the very example of a work that no longer seeks to transmit a certain form of truth but that, on the contrary, produces the disintegration of the idea of truth itself, both through the labyrinthine aspect of its fable and by the fragmentation of the narrative discourse. In Kafka, writes Benjamin, it is the "haggadic" consistency of truth that has disappeared.[32] In this sense, Kafka's work reflects "tradition falling ill." Kafka's genius consisted precisely of making this illness, that is, of the impossibility of transmitting a coherent truth today, the theme of his narratives. Moreover, this impossibility would be embodied in the form of the narration itself. Just like the villagers who, while knowing that the truth of the castle will never be known, persist in spite of everything in reporting their contradictory narratives, so Kafka also "sacrificed truth for the sake of clinging to transmissibility." This is why, wrote Benjamin, "[w]e can no longer speak of wisdom." What remains are only "the products of its decay," and above all, instead of the exposition of truth, "the rumor about the true things (a sort of theology passed on by whispers dealing with matters discredited and obsolete)."[33]

The historical study of the Kabbalah had revealed to Scholem the fundamental paradox governing the Jewish mystical tradition: this mysticism is presented, in its nature, as an *oral tradition*, essentially resistant to all written translation. The social function of this esotericism, that is, the desire to protect a secret doctrine against its disclosure to the mass of nonbelievers, is only the most external aspect of an internal necessity, immanent in the dialectic of the mystical tradition itself. In fact, in principle, that aims less at transmitting a body of doctrine, a content of truth, than at a way of approaching it, an attitude of mind, in other words, a *horizon of reading* or of interpretation. As soon as some direction of reading is clarified or objectified, in a specific text, to be understood, it immediately needs a new key of interpretation. In this sense, in all scriptural fixing, there is an exoteric aspect that is opposed to the oral nature of the mystical tradition. Yet, this tradition is abandoned to all the uncertainties of collective memory; so there is necessarily a moment when, so as not to be forgotten, it must be consigned to writing. But, what had been originally conceived as a horizon of meaning is immediately transformed into a subject of discourse, which then requires interpretation. An endless dialectic, in which the unfathomable nature of the esoteric tradition is expressed: insofar as it basically *means nothing*, cannot be conceptualized or even formulated, what constitutes it as tradition cannot, strictly speaking, be transmitted; conversely, what is transmitted of it never contains it. This is the meaning of the first of the *Ten Non-historical Statements*:

The Kabbalist states that there is a tradition concerning truth and that that tradition can be transmitted. It is an ironic statement, for the truth in question here has all sorts of properties, but certainly not that of being transmissible. It can be known, but it cannot be transmitted; and what, in it, becomes the object of a transmission is precisely what it no longer contains. The authentic tradition remains hidden; it is only in its decline that it relates to an object and it is only in that decline that it becomes visible in all its grandeur.[34]

In this sense, the "illness of tradition" Benjamin spoke of, in other words, the degree of invisibility it has attained today, would be the sign not of its death but, on the contrary, of its retreat to its essence, while, at the same time, it is its transformation into an object of historical study that most clearly indicates its decline.

For Scholem, Kafka's work illustrates in its way the Hasidic lesson told by Agnon, with which he concludes his book *Major Trends in Jewish Mysticism* (from a series of lectures given in New York in the summer of 1938, just as Benjamin wrote him his letter on Kafka):

When the Baal Shem had a difficult task before him, he would go to a certain place in the woods, light a fire and meditate in prayer—and what he had set out to perform was done. When a generation later the "Maggid" of Meseritz was faced with the same task he would go to the same place in the woods and say: We can no longer light the fire, but we can still speak the prayers—and what he wanted done became reality. Again a generation later Rabbi Moshe Leib of Sassov had to perform this task. And he too went into the woods and said: We can no longer light a fire, nor do we know the secret meditations belonging to the prayer, but we do know the place in the woods to which it all belongs—and that must be sufficient; and sufficient it was. But when another generation had passed and Rabbi Israel of Rishin was called upon to perform the task, he sat down on his golden chair in his castle and said: We cannot light the fire, we cannot speak the prayers, we do not know the place, but we can tell the story of how it was done. And, the story-teller adds, the story which he told had the same effect as the actions of the other three.[35]

Unlike Benjamin, Scholem thought that the crisis of the tale (that is, of tradition) reflected in Kafka's work still indicates a certain way of "telling history." "This is the situation we find ourselves in today, and that of Jewish mysticism itself," Scholem noted. All that remains of the vanished mystery is the tale we can make of it; as for Kafka's work, it is the tale of this disappearance: it is through literature that the secret history of the original truths continues to be told (even when they have been forgotten).

*

For Benjamin, Kafka's texts have the formal structure of parables, coded narratives referring to some hidden meaning the reader persists in seeking. But unlike genuine parables (biblical or Gospel), the allegorical form in Kafka is misleading; the doors open onto empty rooms; behind those labyrinthine fables there is no dissimulated truth. Many years later, Scholem took up that idea again, but here, too, translating it into the language of a negative mystique: for him, the absence, in Kafka's narratives, of an allegorical truth becomes the allegory itself of the absence of truth. As Scholem saw it, Kafka's characters perceive the world, like certain Jewish mystics, as a coded text they seek desperately—but always in vain—to decipher:

Mystical exegesis essentially appears as a *deciphering*. The new revelation that falls to the mystic is presented as a key of Revelation. Moreover, even when the key itself has been lost, the infinite desire to see it still remains. This is the situation evoked in Kafka's works, where mystical impulses, referred to that ground zero where they seem to be about to disappear, still continue to manifest themselves with an infinite efficacy. But even one thousand seven hundred years ago, that had been the situation experienced by some mystical talmudists, a situation that one of them, whose name we do not know, sums up admirably and almost clandestinely. In his commentary on the Psalms, Origen reports that a "Hebraic" wise man (probably a member of the rabbinic Academy of Caesarea) had told him the following apologia: the Holy Scriptures are like a vast house with countless rooms; before each room, there is a key, but it is not the right one. All the keys have been mixed up and our task, both difficult and great, consists of discovering for each room the key that fits it. This apologia, which seems to evoke in advance, in the heart of the talmudic tradition at its height, a Kafkan situation par excellence, without however conferring on it the slightest negative connotation, shows us, at the same time, how much, in the last resort, Kafka's world belongs to the genealogy of Jewish mysticism.[36]

This passage is characteristic of the conception of truth Scholem attributed to Kafka and that he already detected at the origin of the history of Jewish mysticism. As in his theory of the "nothingness of Revelation," this is an extreme case of knowledge, in which truth, endowed with an almost unlimited malleability, still continues to form the ideal horizon of all knowledge. Certainly, all the keys have been mixed up; but what is most decisive, keys still exist, and the utopian hope of someday seeing each key fitted to the lock that corresponds to it still defines the ideal end of our efforts. It is still true that, in our experienced reality, this search for truth knows no end. This may be why Kafka's texts, which stage an obsessive pursuit for meaning, also offer an endless work of interpretation. As if Kafka had made that process of infinite search the formal principle of his own work; as if his texts themselves reflected the always resumed process of their own interpretation.

According to Scholem, the search for truth as a desperate enterprise (even if the idea of truth continues to stand out on the horizon of our thought) is the central intuition on which the affinity of Kafka's world with that of a certain Jewish mysticism is based. Is it by chance, Scholem wondered, that it was in Prague of all places that the most radical of these mystical tendencies—that is, the Frankist heresy—left its most lasting traces?

In Prague, a century before Kafka, Jonas Wehle had written (through the intermediary of his son-in-law Löw of Hönigsberg) letters and writings that were never published, but which his Frankist disciples subsequently collected carefully. He addressed the last adepts of a Kabbalah distorted into heresy, that of a nihilist messianism that tried to speak the language of the Enlightenment. He had been the first to raise the following question (and to answer it in the affirmative): when man was expelled from Paradise, wasn't the major victim of that expulsion not man, but Paradise itself? That aspect of the problem has definitely been much too neglected up to the present. Is it the sympathy of souls that inspired strangely close ideas in Kafka, a century later? Perhaps it is because we don't know what became of Paradise that we ask why "the Good has, in some sense, something desperate." In truth, these considerations seem to emanate from some heretical Kabbalah. For better than anyone, Kafka was able to account for that frontier where nihilism and religion meet. This is why his works that express in a secularized form the sensibility unique to the Kabbalah (of which he knew nothing) have, for certain readers today, something of the rigorous splendor of canonical texts, of a broken perfection.[37]

Language and Secularization

In late 1926, Gershom Scholem dedicated this text to Franz Rosenzweig:

This country is a volcano, and language is lodged within it. People here talk of many things that may lead to our ruin, and more than ever of the Arabs. But there is another danger, much more uncanny than the Arab nation, and it is a necessary result of the Zionist enterprise: what of the "actualization" of the Hebrew language? That sacred language on which we nurture our children, is it not an abyss that must open up one day? The people certainly don't know what they are doing. They think they have secularized the Hebrew language, have done away with its apocalyptic point. But that, of course, is not true: the secularization of the language is no more than a *manner of speaking*, a ready-made expression. It is impossible to empty the words so bursting with meaning, unless one sacrifices the language itself. The phantasmagoric Volapük spoken in our streets precisely defines the expressionless linguistic space which alone has permitted the "secularization of language." But if we transmit the language to our children as it was transmitted to us, if we, a generation of transition, revive the language of the ancient books for them, that it may reveal itself anew through them, shall not the religious power of that language explode one day? And when that explosion occurs, what kind of a generation will experience it? As for us, we live within that language above an abyss, most of us with the steadiness of blind men. But when we regain our sight, we or our descendants, shall we not fall into that abyss? And we cannot know if the sacrifice of those who will perish in that fall will be enough to close it again.

The initiators of the Hebrew language renaissance believed blindly, almost fanatically, in the miraculous power of language, and that was their good fortune.

Because if they had been clairvoyant, they never would have had the demonic courage to resuscitate a language destined to become an Esperanto. Even today, they continue to walk along, enchanted, above an abyss from which no sound rises; and they pass on the ancient names and signs to our youth. As for us, we are seized with fear when, amidst the thoughtless discourse of a speaker, a religious term suddenly makes us shudder, though it may even have been meant to console. This Hebrew is heavy with impending catastrophe. It cannot and will not remain in its present state: our children have no other language left, and it is truly they alone who will pay the price for that meeting we have arranged for them, without ever having asked them, without asking even ourselves. The day will come when the language will turn against those who speak it. There are already moments in our own life when this happens, unforgettable, stigmatizing moments, when all the presumptuousness of our enterprise is suddenly revealed. When that day comes, will there be a young generation able to withstand the revolt of a sacred tongue?

Language is name. The power of language is enclosed in the name; the abyss of language is sealed within it. Now that we have invoked the ancient names day after day, we can no longer hold off the forces they contain. Once awakened, they will appear, for we have summoned them with terrible violence. Indeed we speak a vestigial, ghostly language. The names haunt our phrases; writers and journalists play with them, pretending to believe or to make God believe that all this is really not important. And yet, out of the spectral degradation of our language, the force of the holy often speaks to us. For the names have a life of their own; if they did not, woe to our children, who would be abandoned, hopeless, to an empty future.

Hebrew words, all that are not neologisms but have been taken from the treasure-house of our "good old language," are full to bursting with meaning. A generation that takes over the most fruitful part of our tradition—its language—cannot, though it may ardently wish to, live without tradition. When the day finally comes and the force shored up in the Hebrew language is unleashed, when the "spoken," the content of language takes form once again, our people will find itself confronted anew with that sacred tradition, signifying the choice before them: either to submit or to perish. Because at the heart of such a language, in which we ceaselessly evoke God in a thousand ways, thus calling Him back into the reality of our life, He cannot keep silent. this inevitable revolution of language, in which the Voice will again become audible, is the only subject never discussed in this country. Because those who endeavor to revive the Hebrew language did not truly believe in the Judgment to which their acts are summoning us. May the levity that has accompanied us on this apocalyptic path not lead us to our destruction.

Jerusalem, 7 Tevet 5687
(*translated from the German by Ora Wiskind*)[1]

Many aspects of this recently discovered text by Gershom Scholem are surprising. Written three years after Scholem arrived in Palestine, it reveals a profound discouragement about Zionism, at least in its concrete manifestation, and an almost apocalyptic despair about the process of the secularization of Judaism that was taking place before his eyes. For the young Scholem (he was then twenty-nine years old), the most characteristic and upsetting symptom of that development was linguistic: the transition of the Hebrew language from its traditional status of a sacred tongue to its new function of a language of use and communication involved not only forgetting the religious contents of the language, but, what is infinitely more serious, their fall into banality and insignificance, that is, for Scholem, their *desecration*. What is striking here is the passion with which Scholem, a historian of Jewish mysticism, takes the subjects he studies and identifies with them. An identification that, no doubt, casts a new light on the relationship between Scholem the scholar and the man, between the specialist committed to objectivity and the individual engaged in history. In this sense, the 1926 text perfectly illustrates the complexity of the correlation, in Scholem, between the writing of history and the historicity of the historian.

On the other hand, this text is remarkable for the connection it proposes between a philosophy of history and a theory of language. Reflection on the mystique of language in the Kabbalah had preoccupied Scholem since the very beginning of his research; from 1920 on, he planned to write a study on the subject, but it was only after fifty years of work that he decided to carry it out.[2] In that major work, a synthesis of a lifetime of research,[3] Scholem showed that the mystical conception of language, that is, above all the idea that the essence of the real is linguistic and that that linguistic essence is a revelation of the Absolute, is a fundamental element of the Jewish tradition. In this sense, and although it obviously must be studied in its historical evolution, this theory of language in Jewish mysticism concerns the *structure* of the real and not its *history*. In Scholem's work, the study of this theory is part of a vast combination of works devoted, as it were, to the *ontology* of Jewish mysticism.[4] This is in contrast to another area of research explored by Scholem, that of messianism, that is, if you like, of the *philosophy of history* underlying the Jewish tradition.[5] In Scholem's historical works, the analysis of the mystical theory of language and that of the mystical philosophy of history almost never intersect, because in the Jewish tradition itself, they are two clearly separate areas.[6]

However, the idea that these two orders of reality are somehow connected was not alien to Scholem. Moreover, several more personal than scientific assertions indicate the central role played in his thought by belief in a paradigmatic function of language, conceived as an index or a parameter measuring the degree of presence or absence of the divine in the world at any given moment of history. This idea returns as a central theme in his correspondence with Walter Benjamin, especially in letters dating from 1934, devoted to the interpretation of Kafka's work, in which, as we have seen, Scholem discerned both the reversal and the confirmation of the Kabbalistic vision of the world: the evocation through a language structured by forms of negativity of a universe—ours—from which God has withdrawn, and which no longer indicates anything but the "nothingness of Revelation."[7]

These subjects reverberate in certain strategic places in Scholem's work, as, for example, in the last statement of the *Ten Non-historical Statements about the Kabbalah* (1958), which deals again with Kafka, or in the last paragraph of the 1970 study *The Name of God*. But in all these passages, the question is approached from its most general angle, that of the status of language in a world devoid of the sacred. The 1926 text, on the other hand, deals openly with the relationship of the Hebraic language, conceived, in the style of Jewish mystics, as a holy tongue, and the present historical reality, where the Zionist ideal enters the phase of concrete realization. This is the direct confrontation of a central theme of Jewish esotericism with historical reality itself, or more precisely, with an attempt to read that reality—of an unprecedented mutation in the history of Judaism—in light of the most ancient categories of Jewish mysticism.

*

One of the most troubling questions about this text is that of its addressee. Why did Scholem decide to address that meditation on the possible failure of Zionism to Franz Rosenzweig of all people? Or conversely, if he had to write to Franz Rosenzweig, or for him, why choose that subject? Answering these questions—which are by no means purely circumstantial—leads us into the core of the debate echoed by that text, and we must first try to reconstruct the conditions in which it was written. In his autobiography, *From Berlin to Jerusalem*, Scholem tells that one day, Martin Buber and Ernest Simon asked him to "contribute to a portfolio of very short essays which was to be presented to Rosenzweig, who was then already paralyzed and unable to speak." "And I did so," he added.[8] This collection, which was in fact sent to Rosenzweig on his birthday but was never published, is preserved in the Leo Baeck Archive in New York,[9] including the original of Scholem's essay. But Scholem was in the habit of keeping a manuscript copy of the texts he deemed particularly important, and it was this copy that was found among Scholem's papers in Jerusalem.

The history of the relations between Scholem and Rosenzweig is one of fundamental disagreement. Despite the respect the two men had for each other, their conceptions of Judaism and the personal choices resulting from them were too divergent and their personalities too strong to allow a compromise between them. Yet, what they had in common seemed really to have been the essential: the same rejection of assimilation, the same personal route of return to Judaism, and even more specifically, to its religious sources; in short, the same internal course of "dissimilation." But if the point of departure was the same for both, their conceptions of the goal that modern Judaism should set for itself were irreconcilable. Scholem summed up the nature of that ideological discord perfectly in his autobiography:

Our decisions took us in entirely different directions. He sought to reform (or perhaps I should say revolutionize) German Jewry from within. I, on the other hand, no longer had any hopes for the amalgam known as "Deutschjudentum," i.e., a Jewish community that considered itself German, and expected a renewal of Jewry only from its rebirth in Eretz Yisrael.[10]

And in fact, Rosenzweig did accuse Scholem of thinking that "[Diaspora] Judaism is in a state of clinical death and only 'there' will it find life again."[11] As he saw it, on the contrary, Zionism as "a secularized form of messianism"[12] risked stripping Judaism of its religious identity by seeking to "normalize" it at all costs.[13] In the spring of 1922, when Scholem had decided to leave Germany and move to Palestine, he had a long discussion with Rosenzweig about German Judaism that led to a complete break between them. "Thus," wrote Scholem in his autobiography, "I had one of the stormiest and most irreparable arguments of my youth." "I would never have broached this delicate subject . . . if I had known that Rosenzweig was then already in the first stages of his fatal illness."[14]

We know, in fact, that Rosenzweig, afflicted with amyotropic lateral sclerosis, was paralyzed and could not speak from 1923 until his death in 1929. Apparently, Scholem soon regretted the violence of that discussion, yet relations between the two men remained extremely tense: "Scholem projects his bad conscience with regard to me onto me and imagines that I have a grudge against him," wrote Rosenzweig in 1926, a few months before receiving the *Festschrift* including Scholem's text.[15] And in fact, it can be assumed that, if Scholem agreed to contribute to that collection, and especially, if he chose to inform Rosenzweig three years after his arrival in Palestine of his doubts and apprehensions about the future of a Zionism striving increasingly to cut itself off from its traditional Jewish roots, it was, among other reasons, to repair somehow the violence of his words of 1922 and to admit to him (hence the title of the text, "A Confession") that in contact with reality, his own conceptions had come much closer to those of Rosenzweig. Not that he was no longer a Zionist; his critique in that text is an *internal* critique. But his elements are essentially those that Rosenzweig had developed in the name of a religious conception of Judaism.[16]

On the other hand, the problem of secularizing the Hebrew language touched closely on one of the sharpest and most personal subjects of debate between Scholem and Rosenzweig, that is, the theory and practice of the translation of Hebrew texts into German. In 1919, in the review *Der Jude*, Scholem had published translations of Jewish liturgical texts that had attracted Franz Rosenzweig's attention. Two years later, Rosenzweig sent him a translation of the grace after meals he had just finished. Scholem had also translated that text. The correspondence between the two men on this subject reveals a difference of principle concerning the historical implications of those translations, Scholem accusing Rosenzweig of "Christianizing" the spirit of the Hebrew language with his transpositions.[17] This criticism intensified when Rosenzweig published his translations of Judah Halevi's poems in 1924.[18] In a letter to Walter Benjamin, Scholem then wrote of his intention to publish an article in *Der Jude* denouncing "the putting to death of Hebrew poetry in the name of an anti-Zionist philosophy of history."[19] Two years later, even though Scholem did not change his mind about those criticisms, he did seem to be willing to concede to Rosenzweig that the process of secularization and banalization of the Hebrew language in Palestine was just as dangerous for its spiritual integrity as its possible "Christianization" in Diaspora. But more generally, he offered Rosenzweig a text that declares, pace Jewish mystics, the foundational powers of language that must be understood as Scholem's homage to the author of *The Star of Redemption*, which he was later to say represents "a fundamental work of the philosophy of religions,"[20] "one of the central creations of Jewish religious thought in this century,"[21] which shows "as in the Kabbalists, the relationship between language and an authentic theological thought."[22]

*

In a letter to Walter Benjamin dated August 1, 1931, Scholem brought up "the radical difference between [his] concept of Zionism, oriented toward a renewal of Judaism and which [he] accepts after all is said and done to mean qualified by mystico-religious, and empirical Zionism based on the myth of a self-styled 'political solution of the Jewish question.'" "As for me," he added, "I don't think there is a solution of the Jewish question in the sense of a normalization of the Jews, and I don't think the question can be resolved in that sense in Palestine. It has always been obvious to me and what still remains so is simply the fact that Palestine is *necessary*, and that is enough for me."[23] Five years after his essay for Rosenzweig, Scholem here returns to the same key idea that would dominate his vision of Zionism to the end. In the last chapter of his autobiography, he once more repeats that same central idea: "With our return to our own history we . . . wanted to change it, but we did not want to deny it. Without this *religio*, this 'tie to the past,' the enterprise was and is hopeless, doomed to failure from the start."[24]

The text addressed to Franz Rosenzweig can be understood only on the background of the ideological and moral crisis Scholem experienced during his first years in Palestine. A personal crisis, in the first place, provoked by the brutal confrontation between the spiritual ideals that had led the young Scholem to Palestine and the political and social reality he discovered there. But this personal crisis reflected more profoundly the clash between two conceptions of Zionism. One was born among the Jewish intelligentsia in Russia in the late nineteenth century, in reaction to a wave of pogroms, but also as a desire to rescue the Jewish masses of Central Europe from their political and social alienation by bringing them into the world of modernity through nationalism. From the start, Zionism faced the opposition of the spiritual leaders of Orthodox Judaism, who were concerned with preserving the traditional values and lifestyles. And in fact, although Zionism was rooted to a large extent in the most classical representations of Jewish messianism, it was lived, both by its champions and its adversaries, as a radical break with the world of religious Judaism. It was this desire for a break that guided—more or less resolutely, more or less consciously—the construction of a new Jewish society in Palestine by the generations of Pioneers.

It was a movement from a diametrically opposed direction that had led young Scholem to Zionism. In Germany, in the first years of the twentieth century, it was the break with assimilation, the revolt against a social milieu precariously balanced between a Judaism that was already more than half-forgotten, and a Germanness that, though fervently desired, actually remained inaccessible, and the rejection of the illusions feeding that dream of a harmonious absorption into the surrounding society that had led Scholem to seek the spiritual sources of his identity. For him, Zionism meant integration of that personal itinerary into a historical movement that was to end in the spiritual renewal of the Jewish people. In relation to the Jewish religious tradition, the Zionism of the Pioneers Scholem discovered in Palestine was as different from his own as an ideology of rupture can be from an ideology of return.

*

The criticism of the secularization of the Hebrew language, as expressed vehemently in the 1926 essay dedicated to Rosenzweig, can be understood only in light of the Kabbalistic theory of language, to which Scholem constantly refers, either explicitly or tacitly. At that period, Scholem had not yet published the study he dreamed of writing on that subject, but his text already contains the seeds of some of the ideas underlying his major article "The Name of God" forty-five years later. The most fundamental of them is the distinction between two contrary aspects of language: an "external" aspect, where language appears as an instrument of communication, and an "internal" aspect, where its "symbolic" or even "magical" side is revealed. The insistence on the external, communicative aspect of verbal expression characterizes the secular vision of language, while highlighting its symbolic and magical aspect is the distinctive mark of all mysticism. This distinction may be explained if it is compared with Roman Jakobson's differentiation between the communicative and poetic functions of language.[25] In its poetic function, the intention of discourse is not to transmit a message from the speaker to the addressee but concerns the message itself in all its linguistic materiality. This is certainly what Scholem meant in his allusion to the "magic of the verb" as a fundamental human experience, in which "words have an action far beyond the sphere of 'comprehending.'" This experience, he added, is "what makes poets, mystics and anyone savor the sensual wealth of words. This is where the idea of the power of names and their magical use comes from."[26]

In these terms, the distinction between communicative language and magic language does not come from the Kabbalah itself. They are heuristic terms projected by Scholem onto the material he was studying to explain its components. These categories were inspired directly by Walter Benjamin's youthful writings, particularly by the two essays "On Language as Such and on the Language of Man" (1916) and "The Task of the Translator" (1921, published in 1923). The importance for the formation of Scholem's thought of his intellectual dialogue with Walter Benjamin, especially during their stay together in Switzerland from May 1918 to August 1919, cannot be overemphasized.[27] It is certainly at this time that the fundamental categories underlying all of Scholem's work were set. In those two essays, Benjamin developed a theory of language inspired by Johann Georg Hamann, Wilhelm von Humboldt, and the German Romantics; those authors derived many of their ideas from Jacob Boehme, whose theosophical system, according to Scholem, shows strong affinities with the Kabbalah, although no direct historical relation between the two can be proved.[28] In any case, through Walter Benjamin's mediation, these are the classical ideas that informed some of the major concepts used by Scholem to explain the theory of language of the Kabbalah.[29] These concepts also are in the background of his essay of 1926 dedicated to Rosenzweig.

The central idea of that text, that of an almost ontological decline of language when it passes from its magical function to its instrumental function, comes directly from Benjamin's essay "On Language as Such and on the Language of Man." Starting with a commentary on the first chapters of Genesis, Benjamin distinguished three stages in the history of the origin of language: the first is that of the divine language through which the world was created; at that stage, prior to the distinction between words and things, language represents the very essence of reality. That stage, forever beyond human experience, is followed by that of the "paradisiacal language," the original language of humanity, where a perfect accord between words and things prevails: reality is entirely transparent in language, and language captures the very essence of reality with an almost miraculous accuracy. It is this "Adamic language" that was lost when, as a result of the Original Sin, reinterpreted by Benjamin in light of the episode of the Tower of Babel, language became a mere instrument of communication. The appearance of the communicative function of language, the third stage of its primordial history, marks its decline, its fall into the "abyss of prattle." In our present language, its instrumental function denotes its secular aspect, while its magical (i.e., poetic) function indicates the survival in it of its paradisiacal splendor.

It is not hard to discern the echo of this theory in Scholem's essay for Rosenzweig: the Hebrew language that represents the original language of humanity for Jewish mystics preserves in its quintessence the magic potential of language, provided it remains a "sacred tongue," that is, that it survives in its purest form, the one it assumes in the classical texts of Jewish tradition and its liturgy. On the other hand, its negligent misuse in daily practice amounts to a genuine desecration in that the magic or symbolic powers it contains are exposed, stripped, given over to a purely utilitarian use. Hence, the importance of the theme of "names" in Scholem's essay, a theme borrowed both from Benjamin's youthful writings and from the Kabbalah. In Benjamin, the Adamic language is composed of names that, according to Genesis, Adam gave the animals, and, in Benjamin's interpretation, to all things created. This power of naming (which may be said to be the essence of the poet's task) originates, in the Kabbalah, in the divine activity itself.

Among the diversity of names the Bible attributes to God, the rabbinic tradition privileges the Tetragrammaton, which it considers the very essence of all his other names. Jewish mysticism sees the Tetragrammaton not only as the source of all divine names but also as the origin of human language itself. In fact, beyond the patent meaning it conveys, that language contains a level of hidden meaning, structured, in an infinity of combinations and permutations of the letters forming the various divine names. In his interpretation of the Kabbalistic theory of language, Scholem identifies that hidden level with the symbolic, or magic, aspect of all language.[30] There is a superior form of knowledge that can decipher the genuine meaning hidden under the ostensible coherence of communicative discourse, which is nothing other than a logic of divine names. In his presentation of the theory of language of the Spanish Kabbalist Abraham Abulafia, Scholem distinguished between that unveiling of the secret symbolism of all language, defined by Abulafia as "permitted magic" and "forbidden magic," in which the poetic force immanent in language is used for material and selfish ends:

Abulafia is completely aware of the immediate power emanating from words, most of all from words purified to the utmost, which seem meaningless but are actually charged with meaning, as well as their metamorphoses, their "revolutions." . . . Magic does exist for him as that which is non-communicable and which nevertheless radiates from words—this internal and profound dimension of magic remains exempt from the prohibition of sorcery or magic. It is this sort of legitimate magic the prophets engaged in. . . . [But] whoever permits himself, without that status [of a prophet], to intervene, by so to speak technical means, in the Creation, or claims to be capable of such intervention, succumbs to the temptation of mantic sciences, that is, of magic in the usual sense. That discipline, "demonic science," though not without some basis in reality, is a falsification of true mysticism, because it crudely imitates the external aspect of the deeper truth. . . . [The magician] is a man who has sworn his loyalty not to the Lord (*dominus*), but to the devil (*demonas*). For Abulafia, Satan represents the materiality of nature and Kabbalist dethrones him by bringing nature back to its spiritual foundation.[31]

In his 1926 text, Scholem seems to imply that the uncontrolled use of the Hebrew language somehow involves the risk of an involuntary "practical magic." In fact, the symbolic dimension of Hebrew in sacred texts disappears in the modern, for purely utilitarian, language. In our desacralized world, the point is certainly no longer consciously manipulating the magic potentials of language to draw some personal profit from it. But when a whole society turns the language that was that of its religious tradition to purely material ends, when it makes it a simple instrument in the service of its immediate interests, it unwittingly adopts the attitude of the magicians of earlier times. "A crude imitation" of the language of sacred texts, modern Hebrew has emptied ancient words of their symbolic and religious meaning, reducing them to mere signs of material reality. But, for Scholem, those symbolic meanings survive in the depths of the language, or in the unconscious of the culture that tries to deny them. The question is then knowing if someday there will not be a "return of the repressed," when the religious contents will return in a form unpredictable today, but that threatens to be—to use a term Scholem would not have used, but that does convey his thought—that of a collective neurosis.

"The day when the language will turn against those who speak it": that formula in which the mystical theory of language ends as eschatology sums up the intention of Scholem's text dedicated to Franz Rosenzweig. For if, when the symbolic meanings sheltered in the sacred language are exposed, they may seem dire and destructive, it is, paradoxically, because they are in themselves bereft of identifiable content. For Jewish mysticism, in fact, the semantic dimension of language appears only through human discourse; the specificity of meanings is linked to the multiplicity that characterizes the material world in which man, a finite creature, is submerged. The divine language, on the other hand, as revealed in the text of the Torah, and especially in its secret linguistic texture, is so general that it appears most evident in the form of abstract structures (which correspond to divine names and their various combinations). These structures do not transmit a definite and consequently limited meaning but bear an infinity of potential significations, which correspond to the infinity of possible interpretations. To say that the Torah is a divine text means that it is infinitely open to interpretation.[32] Someday, "the names and signs of ancient days," now buried in the unconscious of secular culture, will reemerge, but no one can say how they will be reinterpreted. But, according to Scholem, there is no great danger that after such a long period of collective repression, their return may take the form of an anarchic explosion of uncontrollable religious forces.

*

The pessimism expressed in the letter to Rosenzweig seems to have accompanied Scholem's thought to the end of his life, but was increasingly submerged. In fact, his attitude toward "empirical" Zionism seemed to evolve gradually in two opposite directions. On the one hand, Scholem quite quickly accepted the secularization of Judaism as a historically inevitable stage in what he was to call the "dialectic" of Zionism. Furthermore, it was the concrete experience of the contradictions of Zionism in its phase of realization that taught him the fundamentally dialectical nature of historical processes. A half century after his text for Rosenzweig, he declared again that, among those contradictions, one of the most symptomatic for him had been the one between "the revival of the secular language and the silence overpowering the language."[33] But he added that, for him, the path of secularization was necessary and inevitable: "I cannot free myself from the dialectical lesson of history according to which secularism is part of the process of our entry into history; entry into history implies assimilating to it." And that is why "a direct, non-dialectical return to traditional Judaism is impossible, historically speaking."[34]

The essential question is whether that phase of secularization will *necessarily* be followed by a phase of return to religious values. It is here that the notion of the dialectic in Scholem is radically distinct from the Hegelian or Marxist model. For Scholem, the term "dialectic" denotes the movement of negation or reversal of ideas that survive when they are embodied in historical reality. By extension, he also called dialectics the contradictions that affect them in the course of this process. This reversal that ideas experience when they come in contact with historical reality is in fact necessary. In this sense, the secularization of religious values represents the necessary form of their entrance into our modern history. On the other hand, no necessity dictates their subsequent destiny within history. For Scholem, there is no "meaning of history"; by its very nature, history is random and unpredictable. In particular, nothing guarantees in advance that the religious contents of Judaism will survive secularization and will reemerge in a subsequent stage of history. Or, if they should reappear, no one can predict what form they will take.

But if the historian cannot predict the future, he can analyze at least to some extent the different potentialities in the present. Scholem contrasts a *history of possibles* with Hegelian historical necessity. What is sure, for example, is that Zionism will always face the question of its relationship to the historic past of the Jews. What remains open is the answer the future will bring to this question, from the more or less radical break to forms of a religious renaissance inconceivable today. Yet, the historian, basing himself on the constants he has established, can also try to assess general historical meanings borne by those various potentialities. Thus, in terms of the correlation between the permanence of the Jewish people and its loyalty to its religious essence, which was obvious to him, Scholem asserted, "If the Jews were to become 'like all the nations,' that would be the end of the Jewish people."[35] Like all dialectical reality, Zionism includes a destructive part, that of the "forms of exile existence." The secularization it implies is both "liberation and risk."[36] In that same conversation of 1975, Scholem declared: "I never wished to believe and I did not believe that [Zionism] had to fail. Though neither did I believe that it would necessarily succeed. Maybe it will . . . but there is no guarantee of it."[37]

It is in these texts originally not intended for publication that Scholem gave free rein to his most private doubts about the chances of success of a Zionism that seemed committed to the path of irrevocable secularization. After the 1926 letter to Rosenzweig, such texts include a series of poems from 1926 to 1967, only one of which—the one devoted to a reflection on Kafka's *Trial*—has thus far been published. In a letter of 1931 addressed to Walter Benjamin (like the poem about Kafka) and devoted, among other things, to the problem of Jewish-Arab relations, he condemned the degradation of ethical Zionism into a simple practice of political realism.[38] Later, he extended this questioning of the future chances of an entirely secularized world to all of Western civilization: "When you look at the secularization process, at the barbarization of the so-called new culture, you can perceive grave processes in which it is difficult to discern any seed of future." And yet, he added in reference to a classical category of the Jewish tradition, interpreted by him not as the expression of a law immanent in history but as the rule of one of its possible evolutions: "But who knows? Maybe there is no other way of undergoing crises. One must descend in order to ascend."[39]

It is on the background of this specific conception of historical dialectics that the themes of the 1926 text dedicated to Franz Rosenzweig are summed up in 1970 at the end of the essay "The Name of God":

The word of God, which speaks to us from the Creation and the Revelation, is endlessly open to interpretation and is reflected in our language. The rays of light and sounds we capture are not so much messages as appeals. That which has meaning—sense and form—is not the word itself, but the tradition of the word, its mediation and reflection in time. This tradition, which has its own dialectic, undergoes metamorphoses; it may be transformed into a soft and almost inaudible whisper, and there may be times, like our own, when it can no longer be transmitted at all and falls silent. This, then, is the great crisis of language in which we live, we who are no longer able to grasp even the smallest bit of the mystery that once inhabited it. For the kabbalists, the very fact that language could be spoken at all was due to the Name present in it. What will be the worth of a language from which God has withdrawn? This is the question that must be asked by all who believe they can still perceive the echo of the disappeared creative word in the immanence of the world. In our times, it is poets alone who can respond to such a question; only they have not despaired of language as most mystics have done.[40]

Notes

INTRODUCTION

1. Franz Kafka, "The City Coat of Arms," in *The Complete Stories*, ed. Nahum Glatzer, trans. Willa and Edwin Muir (New York: Schocken Books, 1971), pp. 433–434.

2. Genesis 11:1–9.

3. Kafka, "City Coat of Arms," pp. 433–434.

4. The importance of the critique of historical Reason in Kafka's aphorisms has been underlined by Beda Allemann, "Fragen an die judaistische Kafka-Deutung am Beispiel Benjamins," in *Kafka und das Judentum*, ed. K. E. Grözinger, S. Mosès, and H. D. Zimmerman (Frankfurt/Main: Athanäum, 1987), pp. 35–70.

5. The city of Prague, where Kafka was born and lived, has a fist in its coat of arms.

6. Jorge Luis Borges, "The Secret Miracle," trans. Anthony Kerrigan, in *Ficciones* (New York: Grove Press, 1962), pp. 143–150.

7. Gershom Scholem, *Walter Benjamin und sein Engel* (Frankfort-am-Main: Suhrkamp, 1983), p. 132.

8. Ibid.

9. Ibid.

10. Walter Benjamin, *Gesammelte Schriften*, II, 1, p. 246.

11. Entry of August 1, 1916. I thank my friend Gary Smith of Berlin, who communicated the transcription of that as yet unpublished journal.

12. My interest in models of complexity and randomness was stirred by Henri Atlan over long years of intellectual exchanges. He has my heartfelt gratitude.

13. Franz Rosenzweig, *The Star of Redemption*. And see Stéphane Mosès, *System and Revelation. The Philosophy of Franz Rosenzweig*, trans. Chaterine Tihanyi (Detroit, 1992).

CHAPTER I

1. Walter Benjamin, letter of October 10, 1912, to Ludwig Strauss, in *Gesammelte Schriften*, II, 3, p. 838.

2. Gershom Scholem, *From Berlin to Jerusalem*.

3. Walter Benjamin, letter of January 17, 1913, to Ludwig Strauss, in *Gesammelte Schriften*, II, 3, p. 842.

4. *Berlin to Jerusalem.*

5. Note of August 1, 1916.

6. Franz Rosenzweig, *Der Mensch und sein Werk, Briefe und Tagebücher*, ed. Rachel Rosenzweig, Edith Rosenzweig-Scheinmann, and Bernhard Caspter, Vol. 2, *1918–1929* (Der Haag, 1979), note of April 3, 1922, p. 770.

7. *Star of Redemption*, p. 21.

8. Ibid., pp. 48ff.

9. *Briefe und Tagebücher*, p. 231.

10. Ibid., p. 245.

11. Ibid., p. 250.

12. Ibid., p. 251.

13. Ibid.

14. Ibid., p. 252.

15. Ibid., p. 254.

16. Ibid., p. 279.

17. Ibid.

18. Ibid., p. 280.

19. Ibid., pp. 280ff.

20. Ibid., p. 281.

21. Ibid.

22. Ibid., p. 279.

23. Ibid., pp. 281ff.

24. Ibid., p. 284.

25. Ibid., p. 285.

26. Ibid., p. 287.

27. Ibid., p. 279.

28. Ibid., p. 303.

29. Ibid., p. 305.

CHAPTER 2

1. *Briefe und Tagebücher*, p. 110.

2. *Hegel and the State.*

3. Ibid., p. 9.

4. Ibid., p. 433.

5. *Star of Redemption*, pp. 283ff.

6. *Philosophy of Right*, trans. S. W. Dyde (Kitchener, Ont.: Batoche Books, 2001).

7. *Hegel and the State*, pp. 362–378.

8. Preface to *Star of Redemption*, p. 43.

9. *On the Scientific Study of Natural Right*, in *Werke* (Berlin, 1832–1845), I, p. 373.

10. *Philosophy of Right*, pp. 258–259.

11. Ibid., p. 272.

12. See *Star of Redemption*.

13. *Phenomenology of Mind*.

14. *Hegel and the State*, p. 368.

15. Ibid.

16. *Philosophy of Right*, p. 266.

17. *Hegel and the State*, p. 369.

18. *Star of Redemption*, p. 351.

19. "On the 1930 Publication of Rosenzweig's *The Star of Redemption*."

20. *Letters*, p. 69.

21. *Philosophy of Right*, §347, p. 268.

22. In the Speeches to the German Nation (14th speech, end).

23. *Briefe und Tagebücher*, p. 1139.

24. *Star of Redemption*, pp. 350–351.

25. *Briefe und Tagebücher*, p. 281.

26. *Hegel and the State*, p. 375.

27. Ibid., p. 374.

CHAPTER 3

1. *Star of Redemption*, p. 262.

2. Letter of May 10–11, 1918, to Hans Ehrenberg, in *Briefe und Tagebücher*, pp. 561–562.

3. *Critique of Judgment*, §25.

4. Ibid.

5. Ibid., §26.

6. Ibid., §25.

7. Ibid., §26.

8. *Briefe und Tagebücher*, pp. 551ff.

9. Ibid.

10. Ibid.

11. This development was inspired by the commentary of Elia of Volna on Song of Solomon 2:8.

12. Letter of February 5, 1917, to Gertrud Oppenheim, in *Briefe und Tagebücher*, p. 345.

CHAPTER 4

1. *The Origin of German Tragic Drama*, trans. John Osborne (London: NLB, 1977).

2. *Collected Writings*, II, 1, p. 75.

3. See Thomas S. Kuhn, "Second Thoughts on Paradigms," in *The Structure of Scientific Theories* (Urbana, 1974), I, pp. 459–482.

4. Walter Benjamin, *The Arcades Project*, trans. Howard Eiland and Kevin McLaughlin (Cambridge, Mass.: Harvard University Press, 1999).

5. *Collected Writings*, II, 1, p. 168.

6. Ibid., p. 330.

7. *Origin*, p. 37.

8. Ibid.

9. "Now I should like you to pay close attention to the exact words you used," said Freud to Dora, and added in a note: "I laid stress upon these words because they took me aback." Freud, *Dora—An Analysis of a Case of Hysteria* (New York: Collier Books, 1963), p. 14.

10. *Origin*, p. 37.

11. Ibid.

12. *Collected Writings*, I, 3, p. 935.

13. Ibid., p. 936.

14. Ibid.

15. Ibid.

16. An example of that method will be found in Benjamin's literary hermeneutics: the studied word corresponds to the *phenomenon*; conceptual analysis abstracts a series of motifs from it, which are so many *elements*; these are then reassembled into a certain number of key notions that correspond to *ideas* and constitute the terms of a critical metalanguage, or a metatext that is supposed to represent the truth of the empirical text.

17. *Origin*, p. 34.

18. Ibid.

19. *Collected Writings*, I, 1, p. 200.

20. Ibid., p. 150.

21. Ibid., II, 1, p. 313.

22. *Charles Baudelaire: A Lyric Poet in the Era of High Capitalism*, trans. Harry Zohn (London: Verso), p. 136.

23. *Collected Writings*, I, 2, p. 712.

24. "To the Planetarium."

25. "Brèves Ombres," in *Poésie et Révolution*, trans. Maurice de Gandillac (Paris, 1971), p. 53.

26. *Collected Writings*, I, 2, pp. 149ff.

27. Gershom Scholem, *Walter Benjamin und sein Engel*, p. 62.

28. Ibid.

29. *Arcades Project*, p. 343.

30. Ibid.

31. Ibid.

32. "Some Motifs in Baudelaire," p. 154.

33. *Arcades Project.*

34. "The Work of Art in the Age of Mechanical Reproduction."

35. *Arcades Project*, p. 522.

36. In *Reflections*, pp. 209–210. And see Stéphane Mosès, "Brecht et Benjamin interprètes de Kafka," in *Mélanges Claude David* (Bern: Peter Lang, 1983), pp. 279–302.

37. *Collected Writings*, I, 2, pp. 694ff.

38. Ibid., p. 704.

39. "Some Motifs in Baudelaire," p. 154.

CHAPTER 5

1. *Arcades Project*, p. 298.

2. "The Task of the Translator," p. 71.

3. *Arcades Project*, p. 264.

4. Ibid., pp. 380–381.

5. *Collected Writings*, I, 3, p. 915.

6. Carlo Ginzburg, "Datazione assoluta e datazione relativa: Sul metodo di Longhi," *Paragone*, no. 386 (April 1982): p. 9.

7. *Origin*, p. 27.

8. Ibid., p. 42.

9. Ibid., p. 44.

10. *Arcades Project*, p. 377.

11. *Collected Writings*, I, 3, p. 940.

12. *Origin*, p. 43.

13. Ibid., p. 33.

14. Ibid., p. 38.

15. Ibid., p. 34.

16. Ibid., pp. 35–36.

17. Ibid., p. 35.

18. Ibid., p. 31.

19. Ibid, p. 47.

20. *Collected Writings*, I, 3, p. 929.

21. See Gershom Scholem, "Le nom de Dieu ou la théorie du langage dans la Kabbale," in *Le Nom et les symboles de Dieu dans la mystique juive*, trans. Maurice Hayoun and Georges Vajda (Paris, 1983), pp. 55–99.

22. *Origin*, p. 36.

23. Ibid., p. 47.
24. *Collected Writings*, I, 3, p. 936.
25. Ibid., p. 935.
26. Ibid., I, 2, pp. 701ff.
27. *Origin*, pp. 45–46.
28. Ibid., p. 47
29. Ibid., p. 166.
30. Ibid.
31. Ibid.
32. Ibid., pp. 177–178.

CHAPTER 6

1. *Arcades Project*, p. 688.
2. *Collected Writings*, IV, 2, p. 910.
3. *Arcades Project*, p. 688.
4. Ibid., p. 464.
5. Ibid., p. 389.
6. Ibid.
7. Ibid., p. 324.
8. Ibid., p. 164.
9. Ibid., p. 379.
10. Ibid., p. 391.
11. Saint Augustine, XI, 20.
12. Ibid.
13. *Collected Writings*, I, 3, p. 1237.
14. Ibid., p. 1250.
15. Ibid., I, 2, p. 695.
16. Ibid., I, 3, p. 1242.
17. Ibid., p. 1241.
18. Ibid., p. 1245.
19. *Arcades Project*, p. 402.
20. *Collected Writings*, I, 3, p. 1243.
21. Ibid., p. 1244.
22. Ibid., p. 1236.
23. *Charles Baudelaire*, pp. 195ff.
24. *Collected Writings*, I, 3, p. 1236.
25. Ibid., p. 1243.
26. Ibid., I, 2, p. 702.
27. Ibid.
28. Ibid., p. 704.
29. Ibid., p. 695.

30. Ibid.
31. Ibid.
32. *Arcades Project*, p. 460.
33. *Collected Writings*, I, 2, p. 703.
34. *Arcades Project*, p. 474.
35. Ibid.
36. *Collected Writings*, I, 2, p. 697.
37. Ibid.
38. Ibid.
39. Ibid.
40. *Arcades Project*, p. 478.
41. Ibid., p. 479.
42. Ibid., p. 473.
43. Ibid.
44. *Collected Writings*, I, 2, p. 694.
45. Rosenzweig, *Collected Writings*, p. 67.
46. *Collected Writings*, I, 3, p. 1265.
47. *Arcades Project*, p. 462.
48. Ibid.
49. Ibid.
50. Kafka, *Wedding Preparations in the Country.*
51. *Arcades Project*, p. 119.
52. Ibid., p. 114.
53. Ibid., p. 347.
54. *Collected Writings*, I, 3, p. 1245.
55. *Arcades Project*, p. 471.
56. Ibid.
57. Ibid.
58. *Collected Writings*, I, 3, p. 1245.
59. Ibid., p. 1238.
60. Ibid., p. 1232.
61. Ibid., I, 2, p. 697.
62. Ibid., I, 3, p. 1252.
63. Ibid., p. 1245.
64. Ibid., p. 1236.

CHAPTER 7

1. Gershom Scholem, *Briefe an Werner Kraft*, ed. Werner Kraft (Frankfurt: Suhrkamp, 1986), pp. 23ff.

2. "Open Letter to Zalman Schocken" (October 29, 1937), in *Gershom Scholem: Kabbalah and Counter-History*, ed. David Biale (Cambridge, Mass./London: Harvard University Press, 1979), pp. 31ff.

3. Ibid.
4. Ibid., p. 32.
5. Ibid.
6. Ibid.
7. This thesis was recently challenged by Moshe Idel in *Kabbalah: New Perspectives* (New Haven/London: Yale University Press, 1988), pp. 264–267.
8. *Le Messianisme juif,* p. 66.
9. Ibid.
10. Gershom Scholem, *Fidélité et utopie. Essais sur le judaïsme contemporain,* trans. Marguerite Delmotte and Bernard Dupuy (Paris: Calmann-Lévy, 1978), pp. 257ff.
11. *Le Messianisme juif,* p. 66.
12. Walter Benjamin, *Essays,* I (1923–1934) (Paris, 1983), p. 128.
13. Ibid.
14. *Le Messianisme juif,* p. 78.
15. Ibid., p. 35.
16. Ibid., p. 36.
17. *Midrash Exodus Rabba,* xxv, 16, on Psalm 95:7.
18. Babylonian Talmud, Sanhedrin, 96B.
19. Ibid., 98B.
20. Ibid.
21. *Essays,* p. 35.

CHAPTER 8

1. See Marianne Krull, *Freud and His Father,* trans. Arnold J. Pomerans (New York, 1986).
2. See especially the dreams "Please Close an Eye," "The Uncle with the Yellow Beard," "The Ghetto of Rome."
3. *The Basic Kafka* (New York: Washington Square Press, 1979), p. 215.
4. Ibid., p. 216.
5. Ibid., pp. 217–218.
6. Ibid., p. 218.
7. See *From Berlin to Jerusalem,* chaps. 1 and 2.
8. Gershom Scholem, *Walter Benjamin, the Story of a Friendship,* trans. Harry Zohn (Philadelphia: Jewish Publication Society of America, 1981).
9. *Arcades Project,* p. 378.
10. Scholem, *Story of a Friendship,* p. 171.
11. "Préjugés devant la loi," in *La Faculté de juger,* ed. J. Derrida, V. Descombes, G. Kortian, Ph. Lacoue-Labarthe, J.-F. Lyotard, and J.-L. Nancy (Paris, 1985).
12. Deuteronomy 31:18.
13. Schmuel Hugo Bergman, *Tagebücher und Briefe,* vol. 1 (Königstein/Taunus, 1985), p. 213.

14. *The Correspondence of Walter Benjamin and Gershom Scholem, 1932–1940,* ed. Gershom Scholem, trans. Gary Smith and Andre Lefevere (New York: Schocken Books, 1989), pp. 118–120. English translation © 1989 by Schocken Books, a division of Random House, Inc. Used by permission of Schocken Books, a division of Random House, Inc.

15. Ibid., pp. 123–125.

16. Kafka, *The Trial,* trans. Willa and Edwin Muir (New York: Schocken Books, 1968).

17. *Correspondence,* p. 126.

18. Ibid., p. 142.

19. Benjamin, *Collected Writings,* II, 2, p. 437.

20. *Correspondence,* p. 142.

21. *The Trial,* p. 229.

22. *Franz Kafka: The Complete Stories,* ed. Nahum N. Glatzer, trans. Willa and Edwin Muir (New York: Schocken Books), p. 415.

23. "Offener Brief an den Verfasser der Schrift, *Jüdischer Glaube in dieser Zeit,*" *Bayerische Israelitische Gemeindezeitung* 8 (1932).

24. *Judaica* 3 (Frankfurt-am-Main, 1973), p. 271.

25. *Correspondence,* p. 158.

26. *Story of a Friendship,* p. 171.

27. *Correspondence,* p. 127.

28. *Story of a Friendship,* p. 171.

29. *Le Messianisme juif,* p. 450.

30. *Judaica* 3, pp. 265ff.

31. "The Narrator, Reflections on the Work of Nicola Lesskov," in *Écrits française,* by Walter Benjamin, ed. J. M. Monnoyer (Paris, 1991), p. 209.

32. *Correspondence,* p. 225.

33. Ibid.

34. *Judaica* 3, p. 264.

35. Gershom Scholem, *Major Trends in Jewish Mysticism* (New York: Schocken Books, 1954), pp. 349–350.

36. *La Kabbale et sa symbolique,* trans. Jean Boesse (Paris: Payot, 1980), p. 20.

37. *Judaica* 3, p. 271.

CHAPTER 9

1. Translation by Ora Wiskind, originally published in *History & Memory* 2:2; reprinted by permission of Indiana University Press. Original published by permission of Mrs. F. Scholem in *Archives de sciences sociales des religions,* no. 60–61 (1985), pp. 83–84.

2. See *From Berlin to Jerusalem,* p. 115.

3. "The Name of God or the Theory of Language in the Kabbalah" (1970), trans. Simon Pleasance, *Diogenes* 79 and 80 (1972).

4. See in French, aside from *La Kabbale et sa symbolique, Les Origines de la Kabbale*, trans. J. Loewenson (Paris, 1966).

5. See in French, *Le Messianisme juif; Du frankisme au jacobinisme*, trans. Naftali Deutsch, Stéphane Mosès, and Jean Bollack (Paris, 1981); "Sabbatai Sevi; the Mystical Messiah, 1626–1676," trans. R. J. Zwi Werblowsky (1973).

6. See "Nom et les symboles de Dieu dans la mystique juive / Gershom Scholem," trans. Maurice R. Hayoun and Georges Vajda (1983).

7. *Correspondence.*

8. *From Berlin to Jerusalem*, pp. 140–141.

9. See *Briefe und Tagebücher*, vol. 2, p. 1118.

10. *From Berlin to Jerusalem*, p. 140.

11. Letter from Rosenzweig to Scholem, January 6, 1922, in *Briefe und Tagebücher*, vol. 2, p. 741.

12. Letter from Rosenzweig to Scholem, in *Briefe und Tagebücher*, vol. 1, *1900–1918*, p. 304.

13. Rosenzweig, *Briefe und Tagebücher*, vol. 2, p. 1094.

14. *From Berlin to Jerusalem*, p. 140.

15. *Briefe und Tagebücher*, vol. 2, p. 1094.

16. See "Politique et religion chez Franz Rosenzweig," *Politique et religion, données et débats* (Paris, 1981), pp. 283–311.

17. Letter from Rosenzweig to Scholem, March 10, 1921, in *Briefe und Tagebücher*, vol. 2, pp. 698ff.

18. *Briefe und Tagebücher*, vol. 2, p. 927.

19. *Correspondence*, I, p. 316.

20. *Story of a Friendship.*

21. *From Berlin to Jerusalem*, pp. 139–140.

22. *Fidélité et utopie.*

23. *Story of a Friendship*, pp. 194–195.

24. *From Berlin to Jerusalem*, pp. 166–167.

25. See "Linguistique et poétique," in *Essais de linguistique générale*, I (Paris, 1963).

26. *Le Nom et les symboles de Dieu*, p. 60.

27. See "In Switzerland (1918–1919)," in *Story of a Friendship.*

28. Gershom Scholem, *Kabbalah* (Jerusalem, 1974), p. 200.

29. See the introduction in the French edition of *De Berlin à Jerusalem*, by Arnaldo Momigliano.

30. "The Name of God," p. 71.

31. Ibid., p. 193.

32. Ibid., pp. 179–180.

33. "With Gershom Scholem: An Interview," trans. Moshe Kohn, in Scholem, *On Jews and Judaism in Crisis: Selected Essays*, ed. Werner J. Dannhauser (New York, 1976), p. 36.

34. Ibid., p. 34.

35. Ibid.

36. Ibid., p. 55.

37. Ibid., p. 43.

38. *Story of a Friendship*, pp. 171–174.

39. *On Jews and Judaism in Crisis*, p. 22.

40. "The Name of God," p. 194.

Cultural Memory | in the Present

Nanette Salomon, *Shifting Priorities: Gender and Genre
in Seventeenth-Century Dutch Painting*
Jacob Taubes, *The Political Theology of Paul*
Jean-Luc Marion, *The Crossing of the Visible*
Eric Michaud, *The Cult of Art in Nazi Germany*
Anne Freadman, *The Machinery of Talk: Charles Peirce and the Sign Hypothesis*
Stanley Cavell, *Emerson's Transcendental Etudes*
Stuart McLean, *The Event and Its Terrors: Ireland, Famine, Modernity*
Beate Rössler, ed., *Privacies: Philosophical Evaluations*
Bernard Faure, *Double Exposure: Cutting Across Buddhist and Western Discourses*
Alessia Ricciardi, *The Ends of Mourning: Psychoanalysis, Literature, Film*
Alain Badiou, *Saint Paul: The Foundation of Universalism*
Gil Anidjar, *The Jew, the Arab: A History of the Enemy*
Jonathan Culler and Kevin Lamb, eds., *Just Being Difficult?
Academic Writing in the Public Arena*
Jean-Luc Nancy, *A Finite Thinking*, edited by Simon Sparks
Theodor W. Adorno, *Can One Live after Auschwitz?
A Philosophical Reader*, edited by Rolf Tiedemann
Patricia Pisters, *The Matrix of Visual Culture: Working with Deleuze in Film Theory*
Andreas Huyssen, *Present Pasts: Urban Palimpsests and the Politics of Memory*
Talal Asad, *Formations of the Secular: Christianity, Islam, Modernity*
Dorothea von Mücke, *The Rise of the Fantastic Tale*
Marc Redfield, *The Politics of Aesthetics: Nationalism, Gender, Romanticism*
Emmanuel Levinas, *On Escape*
Dan Zahavi, *Husserl's Phenomenology*
Rodolphe Gasché, *The Idea of Form: Rethinking Kant's Aesthetics*
Michael Naas, *Taking on the Tradition: Jacques Derrida
and the Legacies of Deconstruction*
Herlinde Pauer-Studer, ed., *Constructions of Practical Reason:
Interviews on Moral and Political Philosophy*
Jean-Luc Marion, *Being Given That: Toward a Phenomenology of Givenness*
Theodor W. Adorno and Max Horkheimer, *Dialectic of Enlightenment*
Ian Balfour, *The Rhetoric of Romantic Prophecy*
Martin Stokhof, *World and Life as One:
Ethics and Ontology in Wittgenstein's Early Thought*
Gianni Vattimo, *Nietzsche: An Introduction*
Jacques Derrida, *Negotiations: Interventions and Interviews,
1971-1998*, ed. Elizabeth Rottenberg